Praise for *Dark Nig...*

T0188571

"... [A] fluent, unflaggingly honest sty[...] evocation, this book conveys the impo[...] growth entails darkness as well as light."

"Moore pulls insights from a variety of disciplines and belief systems that one can use when dealing with illness, divorce, joblessness, or the death of a loved one.... He has a gift for recognizing the pain yet encouraging the reader to see the bright spots and move productively through the experience. Easy to read and sure to appeal to intelligent, open-minded readers...."
                                                               —*Library Journal*

"In these reductive and fundamentalist times, Thomas Moore asks us to acknowledge the dark moon within us all, to question the workings of a sun-bright culture which demands our happy, healthy productivity at perhaps the cost of our very souls. This is a wise and timely book, and I cannot recommend it highly enough."
                        —Andre Dubus III, author of *House of Sand and Fog*

"Thomas Moore is one of the profound spiritual writers of our time. *Dark Nights of the Soul* delves into the mystery of human suffering and *really* tells it like it is. We've all been discouraged by neat, tidy self-help dogmatism and Moore refuses to succumb to the commercialism of simplistic, superficial, and subjective solutions."
                —John Bradshaw, author of the #1 *New York Times* bestsellers
                 Homecoming, Creating Love, and *Healing the Shame That Binds You*

"Thomas Moore is the master of conveying the insight that the dark times in our lives are not threats but friends and teachers."
                           —Rabbi Harold Kushner, author of *When Bad*
                                              Things Happen to Good People

"Thomas Moore is a compassionate, wise guide who shows us why walking with God always requires wrestling with the devil. To find out why wholeness always trumps perfection, and why life's ups and downs are joined in an eternal dance, *Dark Nights of the Soul* is highly recommended."—Larry Dossey, M.D., author of *Healing Beyond the Body,*
                              Reinventing Medicine, and *Healing Words*

"... [A]n intriguing, insightful and ultimately seductive book, inviting us below all surfaces into the undercurrents of human endeavor. Amidst every difficulty Thomas Moore is there to offer each of us a very sure and companionable hand, guiding us through the awkward, the unforeseen and the unforgivable."
                        —David Whyte, poet, and author of *Crossing the Unknown Sea*
                                               and *Everything Is Waiting for You*

DARK
NIGHTS
OF THE
SOUL

A Guide to Finding Your Way
Through Life's Ordeals

THOMAS MOORE

AVERY
an imprint of Penguin Random House
New York

an imprint of Penguin Random House LLC
375 Hudson Street
New York, New York 10014

First Gotham trade paperback edition, June 2005
Copyright © 2004 by Thomas Moore
All rights reserved

Grateful acknowledgment is made for permission to reprint the following:

"The Forge" from *Opened Ground: Selected Poems 1966–1996* by Seamus Heaney. Copyright © 1998 by Seamus Heaney. Reprinted by permission of Farrar, Straus, and Giroux, LLC.

"The Forge" from *Door in the Dark* by Seamus Heaney. Reprinted by permission of the publisher, Faber and Faber Ltd.

An excerpt from *The Ink Dark Moon* by Jane Hirschfield and Mariko Arantani, copyright © 1990 by Jane Hirschfeld and Mariko Arantani. Used by permission of Vintage Books, a division of Random House, Inc.

Most Avery books are available at special quantity discounts for bulk purchase for sales promotions, premiums, fund-raising, and educational needs. Special books or book excerpts also can be created to fit specific needs. For details, write SpecialMarkets@penguinrandomhouse.com.

The Library of Congress has catalogued the hardcover edition as follows:

Moore, Thomas, date.
Dark nights of the soul : a guide to finding your way
through life's ordeals / by Thomas Moore.
p.   cm.
ISBN 1-592-40067-1
1. Suffering—Religious aspects.   2. Depression, Mental—Religious aspects.
3. John of the Cross, Saint, 1542–1591. Noche oscura del alma.   4. Spiritual life.   I. Title.
BL65.S85M66   2004   2004003140
204'.42—dc22

ISBN 978-1-59240-133-8 (paperback)

Printed in the United States of America

Book design by Susan Turner

That sweet night: a secret.
Nobody saw me;
I did not see a thing.
No other light, no other guide
Than the one burning in my heart.

JOHN OF THE CROSS
(transl. Mirabai Starr)

Between living and dreaming
There is something else.
Guess what it is.

ANTONIO MACHADO
(transl. Mary Berg and Dennis Maloney)

to my brother Jim

CONTENTS

ACKNOWLEDGMENTS

A BOOK ABOUT THE DEEPEST, darkest, smokiest experiences in a life can't be written alone. I'm grateful to a number of people for their help. As always, I have been sustained by Michael Katz, who is more than a survivor and more than an agent. Bill Shinker showed an amazing trust in me and supported me in a time that could easily have turned into a dark night of the soul. I got to know Lauren Marino, whose patient editing helped me remember that books have readers. Emily Archer has the golden touch, the ability to advise critically and inspire at the same time. Redmond O'Hanlon, my Dubliner miracle-worker and bosom buddy, supported me in ways he knew nothing about. Other friends from Ireland haunt these pages: John Moriarty, the most gifted bard I have ever met; Michael Kearney, a steady friend who knows something of my own dark nights; his brother Richard Kearney, a philosopher with a heart and a teeming imagination; Brendan and Hazel Hester, whose friendship and counsel during this time were precious. In the field of medicine, besides Dr. Michael Kearney, Dr. Balfour Mount and the Reverend George Doebler helped in kind and quiet ways. Dr. Bettina Peyton-Levine is part angel and part human—both parts are evident in this book. Dr. James Guy has been an inspiration to me, someone who navigated his own dark night with amazing grace and whose example leads me on.

Pat Toomay constantly teaches me how to see things and how to write. He also took a major misty journey during the time of this writing and shared it with me.

I want to thank Siobhán and Abe from the Persephonic depths of my heart, and Hanley, my soror mystica.

During the writing of this book, my mother was hospitalized for nine months with a stroke and died just as I was completing the writing. I owe a debt I could never express to my father; my brother Jim; Peggy; and my aunt Betty. About my mother I can only sing a prayer of praise. Her dark night accompanied my writing like a shadow and guided me from an angelic place. Her influence is in every cell of my being.

Finally, I want to acknowledge the splendid people whose stories I tell in these pages. I can't begin to honor them enough and to thank them for giving so much to me.

In the middle of our life journey I found myself in a dark wood. I had wandered from the straight path. It isn't easy to talk about it: it was such a thick, wild, and rough forest that when I think of it my fear returns. . . . I can't offer any good explanation for how I entered it. I was so sleepy at that point that I strayed from the right path.

—DANTE, *Inferno*, Canto I[1]

THE DARK NIGHT

A T ONE TIME or another, most people go through a period of sadness, trial, loss, frustration, or failure that is so disturbing and long-lasting that it can be called a dark night of the soul. If your main interest in life is health, you may quickly try to overcome the darkness. But if you are looking for meaning, character, and personal substance, you may discover that a dark night has many important gifts for you.

Today we label many of these experiences "depression," but not all dark nights are depressive, and the word is too clinical for something that makes you question the very meaning of life. It's time for a different way of imagining this common experience, and therefore a different way of dealing with it. But, I warn you, this business is subtle, and you will have to look closely at yourself and at the examples I give to see how a deeply disturbing episode can be a precious moment of transformation.

Every human life is made up of the light and the dark, the happy and the sad, the vital and the deadening. How you think about this rhythm of moods makes all the difference. Are you going to hide out in self-delusion and distracting entertainments? Are you going to become cynical and depressed? Or are you going to open your heart to a mystery that is as natural as the sun and the moon, day and night, and summer and winter?

If you are like most people, you have gone through several dark nights of the soul. You may be in the middle of one now. You may be in a difficult marriage, have a child in trouble, or find yourself caught in a tenacious and terrible mood. You may be grieving the loss of a spouse or parent. You may have been betrayed by a lover or a business partner or going through a divorce. For some people, these situations are problems to be solved, but for others they are the source of deep despair. A true dark night of the soul is not a surface challenge but a development that takes you away from the joy of your ordinary life. An external event or an internal mood strikes you at the core of your existence. This is not just a feeling but a rupture in your very being, and it may take a long while to get through to the other end of it.

A dark night may not feel like depression. In a long illness or a troubled marriage you may be anxious, but not depressed. On the other hand, a clinical depression might well qualify as a dark night. Whatever you call it, the experience involves you as a person, someone with a history, a temperament, memories, emotions, and ideas. Depression is a label and a syndrome, while a dark night is a meaningful event. Depression is a psychological sickness, a dark night is a spiritual trial.

Many people think that the point in life is to solve their problems and be happy. But happiness is usually a fleeting sensation, and you never get rid of problems. Your purpose in life may be to become more who you are and more engaged with the people and the life around you, to really live your life. That may sound obvious, yet many people spend their time avoiding life.

They are afraid to let it flow through them, and so their vitality gets channeled into ambitions, addictions, and preoccupations that don't give them anything worth having. A dark night may appear, paradoxically, as a way to return to living. It pares life down to its essentials and helps you get a new start.

Here I want to explore positive contributions of your dark nights, painful though they may be. I don't want to romanticize them or deny their dangers. I don't even want to suggest that you can always get through them. But I do see them as opportunities to be transformed from within, in ways you could never imagine. A dark night is like Dante getting sleepy, wandering from his path, mindlessly slipping into a cave. It is like Alice looking at the mirror and then going through it. It is like Odysseus being tossed by stormy waves and Tristan adrift without an oar. You don't choose a dark night for yourself. It is given to you. Your job is to get close to it and sift it for its gold.

NIGHT WORK

You probably know more about the depths of your soul from periods of pain and confusion than from times of comfort. Darkness and turmoil stimulate the imagination in a certain way. They allow you to see things you might ordinarily overlook. You become sensitive to a different spectrum of emotion and meaning. You perceive the ultraviolet extremes of your feelings and thoughts, and you learn things you wouldn't notice in times of normalcy and brightness.

A dark night of the soul is not extraordinary or rare. It is a natural part of life, and you can gain as much from it as you can from times of normalcy. Just look around at your friends and acquaintances. One is going through a divorce. Another's mother is seriously ill. A young child has been hurt in an accident. Another can't get a job. Several are depressed and acting strangely. This is today's list in my own life, and it doesn't even include the threat of war and the fear of terrorism. Each of these involves both suffering and discovery.

If you give all your effort to getting rid of your dark night, you may not learn its lessons or go through the important changes it can make for you. I want to encourage you to enter the darkness with all your strength and intelligence, and perhaps find a new vision and a deeper sense of self. Even if the source is external—a crime, rape, an abortion, being cheated, business pressure, being held captive, or the threat of terrorism—you can still discover new resources in yourself and a new outlook on life. We are not out to solve the dark night, but to be enriched by it.

JOHN OF THE CROSS

The phrase "dark night of the soul" comes from the Spanish mystic and poet John of the Cross (1541–1597). John was a member of the Christian religious order of Carmelites and, along with St. Teresa of Avila, tried to reform that order. Many in the order were so against reform that they imprisoned John for eight months, during which he wrote a series of remarkable poems. His later writing is chiefly commentary on those poems, one of them entitled "Dark Night of the Soul."

John writes about the night of the senses and the night of the spirit. The first phase is a purifying of intention and motivation, the second a process of living by radical faith and trust. John's work is used especially by those who devote themselves seriously to cultivating a spiritual life through community, meditation, and various forms of service. Less technically, the term sometimes refers to depression or to bleak and trying periods in a person's life.

In my use of the phrase, I fall somewhere in between. I see a dark night of the soul as a period of transformation. It is more like a stage in alchemy than an obstacle to happiness. Usually it lasts a while—you wouldn't call a day's worry a dark night of the soul. It doesn't always end happily with some new personal discovery. In fact, we will see several examples of people who committed suicide or succumbed to illness. To appreciate these episodes as transformations in the soul, you can't judge them by any simple, external measure. You have to look deep and close, understanding that you can make significant gains by going through a challenge, and yet it's not always obvious how you benefited from the darkness. Sometimes a dark night makes sense because of what it contributes to others, not what it does for you.

A SPIRITUAL RATHER THAN A PSYCHOLOGICAL APPROACH

I am always slow to label difficult emotions as sick. Usually I would rather see them as trials that make you more of a person. I keep in mind the many men and women of the past I admire, who were complicated, who were neither whole nor healthy. You will find many such people described in this book and held up as models, even though their imperfections and failures showed luminously in their lives. In general, I place a higher value on soulfulness than on health and propriety.

One chapter of my book *Care of the Soul* in particular made an impression on many readers—"Gifts of Depression." I have learned from many sources—ancient medical books, thoughtful artists and writers, and the work of C. G. Jung and James Hillman—to value visitations of melancholy and sadness. I tried to be specific about the rewards that can come from depressive moods. As overwhelming and distressing as it is, what we call depression is, after all, a human experience, tied to all the other meaningful events in your life. You do a disservice to yourself when you treat your feelings of despair and emptiness as deviations from the normal and healthy life you idealize. The dark times, too, like enlightenments and achievements, leave their mark and make you a person of insight and compassion.

This book begins with some strong images from ancient ritual and religion. People of the far distant past knew secrets to dealing with trying times that have been forgotten; the image of the night sea journey, the notion of catharsis, rituals to help with life's passages, and a moon spirit with rather unholy but helpful blessings. Then we look at intelligence and love, how to think and how to be connected, as important lessons to learn from a dark night. Finally, we consider various aspects of ordinary life in which a dark night of the soul might well appear: in attempts to be creative and our need for beauty, in anger and in those times when we "lose it"; in illness and in old age. Each of these experiences might spawn a special kind of dark night.

EMOTIONS IN A MINOR KEY

Emily Dickinson said that her penchant for solitude was like the minor key in music, a refreshing alternative to the brighter major key. Now think of your dark nights. Could they be as useful and even as beautiful as the bright periods? Could they be moods and events in a minor key? Today, books are written explaining how Dickinson was neurotic. But she didn't think of herself as "mentally ill," though she was certainly eccentric. In a similar way, I want to consider our dark nights as out of the ordinary, but not sick.

The dark night of the soul provides a rest from the hyperactivity of the good times and the strenuous attempts to understand yourself and to get it all right. During the dark night there is no choice but to surrender control, give in to unknowing, and stop and listen to whatever signals of wisdom might come along. It's a time of enforced retreat and perhaps unwilling withdrawal. The dark night is more than a learning experience; it's a profound initiation into a realm that nothing in the culture, so preoccupied with external concerns and material success, prepares you for.

When people approve only of major tonalities, they become simplistic, not only in their thinking but in their very being. Today many of the conflicts that threaten the peace, both at home and around the world, stem from raw, naïve, and unintelligent prejudices and reactions. Passions routinely break out in violence. It takes a complex view of yourself and your fellow human beings to hold back on hatreds and fears. A mature person is complicated and has complex ideas and values. The minor tonality of a dark night adds a significant and valuable complexity to your personality and way of life.

UNENDING DARKNESS

Some people speak of their dark night of the soul as though it were a challenge to be dealt with quickly and overcome. "Oh, I've been through my dark night," they say. "But now it's over." To some, what they think is a dark night may be only a taste of the soul's real darkness, especially if it is relatively quick and easy, and especially if the person experiencing it feels cocky for having gone through it successfully and quickly. The real dark night cannot be dismissed so easily. It leaves a lasting effect and, in fact, alters you for good. It is nothing to brag about.

The dark night may be profoundly unsettling, offering no conceivable way out, except perhaps to rely on pure faith and resources far beyond your understanding and capability. The dark night calls for a spiritual response, not only a therapeutic one. It pushes you to the edge of what is familiar and reliable, stretching your imagination about how life works and who or what controls it all. The dark night serves the spirit by forcing you to rely on something beyond human capacity. It can open you up to new and mysterious possibilities.

SHADES OF DARKNESS

We will take note of several people who went through the special dark night of imprisonment, including Oscar Wilde, the Victorian writer who was jailed for his homosexuality. After being released, Wilde wrote to a friend, "My desire to live is as intense as ever, and though my heart is broken, hearts are made to be broken: that is why God sends sorrow into the world. . . . To me, suffering seems now a sacramental thing, that makes those whom it touches holy. . . . any materialism in life coarsens the soul."[2]

Wilde suffered loneliness and the loss of his exciting life, and in some ways left prison a broken man. But this passage shows that he learned a great deal and expresses in perfect language what I want to say here: Being unconsciously absorbed into the values of a materialistic culture "coarsens the soul." The role of a dark night might be to refine your sensitivities and show you how to make yourself into a multidimensional, fine-tooled person.

To live your particular "shade," the first thing you can do is give up clinical language that labels and categorizes. When you describe what you are going through, speak concretely from your own unique experience. Penetrate beneath the layer of language and ideas you pick up from television and magazines about your "problem." Let it show itself for what it is, not for what the therapy industry wants it to be. Medicine and psychology, like many other institutions in modern life, prefer the understandable and treatable case to the irreducible individual. They can imagine restoring you to good functioning, but they can't envision fulfilling your fate and discovering the meaning of your life.

Finally, and this may be the most difficult task of all, give yourself what you need at the deepest level. Care rather than cure. Organize your life to support the process. You are incubating your soul, not living a heroic adventure. Arrange life accordingly. Tone it down. Get what comforts you can, but don't move against the process. Concentrate, reflect, think, and talk about your situation seriously with trusted friends.

INSPIRING EXAMPLES

Some people have to face enormous challenges and go through extraordinary periods of challenge. We can learn from their example to have the patience, the insight, and the courage to endure. In 1987, when he was in Beirut as the representative of the Archbishop of Canterbury, Terry Waite was taken captive as a hostage and kept imprisoned for five years. With his fellow captives, he suffered beatings, isolation, and many deprivations. He was cut off from his normal life, his family, and all supportive human contact.

Waite says that he often called to mind books he had read, and they sustained him during those long years of solitude. One day a sympathetic guard gave him a book about slavery in America. He read it slowly several times and even memorized passages. He thought about the slaves spending their entire lives in captivity, yet without losing their spirit and their humanity. The image of the slave didn't take away his pain, but it made it bearable. He was inspired and sustained by the images of others rising above even worse conditions.

There is a simple secret to dealing with dark nights. You can come through one morally and spiritually, even if to all appearances you have failed. External pressures may get you in the end, but you can still survive with your soul intact. For years, Terry Waite, and others like him, couldn't prevail over their captors and free themselves from their physical torment. But throughout their long captivity, they dominated their situation morally, in their attitudes and in the many ways they gave their experience meaning.

Throughout history, many have been overpowered by their oppressors, but they have triumphed on another level. In the sixteenth century, Thomas More sat in prison for thirteen months before his execution, writing some of his best philosophy. The Marquis de Sade, in some ways the very opposite of a saint, reacted in a similar way. He ranted against his jailers, but he wrote some of his most important fiction under duress. Nelson Mandela prepared himself in jail to be an extraordinary leader and an example for everyone in his time.

This is the secret: Even if you can't be liberated physically, you can still emerge with self-possession, vitality, and character. You can do this with divorce, the death of a child, a serious illness, or a failure in creativity. You can survive morally even if you die physically. We'll see several examples of men and women living this paradox. Your dark night is your own invitation to become a person of heart and soul.

Every dark night is unique. In this book I will tell many stories of people I have known, especially in my practice of therapy. Stories of real people demonstrate the variety of dark nights and the many ways they are resolved. I will delve into many biographies of people who have long interested me, to see how they dealt with or succumbed to their dark nights. You can learn much from apparent failure, and you can glimpse subtle ways in which tragic lives succeed. I also won't hesitate to mention my own experiences of the darkness, for I am no stranger to it.

To deal with these disturbances we also need rich, solid, and useful ideas, rare items in a world of facts and opinions. I get my confidence as a therapist from my studies in religion, mythology, the arts, and depth psychology. The best therapists I know are those who have educated themselves in the great mysteries of love, aggression, and death. They are not the ones with standard techniques and easy answers. You, too, could think through the basic questions, read the best writers, see good films, and educate yourself in the life of the soul. Then, when a dark night comes, you will be ready for it.

PART ONE
PASSAGES

You ask my thoughts
through the long night?
I spent it listening
to the heavy rain
beating against the windows.

—IZUMI SHIKIBU[3]

CHAPTER ONE

THE NIGHT SEA JOURNEY

A DARK NIGHT of the soul may feel amorphous, having no meaning, shape, or direction. It helps to have images for it and to know that people have gone through this experience and have survived it. The great stories and myths of many cultures also help by providing an imagination of human struggle that inspires and offers insight. One ancient story that sheds light on the dark night is the tale of the hero swallowed by a huge fish. The hero, or better, antihero—he is the victim of circumstances— simply sits in the bowels of the fish as it carries him through the water. Because the story is associated with the sun setting in the west and traveling underwater to the east to rise in the morning, this theme is sometimes called the "Night Sea Journey." It is a cosmic passage taken as a metaphor for our own dark nights, when we are trapped in a mood or by external circumstances and can do little but sit and wait for liberation.

Imagine that your dark mood, or the external source of your suffering, is a large, living container in which you are held captive. But this container is moving, getting somewhere, taking you to where you need to go. You may not like the situation you're in, but it would help if you imagined it constructively. Maybe at this very minute you are on a night sea journey of your own.

Sometimes in your darkness you may sense that something is incubating in you or that you are being prepared for life. You are going somewhere, even though there are no external signs of progress. I have sat in therapy with many men and women who had no idea what was happening to them, as they felt pulled away from the joys of normal life. All they felt was bland, inarticulate confusion. Still, most were willing to sit with me, week after week, as, slowly, meaning began to emerge. Some from the beginning had the slightest hint that something creative was at work.

The whale's belly is, of course, a kind of womb. In your withdrawal from life and your uncertainty you are like an infant not yet born. The darkness is natural, one of the life processes. There may be some promise, the mere suggestion that life is going forward, even though you have no sense of where you are headed. It's a time of waiting and trusting. My attitude as a therapist in these situations is not to be anxious for a conclusion or even understanding. You have to sit with these things and in due time let them be revealed for what they are.

THE HERO-SUN AND THE SEA

The classic story of the night sea journey is the Biblical tale of Jonah. God called Jonah to tell the people of the city Nineveh that their evil ways were angering him, but Jonah tried to evade the call by sailing on a ship going to the distant city of Tarshish. A storm came up and the sailors discovered that Jonah was running away from his mission. To save themselves, they threw him overboard, and a great fish swallowed him. He was in the belly of the fish for three days and three nights before it spewed him up on land. Then God called him once more, and this time he responded.

In your dark night you may have a sensation you could call "oceanic"—being in the sea, at sea, or immersed in the waters of the womb. The sea is the vast potential of life, but it is also your dark night, which may force you to surrender some knowledge you have achieved. It helps to regularly undo the hard-won ego development, to unravel the self and culture you have woven over the years. The night sea journey takes you back to your primordial self, not the heroic self that burns out and falls to judgment, but to your original self, yourself as a sea of possibility, your greater and deeper being.

You may be so influenced by the modern demand to make progress at all costs that you may not appreciate the value in backsliding. Yet, to regress in a certain way is to return to origins, to step back from the battle line of existence, to remember the gods and spirits and elements of nature, including your own pristine nature, the person you were at the beginning. You return to the womb of imagination so that your pregnancy can recycle. You are always being born, always dying to the day to find the restorative waters of night.

The great Indian art theorist and theologian Ananda Coomaraswamy said, "No creature can attain a higher grade of nature without ceasing to exist."[4] In the dark night something of your makeup comes to an end—your ego, your self, your creativeness, your meaning. You may find in that darkness a key to your source, the larger soul that makes you who you are and holds the secrets of your existence. It is not enough to rely on the brilliance of your learning and intellect. You have to give yourself receptively to the transforming natural powers that remain mysteriously dark.

A powerful example of this sea journey is the last year or so in the life of St. Thomas More of England. He was a lawyer, theologian, and highly cultured man condemned to death by King

Henry VIII for not formally acknowledging the validity of the king's divorce. To do so would have been to contradict the teachings of his religion. More was held in a small, vaulted room in the Tower of London, a room unfurnished and whitewashed when I saw it, a womblike space that was a concrete metaphor for the terrible vessel in which More found himself. Standing in that room even today, you can imagine it as the inside of a great beast, and in that uterine space More polished his ideas and his conscience.

More's family, especially his dear and highly intelligent daughter Margaret, tried to convince him to agree to the king's wish. In one letter from the tower to her he uses Jonah imagery: "For myself, I most humbly beseech God to give me the grace patiently to conform my mind to his high pleasure, so that after the storm of this my tempestuous time, his great mercy may conduct me into the sure haven of the joyful bliss of heaven."

He wrote to Margaret that he couldn't sleep, thinking about the possible painful deaths he might face. He had "a heavy fearful heart." Yet, in the midst of this nightmare, he felt a deep peace because his conscience was clear. No one else might understand his position in relation to the king, but he had deep certainty based on his religious faith.

I know of no better example of an ordinary, life-loving person, in the midst of a terrible tempest, who could refrain from blaming his enemies and calmly counsel his friends and family. Thomas More was a Jonah figure who had to take time to understand what he was called to do. It went against everything he wanted and against all the affection in his heart. But he found inscrutable peace and grounding in his faith and belief. He took the time of his imprisonment to deepen his ideas and his conviction.

The lesson I take is that there is no loss too great or challenge too overwhelming, provided you are anchored in your vision and your values, while following your destiny. Up to the last minute More was tempted away from his choice, but the honing of his vision in prison allowed him to keep his values clear.

He could be fearful and sad and yet be led by the clarity of his vision.

As with other examples in this book, More was an extraordinary man finding himself in extraordinary circumstances, and physically he didn't survive. You, too, may find yourself in a life-shaping drama of smaller proportions. There, in the midst of a tempest of your own, you may discover how to keep your vision clear and allow your own night journey to define your life.

NIGHT AND DAY

Think of a dark night as part of organic living. To avoid it would be like choosing only artificial food that never spoils. As a natural person, you are going to feel a wide range of emotions and go through many different kinds of experiences. Over the course of your lifetime, parts of you will grow and blossom, some will rot. To be sad, grieving, struggling, lost, or hopeless is part of natural human life. By riding the wave of your dark night, you are more yourself, moving toward who you are meant to be.

For a feeling of well-being, you have to shine, but your sparkle need not be superficial. It can rise up out of a deep place in you that is dark but has its own kind of light. Thomas Aquinas said that a central element in beauty is its splendor, but other writers—Beaudelaire, de Sade, Beckett, Sexton—include a dark luminosity, what the French psychoanalyst Julia Kristeva calls, following an ancient tradition, the Black Sun. Imagine a black sun at your core, a dark luminosity that is less innocent and more interesting than naïve sunshine. That is one of the gifts a dark night has to offer you.

Humphrey Bogart was one of many actors to have this dark luminosity that shone through in his characters. In childhood his parents were alcoholic and addicted to morphine and spent a great deal of time away from him, when he was beaten by his caretakers. Later, as a hard-working contract actor, he played the part of many tough detectives and murderers, transforming his sadness and edginess into a form that worked perfectly for him. His insightful biographer Eric Lax says his effectiveness was due to his ability to "project a sense of something going on beneath the surface." He made his characters Sam Spade and Philip Marlowe "desirable and remote, both too cynical and too honorable to be true."[5] I am not presenting Bogart as the ideal solution to a dark night, but as an example of how a person can at least make something positive out of dark experiences. Bogart once played the lead in a film called *The King of the Underworld*, the perfect image for his fate. He played the social underworld well in his films because he knew the emotional underworld from his childhood.

Both in his childhood and in his servitude to the studio system, Bogart went through strenuous dark nights. Paradoxically, it was the darkness of character created by those torments that made him successful, indeed, made him a figure of myth who endures today. He offers a good example of a person not actually overcoming his captors but outshining them.

Being shaped by your darkness, like the captive Jonah, you become the sun rising out of the night water. You are always being reborn, always slipping back into the sea. Your dark night may feel stagnant and unrhythmical, but it has its subtle movements. T. S. Eliot describes the movements of life and death, light and darkness, as a Chinese jar moving perpetually in its stillness. The movement in your darkness may be difficult to sense, but it may be present nonetheless. You may not be advancing, but you are in quiet motion. There you are, suffering your fate, stuck in some container that keeps your precious life at bay, and there you have a special beauty, a pulse that can be felt only in the dark.

THE SPECIAL LANGUAGE
OF THE NIGHT SEA

In your dark night you may learn a secret hidden from modern people generally: the truth of things can only be expressed aesthetically—in story, picture, film, dance, music. Only when ideas are poetic do they reach the depths and express the reality. In his highly original essay "The Poet,"[6] Ralph Waldo Emerson says that the poet "stands one step nearer to things" and "turns the world to glass." You don't have to write poetry, but you need an appreciation for story, image, and symbol. It would help to get beyond the modern habit of giving value only to facts. You could educate yourself in the arts and in the great stories and images of the world's religions. Bogart fulfilled himself, complete with his anxieties and anger, in front of a camera. You can do it when you find your medium for self-expression. It might be nothing more than telling a good story to your friends. You may discover a talent for a particular mode of expression—an art, a craft, even a sport.

One hundred years after Emerson, another New England poet, Wallace Stevens, described the poet, perhaps borrowing Emerson's imagery, as "a man of glass, who in a million diamonds sums us up." You have that capacity within you to be the poet to your experience. Your dark night may help make you into a person of glass, transparent and readable. You have to learn how to "sum up" your experience in images that convey your personal truth. I do it by writing books on subjects that I wrestle with personally. Many people write songs, poems, and stories. Some, less obviously, make gardens.

Everyone around you expects you to describe your experience in purely personal or medical terms. In contemporary society we believe that psychological and medical language best conveys the experience we have of a dark night. You are depressed and phobic; you have an anxiety disorder or a bad gene. But perceptive thinkers of other periods and places say that good, artful, sensuous, and powerful words play a central role in the living out of your dark night. Consider this possibility: It would be better for you to find a good image or tell a good story or simply speak about your dark night with an eye toward the power and beauty of expression.

Poetic language is suited to the night sea journey, because the usual way of talking is heroic. We naturally speak of progress, growth, and success. Even "healing" may be too strong a word for what happens in the soul's sea of change. The language of popular psychology tends to be both heroic and sentimental. You conquer your problems and aim at personal growth and wholeness. An alternative is to have a deeper imagination of who you are and what you are going through. That insight may not heal you or give you the sense of being whole, but it may give you some intelligence about life.

The quality of your language is significant. In your dark night, try speaking in story and images. Resist the attempt to explain, defend, and interpret. Use metaphors and symbols. Many people say, for instance, that they feel like a volcano about to explode. That is a strong image, but it's a bit overused. Look for your own images that very specifically describe what is going on. A woman once told me that every day she found it difficult to believe that the sun would rise. I have never forgotten that simple image because it conveys so clearly the worry about whether life would continue.

One of the best models for using poetic language for times of dismay is Emily Dickinson. Her letters tell of many tragedies and losses in her life, and almost every one contains a brief poem and a sentence or two that captures the very depth of what has happened. For example, when the friend she loved more than any other, Judge Lord, died, she wrote to her cousins:

> Each that we lose takes part of us;
> A crescent still abides,

Which like the moon, some turbid night,
Is summoned by the tides.[7]

You don't have to write actual poems, but you could learn
from Dickinson to formulate your experience in language that
captures its essence, linking it up meaningfully with the rest of
your life. Dickinson's words about her loss speak to us all. Have
you ever felt as though some slice of you was at the mercy of unknown tugs of feeling, like the moon susceptible to the tides?

American speech is often plain and pragmatic. You probably
use clichés to describe original and deeply felt experiences. An
alternative is to discover the power of strong, descriptive words.
You could also experiment with different forms, until you find
the style that best allows you to say what you feel. Could you create an original letter form, the way Emily Dickinson did? Could
you find a poetic expression that says more about your experience
than ordinary words can?

Dickinson's poems are not easy to understand, but that's because they don't give everything away. They safeguard the mystery of the experience. You may need that kind of language: words
that hold your thoughts and experiences without saying too much.
Poetry is sea-language; it keeps you in the water of your life as it
articulates your experience.

THE SEA AS THE SOURCE

Many poets and artists have created their best work out of their
emotional darkness. Even if you don't see yourself as an actual
artist, you are an artist of your own life. You create your own
story and have your own ways of expressing yourself. I think of
this mystery when I sit in the Mark Rothko chapel in Houston,
which the artist filled with completely black paintings, or at the
Tate Modern in London, surrounded by his haunting and ethereal, more colorful abstractions. His biographer notes that right

after the artist's shock, in his mid-sixties, at having an aneurysm, his "confrontation with death would return struggle and emotional depth to his work, and produce a final artistic advance."[8] A dark night sometimes shocks you back to life and gives you the edge you need to do good work.

One sunny spring afternoon when I was visiting London, I sat in the Rothko room and felt the power of his large, subdued, but colorful paintings. I knew that I was in the presence of a man who had really lived. He knew the bright and the dark, and that knowledge, made part of his very being, shone through in his canvases. In return, I could recover a sense of my own darkness and depth, a direct gift from him to me. Some artists and actors disappoint because, no matter how good they are technically, they don't have the personal depth required to make real art. I find that as I try to incorporate the substance of an artist like Rothko, or Samuel Beckett, who is my ideal of the honest and visionary artist, I lack their edge and their imaginative muscle, but still something of their dark force works itself subtly into my words.

In your darkness, you are in the belly of a whale with nothing to do but be carried along. In tales of the fish-womb, the hero, swallowed by a great sea monster, loses his hair in the inner heat, a sign of profound transformation, akin to the monk who shaves his head to mark the change from ordinary life to a life of holiness. Monk and infant, bald, precursors of every man and woman who returns to a state before birth in certain dark nights of the soul.

When you sense that your dark night is one of pregnancy and oceanic return, you could react accordingly and be still. Watch and wonder. Take the human embryo as your model. Assume the fetal position, emotionally and intellectually. Be silent. Float in your darkness as if it were the waters of the womb, and give up trying to fight your way out or make sense of it.

There is something Zen-like in this recommendation. Shunryu Suzuki, in his usual simplicity, taught "one-act Samadhi."[9]

He said you should limit your activity and be concentrated on what is happening at this moment. In this way you can express yourself. You are not wandering all over the place. He says, when you bow, bow; when you sit, sit. I would say, when you are on a night sea journey, be taken. Don't try to have it finished. Don't try to figure it out. Don't try to outsmart it. You wouldn't interfere with the natural birth process, so don't fidget your way into the journey of soul that will make you more of a person and reveal your destiny. Be in one-act darkness.

THE BELLY OF THE WHALE

Remember how Jonah got into the whale in the first place. He refused the call to speak to a thoughtless people. He has been seen as an antihero, a common man who doesn't feel he has the stuff to become more than he is. Here lies another theme in this popular story: The dark night saves you from being stuck in your small life. It makes you a hero. It grows you into your fate and into being a responsive member of your community. In your mother's womb you were becoming a person. In your womb-like dark night you are becoming a soul.

The whale's belly is *sunyata*, fruitful emptiness. Jonah sits in the whale doing zazen, meditating like a monk. He sits, not literally but figuratively. His status as antihero is given place and becomes intense, and meanwhile he moves closer to his fate. He is like a Beckett character, having no control over his situation and yet mysteriously getting somewhere even as he doesn't move. He is also like a person in therapy. "Why do I keep coming?" people ask, since change is usually not obvious and dramatic. You sit there week after week like a Chinese jar, imperceptibly in motion.

In the dark place you may ask the basic questions: Who are you? What is this world? What kind of family do you come from? What are your origins, your early experiences? Deep down, what do you want? What do you fear? In the belly of the whale you are given the chance to start over. The sun-fish rises once again in the east. You get another morning in your life.

In the Biblical story, Jonah, sitting in the whale, sings a song in praise of the Lord. His words would be familiar to anyone suffering a dark night: "Waters choked me to death; the abyss whirled around me." There is only one psalm to sing in the dark night: the song that praises the dark. This is the song John of the Cross sings, and this is what Mark Rothko put on canvas and what Anne Sexton, the suburban homemaker turned poet, wrote on paper. The way you speak, the way you live, the ways you express yourself—these are all highly significant in dealing with your dark night. If you sing against the darkness, a tactic few real artists take, you may be in an impasse with it forever. But if you can find some way, suited to your talents and temperament, to express your situation poetically, you will be singing a psalm to the God who is your ultimate darkness.

You don't have to be a trained artist to do this. From your dark night you can speak with unusual clarity and passion, from the depth of your feeling instead of from some habitual, superficial place. Many times I have seen people find a new way of communicating their feelings and thoughts from the darkness. This expression of yourself is essential to the experience and to whatever transformation is possible.

Society, too, prefers to sings its blues rather than to state them plainly. The poignant song gets through to us and charms us even as it portrays memories of sadness and loss. Whatever impulse moves us to create or to listen to a mournful song is the same impulse that begs for poetic expression of our dark feelings.

SPIRITUALITY OF THE DEEP

The language of psychology may not say enough about the darkness and therefore may not get you through. With its therapeutic goals, psychology reduces experience too far. Its mission is to re-lieve you of your suffering. It is not philosophically or theologi-cally attuned for helping you find meaning in the dark. And so it isn't sufficient.

Religion, too, often avoids the dark by hiding behind plati-tudes and false assurances. Nothing is more irrelevant than feeble religious piousness in the face of stark, life-threatening darkness. Religion tends to sentimentalize the light and demonize the dark-ness. If you turn to spirituality to find only a positive and whole-some attitude, you are using spirituality to avoid life's dark beauty. Religion easily becomes a defense and avoidance. Of course, this is not the real purpose of religion, and the religious traditions of the world, full of beautifully stated wisdom, are your best source of guidance in the dark. But there is real religion and there is the empty shell of religion. Know the difference. Your life is at stake.

Flight from the dark infantilizes your spirituality, because the dark nights of the soul are supposed to initiate you into spiritual adulthood. You have to be exceptionally alert in the sphere of re-ligion, because, for all its beauty and substance, it can be full of traps. Even those who perpetrate religious nonsense don't seem to be aware of what they are doing, and that makes it only more difficult for the susceptible seeker of spiritual wisdom. You have to use your intelligence every step of the way.

The spiritual life is both deep and transcendent. It shouldn't whisk you away from your daily challenges but should offer you an intelligent way of dealing with all the complexity involved. It should make you a person of character and discernment, emo-tionally tough and intellectually demanding, as well as loving and compassionate. It should give you insight into the deepest of your questions and problems, and give you a vision that extends beyond the everyday issues. Religion often fails to explore the depths and only offers the vision, but then the transcendent pos-sibilities lack depth and in the end hurt more than help.

One of the strongest voices of religion in the face of death, and yet another compassionate and talented person speaking from prison, is Dietrich Bonhoeffer, a theologian and pastor, sentenced for participation in a plot against Hitler. In his last letters from prison, he tries to describe a kind of religiousness that is exactly the opposite of what it once was for him. "The world that has come of age," he writes, "is more godless, and perhaps for that very reason nearer to God, than the world before its coming of age."[10] What he means, I think, is that in the old days religion called on God as a power outside of life to solve our problems. Today, Bonhoeffer says, we have to face our problems directly, and having lost the option of a God coming like the cavalry from the sky, we discover the real meaning of religion, an openness to the mysteries that are playing themselves out. Bonhoeffer wrote this toward the end of a dark night of the soul that was, by all accounts, not at all depressive. He kept his hope alive, but he also turned the very idea of religion upside down. He was another who won the battle morally, but lost it physically. He was hanged, but his letters now inspire a new and "ultimately honest," to use his phrase, way to be religious. He wrote from the heart of his darkness, and there was an inspiring luminosity and energy in his thoughts.

JONAH'S CALLING

Jonah's resistance to the call of God could be seen as resistance to the other will that rises from within. Most of our decisions involve an interior dialogue: Should I take this job or that job, stay home or travel, get married or remain single? Circumstances may solve the question, but often you are torn between two sides of the issue, two voices trying to persuade one way or the other. From ancient times, the inner urge, which can be both guide and tempter, has been called a *daimon*.

The ancient Greeks used the word to describe any unnamed spirit having an impact on someone. Plato spoke of love as a daimon. Later, Jung described it as a spirit with a degree of autonomy, having a strong influence on your interior life. The existential psychiatrist Rollo May wrote frequently about the daimonic, describing it as a strong push, an urge like sex or hunger. He said to keep this daimon from overtaking a personality, it needs dialogue. You need to talk to people about it and maybe even, as Jung did, converse with it. As I see it, the daimon is a strong drive found either within you or sometimes in the world that urges you toward some action. You have to spend time with this daimonic force before you discover how to give it a creative place in your life.

When you feel an urge to take a major turn in your life, that is the daimon waking you up. When you find unexpected strength in your voice or in your work, that is the daimon empowering you. When you want to go in one direction, and something in you pushes strongly in a different direction, that other voice is the daimon. It is an ancient idea, but it also lies at the heart of the work of the Greek mystic Heraclitus, C. G. Jung, W. B. Yeats, Rollo May, and James Hillman. You live with your daimon when you take your innermost passions into account, even when they go against your habits and standards. You need dialogue so that you can work out a livable connection with this challenging but ultimately creative power.

In the best of cases, over time you get to know your deep passions. You come to recognize the voices that speak deep in your imagination. You sort out the devils from the angels, the voices of fear from the voices of hope. You may get to the point where you feel in harmony with yourself because you are in dialogue with these other presences. A psychologist might call them fantasy figures and warn against giving them too much reality. But in spite of the dangers, you can bring them into the equation and consider them carefully.

Anyone may feel an inner urgency that goes against all that is reasonable and intended. It's not unusual to see a person craving something for himself, and at the same time something inside desperately wants just the opposite. In his early years, John Keats wanted badly to become a doctor, but the daimon poet in him won him over. Marilyn Monroe wanted to be a serious actor, but the spirit of sexiness and physical beauty got in the way. Today she is still, for the older generations anyway, a figure of cultural myth, a "goddess" more than an actress.

Heraclitus said that daimon is fate. That spirit in you that often moves strongly against your will may be the force that leads you to your fate. Keats and Monroe may have settled for their own vision of who they could be, but something more powerful inside them gave them a much greater presence in the world. The same is true for all of us: the hopes and plans we have for ourselves may be nothing compared to the possibilities. We have to allow this other self to have room to make us into who we might be.

The daimon also plays a role in relationships. In therapy, sorting though love triangles and difficult partnerships, I thought I saw something much greater at work than relationship. The issue was not, how can these two people be together happily, but what are they fighting? What is their fate, in the largest terms, that they are trying so desperately to avoid? I could see in their marriages the validity of Heraclitus' comment. They were avoiding the daimonic, which was showing itself dramatically in their lives together, and therefore they were saying no to their fate.

Today people often seek the right and healthy way to be in relationship, and they forget about the importance of their individual callings. They try to blend their lives together rather than live shared individual destinies. I knew one young man who spent years trying to be married successfully. In the meantime, he neglected his talents and wasted his life away at jobs far beneath him. He would come to me in times of distress, when yet another marriage was heading for the rocks. Finally, in his mid-fifties, he made the radical decision to finish his education and launch his career. Miraculously to him, his current marriage grew strong and happy. He had a life of his own, and therefore he could be in a shared relationship.

Consciously a person might insist that a certain marriage or partnership take place, but another will, from within the same people and couple, may want otherwise. This struggle against a deep inner urge is responsible for much of the distress and many of the dark nights associated with love and partnership. You think you know what is best and what has to be, but life itself, more mysteriously, works in a different direction. The prolonged struggle, which usually has both interior and external dimensions, becomes a dark night.

A dark night of the soul may involve a long, difficult contest between one will and another will, both of which act within the same person or the same couple. Even when the outer life is settled, and the couple get married or settle down, the battle may continue. You may learn that this incessant argument is not necessarily destructive and in fact gives life to the relationship. And, as Jung says in his essay on marriage, you may learn that you have married your partner's daimon as well as her person, and she has linked her fate with your inner self as well. It all makes marriage and other partnerships fascinating, but not easy.

A VOCATION FOR TRANSCENDENCE

You may be blind to the very thing that will make your life feel worth living. You may be repressing the very source of your deepest satisfaction. You may be gullible, taking in the world's insidious lessons in superficial satisfaction. Therefore, you have to dig deeper. Discover who you are and who you want to be. Don't be dissuaded from that objective by the illusory promises of commercial life. Instead, be yourself.

That is the point of the night sea journey—to be born into yourself. There, you are in the amniotic fluid, in an alchemical substance once again. You are journeying toward your own life.

You are preparing for your fate. The promise is exhilarating, but the dangers are extreme. You have to avoid being just one of the crowd and instead take the chance of being born an individual.

Jonah didn't think he had it in him to realize his destiny. He tried to escape it by boarding a ship headed away from his God-given orders. But this ship took him out to the environs of the whale, which would prove to be the uterus of his becoming. His escape turned into his vehicle of self-realization.

Look deeply into your fears. Take serious note of your defenses. See where and how you elude the demands of your existence. Maybe now you will see the cosmic wisdom in your dark night. You have to change course and rediscover your own direction. You have to surrender to the steaming motion of your self-realization.

Jonah was called by God to speak on his behalf, which is a point of view directly opposite the one explicitly or subliminally presented in all forms of media forced on you today. Your dark night is preparing you to be yourself. It is reenacting your birth as a person. It is offering you an alternative to absorption in your manipulative culture.

Your dark night is forcing you to consider alternatives. It is taking you out of the active life of submission to alien goals and purposes. It is offering you your own approach to life. You can sit with it and consider who you are and who you want to be. You can be fortified by it to stand strong in your very existence. You can be born again, not into an ideology that needs your surrender, but into yourself, your uniqueness, your God-given reality, the life destined for you.

Needless to say, by emphasizing self-realization and individuality, I am not speaking against fellowship and community. A community thrives when it consists of true individuals, accepted for their own contributions and ideas. You are in the belly of the whale to get to Nineveh, to become part of the world, to add your important voice to its song. The people are waiting for you to be offered into society. They need you, and you need them. But you have to be prepared by your dark night, which is both your pain and your deliverance. It is the great obstacle to getting on with life, and yet it is the best means of entry into what fate has in store for you.

CHAPTER TWO

RITES OF PASSAGE

L IFE CONSTANTLY FERRIES US to a new level of maturity. Each of us is like a boat passing through a long series of locks that lift us up or take us down to a new plateau. We go from one phase to another, each change a challenge. Becoming an adult, getting married, going through divorce, getting old, changing jobs or careers, becoming a parent, giving birth—in our own way we all go through passages that leave a lasting mark. These deep-seated shifts shake us up and reframe our world. For that reason, they can be threatening. We may resist the needed change. We may get married without dying to the single life, or become a parent while trying to preserve our old childless way of life. We may fear the dark night that presses, but we will be better off if we go through it.

Today, with a therapeutic mindset, we no longer appreciate initiations and passages. We expect people to deal with change, and if they fail, we provide them with therapy. We lack powerful communal rituals that would offer support and guidance. Our developmental models of a human life account for progress but not major shifts in being. Linear thinking, so much a part of modern life, affects the way we understand our very lives. We evolve and develop, but we don't transform. We imagine growing like a skyscraper under construction, reaching to the sky, not like a caterpillar turning into a butterfly.

People talk about being reborn Christians, but what about being reborn humans? We need to be born again and again further into our humanity, discovering in increasingly sophisticated ways what it means to be a person in a community of persons. Archaic societies understood this point better than we do: Fundamental shifts in perspective are essential and they are best imagined on the model of birth. The metamorphosis of the self never ends, and we need effective means to get through each phase successfully.

When you get married or become a parent, you become a different person. But sometimes the sign of a deep change isn't so obvious. It may be a single transforming event in everyday life. Reflecting back on the moment when he met the woman who would define his life and haunt him for years, W. B. Yeats wrote, "A hansom drove up to our door at Bedford Park with Miss Maud Gonne, and the troubling of my life began."[11] This relationship affected Yeats the whole of his life, bringing him both happiness and frustration. He was a highly perceptive man, and he understood that a single moment, a meeting with a strong and remarkable woman, could shake his soul to its depths.

You must have a similar story of a decisive moment, perhaps, like Yeats, a turning point that made all the difference in your life. I had two life-defining moments in my childhood. One was the day when—I must have been twelve years old—I saw a brochure telling me that I could be a monk and live in the simple, sparse room they showed in a photograph. That little booklet spun me around, and I haven't exited that spin since. The other, more mysterious, was the day I clung to an overturned rowboat in a large Michigan lake, as my grandfather desperately struggled to save me. I don't know exactly how this near-death moment affected me. I think it was preparation, too; a meeting with death and an early invitation to take life seriously.

Some turning points in life may cast a dark shade on your future. When you get seriously sick, your illness is not just physical; it forces you to see yourself and your world in a different way. It, too, is a rite of passage. A serious bout of jealousy can affect the way you deal with people and prepare you to be a good partner, able to deal with the complexity of marriage. A strong mood or an overpowering emotion might raise you up a level, causing a shift in your very nature.

Grieving the loss of a loved one, too, can transform you at your core, for grief is more than an emotion. It can be a painful restructuring that forces you to alter your basic views and values. A loss may cause you to reconsider the whole of your life. You may be inspired by the death of a person you admire, and you may imagine new possibilities for yourself, discovering that the only way out of the pain is to re-imagine your very existence. Your healing may be a direct outgrowth of your suffering.

ANCIENT RITES OF PASSAGE

In the distant past people did things very differently. They made high drama of the passage from one state to another, creating powerful rites that mimicked birth, teaching a person emotionally and symbolically that to change is to be born again as a person. They sacrificed animals, frightened their young initiates with displays of aggression, and used drums and howls and body paint to make the point chillingly that a change in life is serious business.

Powerful communal rituals dramatically helped young people shift from one phase of life to another. A boy or girl might be buried in the ground and made to crawl through a tunnel, walk around blindfolded, or speak in baby talk—all to symbolize the birth into a major new phase. Victor Turner, the anthropologist, tells of a man in a certain tribe who was to become king. In the initiation rites people spat on him, beat him, kicked him, threw disgusting things at him, and cursed him. Turner was shocked, until someone said to him, "He isn't our king yet. For a little longer we can do what we want with him, but soon we'll have to do his will." Frightening, graphic rituals, incisions, and sacrifices left a mark on the young person, and he or she was forever after changed.

Shocking and disturbing rites make emotional sense. You get advice every day, but how much of it sinks in? At key moments, you may have to go through painful, disturbing experiences, just to grow up, to realize who you are and how life works. A car accident, an illness, a divorce—these are not only tragedies, they may also be rites of passage. They can take you, step by step, into your own undiscovered reality, making you a real person. Ancient rituals teach us that our ordinary pains and shocks can stir us into awareness.

MODERN RITES OF PASSAGE

Even today you may have to go through an emotional tunnel on your way toward adulthood or becoming a wise, experienced person. Leaving school, getting married, retiring from a career, you may be scared to death and enter the pits of despair. The key is to understand the importance of such passages and let the initiations happen. You could understand that being disturbed at certain turning points is natural and to be expected. You don't have to fight it; you can open yourself to change. You may experience considerable anxiety and may even have physical symptoms. Going through a divorce, I developed painful blisters on my tongue—symbolic, perhaps, of the difficulty I had in uttering the words of separation. I have seen skin problems, stomach upsets, and other physical symptoms in others going through major life changes. The religion scholar Mircea Eliade says that illness, too, can be seen as an initiation, a painful passage that has the power to remake your personality and your life.

My first real initiation took place when I was a very young thirteen—my follow-through on the pamphlet I had read. I still feel many of the emotions from the time when I left home to enter a Catholic seminary and monastery. In September of 1954, I moved from my hometown of Detroit to go to school in Chicago. I remember well getting out of bed at five in the morning to go to the old train station downtown. Several members of my extended family joined me there to see me off. I never really returned to the family, except for summer and Christmas vacations, and the homesickness I felt during those years was so painful that I'm surprised now that I stuck it out.

Even today the smell of autumn leaves and the chill in the air, so beautiful and calming to many people, gives me nausea. If I were to be in Chicago in the fall, though I love the city, I don't know if I could handle it. The homesickness hasn't gone away completely, after all these years. Now I am more aware of the cost to my family and to my own future life of following my youthful enthusiasm. Of course, it had its rewards, but it also led to a long and sad dark night of the soul that still hasn't ended.

Moving physically, especially separating from your family and friends, is one way to advance on your soul's journey. Yet, it can be a deeply disturbing development. At one level you want change, but at another it's the last thing in the world you would choose. That is how I felt, completely divided between the self that wanted an exciting future and the self that craved the warm comforts of home. Sometimes a dark night begins to brew when you are caught between two incompatible wishes, when some powerful necessity rubs up against your security and comfort.

A PHILOSOPHY OF THE NIGHT

A rite of passage marks a change in the way we sense ourselves and our reality. The transition may last only a day, or it may take a lifetime to play itself out. Some lives are nothing but a dark night of the soul, while others give hardly a hint of distress and disorientation. Fate plays a crucial role in most dark nights, and it pays to have respect for the role of fate and destiny in our lives. We are not entirely in charge. Sometimes it may be our task to cooperate with signs of our destiny, even when we would rather move in a different direction.

A dark night of the soul is dark because it doesn't give us any assurance that what is happening makes sense and will ultimately be beneficial. We can't understand what is happening to us, and if we are in the habit of always wanting to know what is going on, this aspect of the dark night will be maddening. We can find meaning in these times of change, but we have to think differently about our lives, be less psychological in our approach, and more philosophical and spiritual. Bonhoeffer had no assurance that his plotting against Hitler was morally proper and would be received positively by the people for whom he was pastor and theologian. He had to take a risk, but he found confidence in his religious thought, in his theology.

John Keats, the English poet, surely one of the most sensitive and emotionally intelligent persons in history, had just turned twenty-six, when his tuberculosis put him on his deathbed. His physical pain was great, but more difficult for him was the separation from the woman he loved, Fanny Browne. Four months before his death and in one of his last letters, he writes to his friend Charles Brown: "I can bear to die—I cannot bear to leave her. . . . Where can I look for consolation or ease? . . . I fear there is no one can give me any comfort." [12]

Yet in the next letter, his last, he still has his good humor, and he makes a simple but important statement. "You must bring your philosophy to bear—as I do mine, really—or how should I be able to live?" Keats, a young man of remarkable maturity, had developed a philosophy of the soul by which he could live. He could say that beauty is truth and could claim the value of "negative capability," that is, "when a man is capable of being in uncertainties, Mysteries, doubts." This idea of being able to hold uncertainty and doubt has inspired many who have learned from Keats, and in his own life this capacity was tested in him right up to the last moment. Like Bonhoeffer, his worldview and deep reflections gave him peace and assurance.

Keats had nurtured his vision carefully throughout his short life in his poetry, in thoughtful letters to friends and family, and in meaningful conversations to which he often alludes. He was in the ultimate passage, about to die, and yet could speak with grace and optimism. His spirit was rich and strong and radiated through the physical hopelessness.

In a key letter, written to his brother and sister-in-law when he was twenty-three, he said that being intelligent is not enough. Your intelligence has to be converted into a soul. "Do you not see," he wrote, "how necessary a World of Pains and troubles is to school an Intelligence and make it a soul? . . . Call the world if you Please 'The vale of Soul-making.' " This single letter is a major resource for us all as we try to understand the place of suffering in our lives. As so many have said, but perhaps few as insightfully as Keats, suffering is a great teacher.

Keats converted his emotional and physical suffering into a highly intelligent and sensitive soul through his letters and his poems. As an alchemist would say, you need a vessel, a medium in which this important transformation can take place. One difference between depression and a dark night of the soul is that depression is a mood you endure and try to get through, while a dark night is a process in which your coarse soul is refined and your intelligence deepened. How you imagine your ordeal makes all the difference.

Creating a carefully constructed and passionate philosophy

of life is not something modern people do. Today many blindly follow their clergy, their ideologies, their political leaders, and the press. Many get their life guidance from television and rarely have original thoughts about their experiences. Others may have many opinions based on the latest studies but generally have not worked out a deep vision. They are informed, but they haven't thought deeply enough.

DEVELOPING A PHILOSOPHY OF LIFE

Without a philosophy of life, you may be swamped by your emotions and believe that life is meaningless. You see the chaos in and around you, and you assume that it could never make sense. With this attitude it is easy to latch onto simplistic explanations, which are never far away. An entire industry of counselors, preachers, psychologists, coaches, and gurus of all stripes are eager to tell you how to live. But these borrowed and purchased strategies aren't enough when a dark night has really taken hold of you. You need to work out a system for yourself. You have to prepare yourself for challenges that could be far more radical than you expect.

How do you create a supportive and livable philosophy? First, you take your life seriously. You don't have to be morose about it, but you must realize that you can't pass on the responsibility for your life to anyone else. Today, people don't always feel the weight of their existence. They live by superficial values and naïve ideas. Instead of pursuing deep and solid pleasures, they lose themselves in light entertainments, legal and illegal drugs, and general unconsciousness. The only time they feel any emotional weight is when they are depressed, but then it is only symptomatic and painful. Depression may stand in for real sadness and despair. Depression is a strong emotion, but a dark night is a slow transformation fueled by the deep issues at work defining the very meaning of your life.

Sometimes what matters to one person may seem superficial to someone else. The Mexican painter Frida Kahlo lay in her hospital bed after an accident that tore her body apart and wrote to a friend, "I sincerely want to die, because I can't stand it anymore. It's not only the physical suffering, but also that I don't have the least entertainment. I never leave this room, I can't do anything, I can't walk."[13] It's difficult to know what gives a person the will to live. It might be toys for a child in poverty or entertainment for a vivacious woman in a hospital bed. What appears to be trivial and insignificant may make a person feel that life is worth living.

Unconsciousness is like junk food. It's an easy way to go through life, but it doesn't give you the nourishment you need. You don't have to bother with sorting things out or with thinking at all. In small portions it is worth pursuing for relaxation, but as a way of life it can lead to extreme passivity. It may seem painful to think and reflect, but bringing your own intelligence to bear on everyday experiences can add an essential dimension that gives its own kind of pleasure.

A philosophy of life begins to take shape when you educate your heart and cultivate your life. You read, you talk, and you think; you don't just act. You consider your experience and take lessons from it. You may need to write these lessons down in a journal and talk about them with friends. Deep conversation is a valuable way of cultivating an intelligence about life. Many people in the past used letters, written thoughtfully and honestly, as a way of self-education. In these people their philosophy of life came into being through the process Keats called "soul-making," an alchemy that transforms raw experience into an ever-deepening personality and a rich way of living.

Henry David Thoreau lived in a tiny cabin at Walden Pond outside Boston for over two years to practice a life of reflection, to help him move more consciously into his life. For him it was clearly a way to make an important shift, a concrete rite of passage. About this experience he wrote, "I went to the woods because I wished to live deliberately, to front only the essential facts of life, and see if I could not learn what it had to teach, and not, when I came to die, discover that I had not lived." You can prepare for your dark nights in the same way, by finding your own style of retreat and reflection, developing a vision that supports and inspires you. Everyone needs a "Walden Pond" of his own, a real or metaphorical place where you can take stock of your life and find a sense of purpose and values by which you can live.

A philosophy of life is a bundle of wisdom you have gathered from your reading and experience. It is not a rigid ideology that allows no development and complexity. It's a living thing, a developing idea about life that belongs to you alone. You may want to share your insights and may even wish that the rest of the world would adopt some of your principles. But essentially it is your special source of comfort and understanding. It allows you to be yourself, to judge yourself with reference to an absolute and not against the opinions of other human beings.

Your philosophy of life may be highly influenced by your time and place; on the other hand, in some ways it may go against conventional wisdom. It may include ideas about how the world came to be, what life is all about, how to treat people, how to make life meaningful to you, and how to contribute to the welfare of humanity. It may incorporate ideas about death and afterlife. You build this philosophy from study and experience. Again, contemporary America values opinion over reflection. It always wants to know who is right, and not who has the most interesting and suggestive ideas. Who goes to school today for a real education, to become a thinking, cultured person? The tendency is to be trained for a successful career, and it is almost impossible to educate a person within the context of training.

A philosophy of life elevates and airs out what might otherwise be an emotional swamp. Feelings are wet and damp, inundating us and preventing us from thinking clearly. Ideas are drier and allow a vision to emerge from a sea of feelings. The Greek philosopher Heraclitus said that a dry soul is a wise and wonderful soul that steps back from the torrent of events to glimpse the eternal realities. A philosophy of life sublimates our thoughts and prepares us to deal with challenges before they appear.

The work of psychotherapy, too, aerates a soggy soul. You consider your overwhelming emotions and sort them through until an idea appears. This idea may not be a solution to your problems, but it may mark a first step in drying out. I have seen people in therapy swamped in love, drowning in passion, and deluged with feelings. Simply talking about the emotions offers relief and begins a process that leads to a less compulsive lifestyle.

Over the years, I have noticed that people who come to therapy have either rigid opinions that they picked up in religion or family, or they seem completely at sea. The alternative is to develop complex and flexible ideas. For all the talk of mind and body in contemporary medicine, there is little emphasis on the mind as a home to ideas and consideration. Dark nights ask for intelligence and deep thought on our part, not just emotion.

BIRTH AND REBIRTH

Physically, we are born once, but the soul is involved in an eternal, continuous birth. From a purely human point of view, baptism, naming days, and other infancy rituals symbolize the ongoing birth of the person. In school, a child goes through many initiations, some of them marked by ceremony. In the Waldorf school my children attend, each school year begins with a Rose Ceremony. The eighth-graders individually present the new first-graders with the flower, symbolically showing the tie between the end and the beginning of the process. The rite is simple but powerful, and parents make every effort to be present for it.

Weddings, funerals, anniversary and birthday parties, and special dinners help the individual and the family make the changes in life that affect them all. The spiritual life is not abstract. It thrives on ritual, art, good words, and symbolic acts. These concrete actions bring the transition home physically, emotionally, and intellectually. In this way, you know you have gone through a change, and you can adjust accordingly.

These rites encourage a kind of birthing. To be born in soul again and again is a positive experience, but it also involves pain. It means entering a new kind of life just when the old one might have grown comfortable. Familiarity can bring you tranquillity, but you also need the sting and chaos of the new. To be alive entails both of these qualities, the yin and yang of peace and pain.

In Freud's groundbreaking book *The Interpretation of Dreams*, he presents a beautiful little dream told by a woman patient: "At her summer holiday resort, by Lake ____, she dived into the dark water just where the pale moon was mirrored in it."[14] Freud contorts this Zen-like dream to fit his theory, but I would accent the need sometimes to go into the water in order to be born again, a baptism of immersion into the lunar light. Freud concludes that the dream is about the patient's wish to keep going to therapy, but surely such a powerful dream has to do with a profound change in her soul, perhaps the discovery of a deeper wisdom. She isn't being born, but she is returning to the source from which she may be reborn.

Life is a continuous cycle of births. Imagine yourself as made up of three parts. One part arrives at birth and never changes, the eternal self. At that level, you are eternal, and throughout your life you recognize that unchanging self in the midst of developments, a quintessential star ever shining in the deep interior of the soul. A second level is so completely defined by events and environment that it changes all the time. This is the self that tries to survive and thrive in the everyday world, the practical self. Yet a third level is the caterpillar-and-butterfly part, the unfolding self. This self is always becoming, always evolving, unless it is blocked, and goes through deep transformations. It is the go-between that links the eternal with the everyday. Ancient societies focused their attention on the unfolding self, while we favor the practical self. At every moment, we are a star, an agent, and an emerging butterfly.

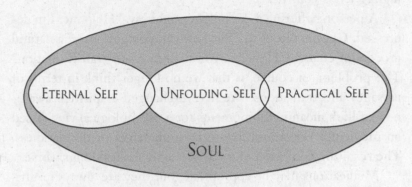

To keep the unfolding self alive, you have to open yourself to change, every step of the way. Of course, there are times when it is appropriate to step back, settle down, and maybe not move for a while. But to be a person means to be faced every minute with the decision to live or to die, to accept the invitations for yet more vitality or to decline them out of fear or lethargy. Dark nights of the soul seem to seek out this unfolding self and create a mood in which the necessary developments can take place. You may not go through the deep initiations when you're busy or carefree.

THE DARK NIGHT AS RITE OF PASSAGE

A life passage, such as the birth of a child, getting married, the loss of a spouse, or illness, might be the occasion for a dark night, but dark nights may also serve as rites of passage. Not every transition in life has a ceremony or occasion connected to it. You may be the victim of a powerful mood. For instance, you may feel like a failure, and wonder if you are ever going to accomplish anything. Friends may try to talk you out of this slump, telling you how much you have done and how great your potential is. But the mood itself could bring you to a decision, a turning point where you suddenly begin giving your life meaning. The dark night itself is your passage.

A person suffering a dark night might say, "Help me. I'm depressed. Get me out of it." But how can you get out of a natural process of change? How can you medicate self-transformation? The problem, of course, is that we no longer think in terms of passages and transitions. We have exchanged a spiritual awareness of life's meaningful moments for a psychological view based on medicine. We would like to cure ourselves of the darkness. The resulting confusion of categories only makes things worse.

Medications may be appropriate, but they are always insufficient. Medicine plays an important role in all suffering, emotional and physical. The problem is that medicine itself has become materialistic and only recently has been searching for ways to include a spiritual dimension. It treats the body as only physical and neglects the full range of connection between meaning, emotion, and our physical state. Until medicine and professional psychology abandon the now outmoded secular philosophy altogether and recover an appreciation for the absolute depth of human life, they will not be useful for our dark nights.

The religion scholar Mircea Eliade notes in his journals that "today the sacred is camouflaged in the secular." Ancient, traditional themes appear in the most ordinary circumstances, and all it takes is an eye for the sacred to see them. The clearest place where this is true is in sports. There you witness a dramatic battle between self and other, and home and visitors. Sports bring out the basic themes in any human life: facing difficult odds; struggling, advancing and retreating; winning and losing. A ball game takes place within certain bounds and according to strict rules, which keep the game separate from real life. These rules are like the rubrics or instructions for ritual: They allow a certain kind of athletic theater to take place, where both players and spectators experience in imagination the tensions they feel more meaningfully in everyday life. The spiritual element in sports appears in language such as "miracle plays," "super bowls" and superstars—"super" is a word for transcendence—and in the pageantry and rituals of various games. In professional American football, the Super Bowl is for some a powerful rite of civil religion, a compelling ritual process for a large segment of the culture.

In your dark night, you could see issues that go beyond the sphere of psychology: matters of meaning, rites of passage, mortality, and values. Psychology doesn't explore these concerns except in a distant, analytical way. You need a spiritual point of view to appreciate them and deal with them. You may not be drawn to an organized religion, but you probably need a spiritual point of view to keep these issues in mind.

During a dark night you may feel the need to be quiet, even silent. You may find talking difficult, and you may seek out a quiet place. I remember one man who would go to bed for a week or two and not leave his house during particularly intense periods. Similarly, you may not feel like eating, and so fasting becomes a natural part of your passage. In a religious setting, you would fast according to traditional rules. Without the support of religion, you may think of your loss of appetite as physical, maybe even a need to seek medical attention, and your silence simply as a strategy. But these are spiritual techniques that have been used for centuries.

You may feel the need to be alone, or at least to avoid certain kinds of socializing. You may disappear for a while, and your friends wonder what has become of you. You may need a room of your own or a solitary place to seek out. This may be a simple form of retreat, another traditional way of marking a rite of passage, and it may help you with your dark night. Without knowing it, you may have become a monk of sorts in your own way. I know several men who go on retreat in monasteries, but I know another who simply disappears. No one knows where he goes, but he always comes back refreshed.

Ritualizing the natural impulses of the dark night is a way of responding to the situation spiritually and in tune with your feeling. Ritual, like art, brings imagination to the scene, which allows both participation in the event and the distance of reflection. Locking a door can be a ritual act in service of your privacy, which you may discover is necessary for the care of your dark night. You may need a quiet dinner with a friend or a walk alone near water. You may benefit from watching an old familiar movie or reading a favorite poem aloud. You may pay a visit to a family member or go to a place in nature that reflects your mood—the desert, the woods, a cave.

THE PHASES OF PASSAGE

Arnold Van Gennep, an early expert on ritual, said that every rite of passage has three phases: separation, liminality, and reincorporation. You don't have to be rigid in accepting a formula like this, but it may help you understand what is going on when you feel the darkness of transition. The pattern is similar to the one Joseph Campbell ascribed to the hero's journey: departure, initiation, and return.

Separation

When going through a dark night, at first, you may feel cut off and alone. Clients in therapy often say they feel isolated and have no one to talk to. They may come to therapy specifically to deal with their isolation. They may wish for deep human connection, but instead they find a different and more effective kind of solitude. Therapy, too, is cut off from life, but it mirrors the necessary isolation of a rite of passage.

The separation you experience in a dark night is not simple.

You may be lying in a hospital with a sick person in the next bed, nurses and orderlies visiting you all day long, family and friends stopping by to say hello, and voices and buzzers sounding around you. Still, your illness may make you feel cut off from the human family. Anatole Broyard, a writer and a very articulate patient, spoke of these feelings.

"I see no reason or need for my doctor to love me—nor would I expect him to suffer with me. I wouldn't demand a lot of my doctor's time: I just wish he would *brood* on my situation for perhaps five minutes, that he would give me his whole mind just once, be *bonded* with me for a brief space, survey my soul as well as my flesh, to get at my illness, for each man is ill in his own way."

Broyard wants a real connection, and his plea is an important one in the cool, often remote world of medicine. But, though friendship and visits are important, there is a place where the solitude cannot be penetrated. Being ill in your own way is to be alone in your own space. I'm not sure that any doctor could completely take away the sense of isolation brought on by the sickness. The same is true of other forms of dark night.

Liminality

Your dark night may make your familiar world inaccessible, but it also puts you in touch with an unfamiliar realm, perhaps a new kind of existence altogether, and it may make you feel you are living in-between two places, the known and the unknown. This condition is often called "liminal," meaning "on a threshold," not quite in and not quite out. Religions focus on liminal conditions as being especially valuable for spiritual experience. When you are distracted from the "busyness" of your life, you may be open to other kinds of influence. You can meditate, pray, and entertain some intuitions.

The anthropologist Victor Turner gave special importance to the middle phase of liminality. He said, "It is like death; like being in the womb; like invisibility, darkness, bisexuality, the wilderness, and an eclipse of the sun or moon." Any of these qualities may make your dark night seem unusual, even uncanny. Your external life may or may not have changed, but suddenly you find yourself in a twilight zone. Turner describes how, in traditional societies, where rites of passage are carried out in graphic form, the initiate may be naked or dressed in simple, skimpy clothes. Eliade describes old rites in which the initiates return to their village acting like infants, not able to feed, wash, or dress themselves, naked, and forgetful.

These ancient religious rituals have echoes in common experiences of passage today. People in transition often disregard their appearance. They may let their hair go and not wash or shower. The elderly in hospitals often experience dementia, a profound forgetting that makes them dependent on the staff for their most basic needs. It's as though their attention to this life has gone into eclipse, as they get to know another dimension. Their loss of function is, of course, due to physical degeneration of the brain, but still, their families now relate to a person in profound transition, and it might help those families to understand dementia as a form of passage.

You may have to allow this kind of transition in yourself and in others. It's all right to disregard certain activities, like bathing and dressing well. When you're going through a significant change of life, your good habits may fall apart. You may do things that distance you from your family and community. The insanity of a dark night makes some people less civil and controlled than they were in the healthier days, and yet, at the same time, in spite of all the limitations of this dementia, they may be more present, less defended, and communicative in other ways.

The writer Annie Dillard says that in the creation of a particular book, "I let all the houseplants die. After the book was finished I noticed them; the plants hung completely black dead in their pots in the bay window."[15] Writing a book, or doing anything creative for that matter, can be a kind of dark night. Many people say that at these moments they feel compelled to keep up their ordinary rituals of walks, solitude, and coffee, just to maintain a sense of normalcy. But they may also neglect their chores and duties. When you are in a liminal place, you may forget your usual environment and habits.

The disorder typical in a rite of passage may be determined from outside. Brian Keenan graphically tells of the mayhem of being a hostage in Beirut. His hair and beard grew wild, and he often went without clothes. He describes having to defecate and urinate in the room in which he slept. His reflections tell of his liminal state, the loss of his familiar world: "My thoughts were frequently occupied by the loss of my humanity. What had I become? What had I descended to as I sat here in my corner? I walked the floor day after day, losing all sense of the man I had been, in half-trances recognizing nothing of myself. Was I a kind of Kafkaesque character transformed out of human form into some animal, something to be shunned and locked away from the world?"[16]

Keenan's language echoes that of anthropologists describing tribal rites of passage. As we go through this particular kind of dark night, we might descend in different ways toward our animal natures, as though we were returning to origins. Keenan says that he and his prison mates didn't speak of their sexual lives with their partners, but they did use foul language in the extreme. To avoid self-pity and defeat, he says, they relied on anger and rough humor.

A dark night may take you away from the cultivation and persona you have developed in your education and from family learning. You may slip back into a degree of wildness that allows you to start over, perhaps at a new level. Teenagers sometimes make a lifestyle out of personal disregard. They are going through one of the most prolonged and serious rites of passage they may ever experience. It may not feel like a dark night of the soul to them, but their families see it for what it is. Here, too, we have to allow considerable latitude as the boy or girl leaves childhood behind and takes a while to achieve adulthood.

This applies to all transitions to adulthood, which can take place at any age. Becoming an adult may not happen on schedule. Many of us take a lifetime to grow up. I spent my teen years in a monastery school and didn't experience the major transition of adolescence until I was nearly forty. I knew little about money, sex, relationships, politics, and work in my early years, but finally at the end of a too innocent and too unrealized marriage, I began to learn the serious lessons in life. You can't make hard rules about what will or should happen to anyone else.

Re-incorporation

Coming back into normal life after a dark night may not be as easy as you expect. You will have changed. People will wonder about you. Old relationships will have to be renewed, and you will have to invent new habits and ways. People are basically conservative and don't like their friends to change. When you go through a rite of passage, your friends and family need to adjust, too.

You can stand firm in your newly found reality, but you can also offer assurances and make it easier on the people around you. Modern counseling psychology sometimes stresses the need to assert yourself in the face of misunderstanding, but there is also a place for graciousness and manners. This is especially true in marriage, where the slightest changes in personality can be threatening to a partner. You don't have to be defensive about your fledgling new self but can gradually introduce your partner to the new life you are discovering.

People don't often realize how effective a few straight-forward, honest words can be. If you have gone through a long ordeal and have changed because of it, you can tell those who are close to you exactly that: "I've gone through something powerful. I feel different somehow. I may appear like a stranger to you. I don't want to distance you, but I don't feel quite myself, or my old self, anyway." These simple words might be more powerful than excuses, avoidances, and halfhearted explanations.

Some people wait for their families and communities to receive them, when they might be better off taking the initiative themselves. If you are seeking re-incorporation, you may have to take the lead and help those whose acceptance you desire. In any circumstances, waiting for someone else to do the neighborly deed is a manipulation, a way of buttressing your ego. You may have to take a risk in presenting yourself so clearly to others, but it is worth the risk to take the initiative instead of expecting them to be understanding and accepting.

The return to the marriage, the family, or the community is an important step in the process of transformation. You are not complete until your relationships have been cared for. Your dark night is important not only for yourself but for those around you. You may not realize it, but they have been enduring your dark night, too. They need at least a small rite of return, some signal that night has ended and new life can get under way.

RITUALS FOR OUR TIME

We have our own versions of what in primitive societies would be graphic, embodied rites of passage. In an old society, you might be blindfolded, to symbolize your role as an infant just coming into the world. In a society that has forgotten the power of symbols, you simply act like a child and don't see what's going on. In an older society you might be exiled from the community for a period of time and allowed to wander in the wilderness. In our society you may find yourself in a boarding school, away from home, where rites of initiation can be powerful and painful. Some therapy programs send city kids into the country, believing that the relative wilderness there can help the young person grow up and mature.

Many people today are asking how they might restore old

ways or create new rituals. It's a difficult problem because the powerful imagery in ancient rituals reaches deep into the collective, communal imagination. You can't just invent spiritual images from the top of your individual head. But there are things you can do to bring more of a ritual life to your dark nights.

You can join a spiritual or religious community where the rites are practiced with care and knowledge. You can also borrow rites from traditions you will never know thoroughly. You can study rituals from around the world and adapt them to your life. You can use your imagination to create simple rituals that address your situation. Or, you can do all of these things at the same time. The most important thing is to become more acquainted with the realm of art, religion, and dream, where images are not merely cerebral but are rooted in the human imagination and in deep-seated emotions.

Admittedly, there is something not quite "true" about borrowing or restoring old rituals in the modern context. They often seem sentimental, superficial, and not quite serious enough. But if you can't borrow old and foreign rituals and can't make up new ones, what can you do? One possibility is to internalize the rites or experience them less visibly, less literally. For example, I grew up as an altar boy, smelling the beeswax of the official candles used at Mass. Today, I light a candle on my desk as I write, and as often as possible I use pure beeswax. A scented paraffin candle simply doesn't work. I need a small vestige of my past religious practice, reminding me constantly of my devotion and tradition.

My book *Meditations*, on how to live the monk's life in our daily, secular existence, is full of ideas for translating traditional practices into ordinary gestures of a sacred existence. For instance, I mention that sweatshirts that have a hood on them hearken back to the monastic cowl, or special part of the monk's robe that shrouded his head in an act of reverence. Thick wood doors and bells and wide belts—all are reminiscent of the monastic style. If, like me, you enjoy the persona of the monk, you could wear these sweatshirts and belts, not make a big deal of them, and secretly transform yourself.

If you choose not to become involved in ritual, some form of compulsive, repeated behavior will probably enter your life anyway. Drinking, gambling, philandering, drugs—they are all full of rituals that you may feel compelled to perform, but they don't have the effect of transforming you. You may go to a particular bar on a regular schedule and have drinks that are symbolic—beer for the common person, single-malt scotch for the sophisticate. Having an affair, you may find yourself slipping into patterns of secrecy: using a false name, lying about your whereabouts, buying unusual gifts. Gambling is a highly defined ritual where the games, the winning, and the losing are all symbolic and perhaps displaced ways of feeling alive and having substance.

Ritualism, the fall into unconscious and often compulsive rituals, is a symptomatic form and usually does more harm than good. It's interesting how people who lose touch with their souls become ritualistic in ways that are destructive. When you find yourself engaged in empty rituals—repeated patterns centered on certain objects and substances, such as alcohol or money—look for ways to restore solid, spiritual rituals to your life. Find a church where the ritual really raises your mind and heart. Go regularly into nature. You will be reminded what is important and essential. If you are living a disordered life, begin to take special care with food, dress, and your home. The spirituality of everyday life is at least as important as what goes on in church or temple.

Any act becomes a ritual when it is done for the imagination and the emotions rather than merely for effect in the physical world. You can garden because you need vegetables or because you need to be connected to your roots in nature. To direct your actions toward the soul, you may add some touches of ritual. In the monastery, we used to walk in procession through the fields and bless the crops. At the biodynamic farm next door to us, one day each year the local community walks the fields and sings to the cows. You could place a simple piece of sculpture—we have a simple stone Buddha—somewhere, or use a particularly fine tool.

A common way to mark passages is to make music out of time and do things on a rhythm. Going to the same spot on a lake every July may give your action an added layer of meaning. Another way is to bring some art to the deed. Simply dressing up for a dinner can make it special, speaking to the emotions as well as the stomach. I write in a room that has arching wooden beams, reminding me of my days in a monastery. The symbolic dimension draws out certain qualities in my personality and memory as I work.

The spiritual and religious traditions teach that rituals are acts done on a certain schedule, are often set apart from ordinary activity, and have a strong symbolic component. They are often designed for key turning points in a person's life or in the experience of a community, times, that is, that are naturally liminal.

Your dark night may be a rite of passage. It may be offering an opportunity to make a significant turn in your life. It isn't easy to make these turns, largely because they demand that you enter the unknown. You may have to dig deep into your resources— your past experiences, your learning, the personal qualities you've already developed—so the dark night takes you deep.

LIFE IN A JAR

Your dark night is liminal, an in-between place, and that explains in part why it is so uncomfortable. It is neither here nor there. It seems to take you out of life rather than further into it. It becomes difficult to find words for your experience, and you may hesitate to describe it to friends because people usually want good news. They don't know what to do with a person in the dark.

As Jung might say, you are in a vessel and difficult to contact. A classic alchemical illustration from the seventeenth century shows a "retort," a tall-necked vase, completely black and labeled "putrefaction." This is the alchemical night associated with a process known as *nigredo* or "the darkening." You don't know what's going on. Nobody around knows what is happening to you. But something is taking place, some deep process dissolving you and remaking you into something new.

In Samuel Beckett's mesmerizing theater piece called *Play*, three people sit in large jars discussing their bitter love triangle. They speak only when a light shines on them, and they talk fast. There are moments when we are all like that—stuck in a jar, trying to figure things out. The dark night itself is a kind of vessel that allows our putrefaction, the breaking apart of a life that once made sense but needed reviving.

If the dark night is indeed a rite of passage, your job is to let the transformation take place. Be sculpted, renewed, changed. You are the caterpillar becoming a butterfly. Your task is to let the change happen. Do what you can to participate in and cautiously and artfully further the process. Discover the very point of personhood: the process of constant renewal.

You may imagine your life as a continuous line from birth to death. You may think of yourself as either growing or being stagnant. Another way, the traditional rite of passage approach, is to see life as a series of transformations, in which you become a person with new capacities and talents. Each of these steps might have its own dark night. To be a person means that you are always becoming, and a dark night of the soul is one sign that you are alive.

CHAPTER THREE

SORTING OUT AND
STARTING OVER

A s YOU GET OLDER and have many new experiences, life gets complicated. Challenges, failures, and entanglements multiply. Since experience hasn't kept up with your ideals, you may begin to doubt your wisdom and abilities. A dark night may help clear out your mind and heart and allow you to start over. As we have seen, John of the Cross, the master of dark nights, saw them primarily as a process of purification. But you have to cooperate with the feelings and find concrete ways to thin out your life.

As life goes on, you may become more thoughtful and less preoccupied with yourself. You acquire a broader, deeper vision, and your heart is capable of opening beyond self-interest and toward the needs of people around you. As many religions teach, the self is a big obstacle to the spiritual life. To diminish the self, you sort out the important from the trivial and focus your energy. As you focus and reflect, experiences change you. You become more refined, more thoughtful and sensitive. You see through the many events of your life to their meaning and significance, and your conversation accordingly becomes more substantive and sharp.

I have a friend who taught me important lessons in this personal purification. She is a nun of considerable standing in her order and was a high school principal when I met her. We could play and clown together, but our conversations were always acute, substantive, and to the point. She could go from fun to deadly serious in a flash, and she would tolerate no fudging or self-indulgence. At school meetings, she would always have her ornate Spanish dagger, which she normally used as a letter-opener, and during dull and disappointing moments she would catch my eye and dramatically "stab" herself with the dagger. When I left that school, she made me a gift of the dagger, which to this day rests on my desk, a reminder always to "cut the crap" and live with an edge.

It helps to clear out the theories and dogmas you picked up from your family, school, and religious upbringing. To be an independent and mature adult, you may have to dump all kinds of things that get in the way. Then your thoughts and judgments become leaner and clearer. You realize that much of what has preoccupied you is not essential. You can live happily and sensuously in this rich and promising world without being caught up in many of its dehumanizing values and empty distractions.

The writer Lee Stringer tells the passionate story of his life on the streets of New York, where he was hooked on alcohol, cocaine, and crack. He had gone through a highly disillusioning failure with an import company and took to living on the streets. Eventually he discovered that he could write. He began writing for a newspaper for street people and soon became its editor. Then he went on to write bestselling books. Reflecting on his experience, he says that he could have gotten back on his feet through professional help, but he believes in learning through "hard knocks."

His conclusion could well be a summary of this book. "It has occurred to me since that perhaps what we call depression isn't really a disorder at all but, like physical pain, an alarm of sorts, alerting us that something is undoubtedly wrong; that perhaps it is time to stop, take a time-out, take as long as it takes, and attend to the unaddressed business of filling our souls."[17] Here is a key idea: stop thinking of your dark nights as problems and begin to see them as opportunities for change.

A dark night of the soul often forces us to start thinking. Our greatest strength as human beings is the capacity to think things through, but emotional preoccupations can get in the way. Narcissism is one of the most common: to be so worried about image or identity that we can't entertain fresh ideas, or to be so insecure that we stick close to our tightly held opinions and biases. Ask people about some important contemporary issue, and what you often hear is more emotion than thought. Spiritual people in particular have a tendency to speak their beliefs without thinking them through, clinging to them with strong feelings but little thought.

As you purify your attention and focus more clearly on the things that matter, you are more open to events and feel more alive. The first part of life is naturally more directed at the self, at becoming somebody and emerging from the collective as a creative individual, but eventually that focus may diminish, giving way to a concern for the world around you and a deeper understanding of what life is all about. Narcissism is a concern for self that stands in the way of experience. As your heart expands, you learn to love a world that needs your affection and service, and, paradoxically, your sense of self intensifies.

Addictions of all kinds signal that life is stuck and blocked. If you find yourself in a troubled marriage or struggling in other kinds of relationships, or feel driven to succeed socially or financially, you may need a cleaning out. You could imagine all these problems as being merely psychological, in need of good therapy, or, like John of the Cross, you could understand that they are symptoms of spiritual constipation. It might help to concentrate on developing a vision and strong sense of values rather than on the usual psychological issues of emotion and relationship.

A spiritual existence requires constant cleansing, because the spirit by nature is less involved in day-to-day issues and more focused on the core, the universal, and the eternal. The soul should be stuffed with issues and relationships and even problems, but it needs a degree of regular thinning, a process that can be the fruit of a dark night. To do this important work, we need the wisdom of a good spiritual guide who can keep attention to the spirit without ignoring the deeper soul.

THE PROCESS OF CATHARSIS

You may think of catharsis in the popular sense as a purging of the emotions. A primal scream or voicing your anger may offer some relief from pent-up feelings. But catharsis also means having sharper ideas, clearer feelings, and a more defined sense of purpose. It clarifies and winnows, and in that way is well suited to the work of a dark night, which by its nature is an emptying process. John of the Cross speaks of the dark night as "empty and unburdened," a good alternative to what he calls a "crowded soul."

Spirituality and clarity go together. Spiritual practices aim at expanding the mind and the heart, and most spiritual teachers recommend some form of contemplation as the core of the practice. It may be yoga, sitting, insight, or a method more tangible and sensuous, such as music, painting, flower arranging, or dance. You can learn a great deal about contemplation from one of the ancient systems of meditation, but you can also be contemplative in ordinary ways adapted to your personal lifestyle.

My favorite kinds of contemplation include playing the piano, walking in a forest, sitting quietly in a church or house of worship, and even window-shopping. I understand that the highest forms of meditation are pure and still and aim at an awareness free of distraction. But I also value the spirituality to be found in the concrete, everyday world. Walking through a store, my attention is caught by beautiful things, and I can easily fall into deep reverie just looking at them. I find this a good way to be spiritual without criticizing ordinary life or the physical world. I favor an incarnational theology and spirituality, one that is profoundly rooted in experience.

The general aim of catharsis is creative tranquillity, a condition in which you are free from pressing practical concerns to consider the bigger questions. The actual practice of contemplation may vary from one person to another, but some physical quieting helps start the process. Nature can help by providing an environment that stills a hyperactive mind. Many people find that a walk in a forest or a quiet moment by a river cleans them out and prepares them to face the world with a fresh attitude.

When Oscar Wilde was released from prison, his first act was to meet up with two close friends at a seaside village. He quoted Euripides, "The sea washes away the stains and wounds of the world (*Iphigenia in Tauris*)." An ordinary person, materialistic and unconscious, might vacation by the sea for sheer comfort and luxury, while a more spiritual person might understand that being near water can cleanse your heart and mind. There is nothing wrong with comfort and luxury, but the spiritual dimension completes the picture and satisfies even more deeply.

Architecture, too, can make a big difference, and so it makes sense to step into a church or house of worship, or to find a room or space that effectively calms you. When I lived in Ireland with my family, every afternoon I walked to the school, about a mile away, to meet my young daughter. The walk was calming, but frequently I arrived early and spent fifteen minutes in the church connected to her school, where I sat or knelt and let the peacefulness permeate me. Looking back on that school year, I realize how precious those moments were and how they helped me sort myself out.

Even such a simple practice, requiring almost no effort beyond remembering to do it, felt like the groundwork for a cleansing of my life and soul. Rather than face problems directly and psychologically, I was trying to nurture my spirituality in a simple and ordinary way, one that was directly connected to a simple everyday chore. Over the course of a school year, those fifteen minutes amounted to a considerable amount of time given to contemplation.

Other spiritual practices may also clear out a crowded life. Religions teach fasting, retreat, vegetarianism, a spirit of poverty, neatness, cleanliness, moderation, and solitude—these familiar practices can be part of the busiest person's life and give that life a spiritual dimension. In this sense, making your bed every morning can be a spiritual practice. This natural spirituality I am describing deepens the place from which you live and allows you to open your heart both to receive more from life and to give to others.

I learned strict meditation practices early in my life, and now I prefer the "incarnational" methods. But I find that I still have skills, if that is what you should call them, from my early days. If someone tells me now to close my eyes and focus my attention, in a matter of seconds I feel deeply absorbed and relatively free of distracting thoughts. I find so much pleasure in that "disappearance" that usually I don't want to return to ordinary awareness. So, even though I advocate a contemplative way of life in the world, I can fully appreciate methods that teach you how to evoke deep ecstasies and interior journeys.

A soulful life is full of rewarding complexity, and that is as it should be, but the soul also benefits from a sorting through of all the many experiences. Both the openness to experience and the clarifying of that experience will serve you. You can become both too burdened with experience and too clear in your values and concepts. The ideal is to be both engaged in an active life and withdrawn in contemplation. One approach serves the other.

CLEAN UP YOUR LIFE

The general goal is to link soul and spirit, the vitality of everyday life with the interiority that comes from contemplation. Notice how my story links a walk to pick up a child with a visit to a church. Spirit and soul work best when one is connected to the other. This doesn't mean that exceptional spiritual activities, like yoga, pilgrimage, and sustained prayer, don't have a place, but they need grounding in ordinary life so that they don't become too precious and self-serving.

Opportunities for various kinds of spiritual retreat pop up in every sphere of life. The loss of a job could prod you to sort out your life. If you are feeling lost and worried, instead of simply doing nothing in the time suddenly at your disposal, you could reflect on your past work, your sense of calling or the lack of it, and other people's experience of work and loss. You could transform plain joblessness into spiritual retreat. You could get more serious about your vocation and, instead of just job-hunting, you could ask yourself what gives you a sense of purpose. You could go further into the darkness, rather than looking for ways to avoid your anxiety.

Aristotle described catharsis in the context of the theater. Today he might talk about going to a movie. You get absorbed in a fictional story, and vicariously you work out your own emotions and ideas. You think about the story in relation to yourself. Discussing the film, you sort out your own world. Maybe you relate it to your experience or tell your own related story. Commenting on Aristotle, the philosopher Richard Kearney sums up catharsis as a matter of "acknowledging painful truths."[18] This is a simple idea, but it gets to the heart of what it takes to clear out the soul.

DEWORLDED

Kearney also says that catharsis "stops us in our tracks, throws us off kilter, deworlds us."[19] To a person intent on getting somewhere, these are not appealing developments, but to the human soul it is important to get out of the busy life, to be dissuaded from familiar activities, and to step outside the paradigm that has become habitual and taken for granted. To be "deworlded" means to have a rare opportunity to consider a different way of life. You can't renew life without stepping out of the pattern that is in place.

If you can appreciate this aspect of the dark night, its power to cleanse your life, your personality, and your world, then you might be less inclined to get over it quickly. You might be able to enter it with your imagination at work, knowing that the point is to clear away much of the debris that has shielded you from important realizations. The next step might be to express yourself with your new clarity, being more straightforward and honest.

During my mother's sickness, which coincided with the writing of this book, I felt a new kind of communication within my family. Every word mattered. We discussed our feelings and thoughts with unusual clarity. At times, I could hardly believe we were the same people. My father characteristically asked tough questions and tried to keep us all alert and prepared. My brother spoke for the internal life of the family and kept us emotionally clear. The rest of the family expressed their love and support directly and concretely. We had been deworlded by events and were compelled to draw on all our resources to unite as a family and care for each other.

The rinsing of conversation and language—no indirection or hesitation—was a form of catharsis. A woman we all loved was disappearing before our eyes, and that emptiness invited us to join together in a new way. Our anxiety and sadness made a community of the family. Consider how many times each day you indirectly and obscurely avoid the full impact of the situation in which you find yourself. Now, imagine what ordinary life would be like if we all related to each other at home and at work so directly and cleanly. Imagine what the world would be like if leaders spoke to each other and to us with absolute candor.

Death, of course, is a major clarifier. When my mother died, my father asked me to go through her things. I didn't enjoy intruding into her private world, revealed in the clothes and jewelry and notes she left that day when the stroke happened. I couldn't help comparing the full life, represented by the interrupted, somewhat cluttered state of her closets and drawers, with the streamlined life she led in the bare hospital room. At the same time, I was struck by the simplicity of her life. She was a very spiritual woman who lived lightly on the earth. Her family relationships were far more important to her than any possessions, and when she died she left little of financial value behind.

The dark night may be a kind of dying. It washes out a cluttered life, just as God in the Old Testament cleansed the whole of existence with a flood. The Greek dictionary says that the word "catharsis" was used for the pruning of trees and purgative medicines, among many other forms of cleansing. Think of your dark night as a pruning of your tree of life. You may be overgrown. Your juices may be wasted in unnecessary shoots and branches. You may need a clearing out to make room for proper growth.

You can thin your life effectively by taking the lead of your dark night. Go with developments, rather than against them. If you feel lost, be lost in ways that suit you and make you feel like a participant in your life. If you feel empty, empty out your life where it needs it. If you feel sad, let sadness be your dominant feeling. Being in tune with your deep mood is a way of clarifying yourself. Speak for it. Show it. Honor it.

Life has its ebb and flow. It builds up, and then it clears out. You need this rhythm, just as you need to breathe in and breathe out. Like your body, your soul gets filled with pollutants. Dark moments are part of the rhythm by which you fill up and empty out. Contemporary writers often emphasize growth and advance. Someone should also speak for being still and not getting anywhere. The entire rhythm is crucial.

TELL YOUR STORY

Aristotle understood that drama and fiction can clear out a cluttered and confused soul. Going to the theater or to a movie can be a form of catharsis, but telling the stories of your own experience can also cleanse and purify. Psychotherapy is nothing more than one person telling stories and the other listening well. Ordinary conversation, too, is full of stories that play a central role in developing an imagination for life. The repeated telling of a story gradually allows the pieces of life experience to find their relation to each other.

Not only the listener, but the teller of a story, too, experiences a catharsis in the telling. If you can find good words and style for your story, you may feel cleansed by it. A story of what you are going through gives your experience form, places it outside yourself for consideration by yourself and others, and gives the aesthetic pleasure that a good story offers. Whether it is an artful story or a simple report on a life experience, a good story requires a certain clarity that comes from honesty and the willingness to forego excuses, caveats, and explanations.

Some say that a person going through a dark night may not feel like making a story of it. He may feel so empty and confused that it is impossible to turn it into a narrative. Some would rather sit vacantly and wait for someone else to initiate some action and make sense of their plight, but it is also important to find a form of expression that suits the individual. I remember one woman who got tired of repeating the same complaints and the same personal histories and felt vaguely angry at the whole process, until one day she brought me a series of letters she had written to a close friend. She couldn't wait to read them to me and obviously never thought of them as something she should do for her therapy. Clients in therapy often seem to groan their way through the narration of their life histories, but when they show you a photograph or a painting they have done, they become animated and involved.

My patient's letters were very revealing. They showed clearly what she desperately wanted and what frightened her. In archetypal psychology we ask: What does the soul want? Answer that one and you are well on your way toward healing. Note that the question is not, what do *you* want, but rather, what *is wanted* at a level beyond and beneath your consciousness. From my client's letters we learned about her deepest longings and fears that kept her locked away within herself. She enjoyed reading the letters to me, as much for their form as their content. I'm sure if I had asked her directly what she feared and what she wanted, she would have sunk into her vacant, disinterested self.

Telling your story is an essential tool for genuine catharsis, but the storytelling may take any number of forms. One man brought me paintings every week. He would spread them out on the floor and tell me about them. He didn't exactly interpret them, and he didn't relate them directly to his dark mood, but he talked about them with enthusiasm. He was trying to sort out his emotions in a way that best suited his temperament. The impetus to do the paintings came entirely from him, and I would join him in commenting on the images. He led the little ritual of presenting the paintings, contemplating them for a few moments, and then drawing out implications. Once again, the pleasure of the form hinted at its usefulness to the soul.

Photography is a contemporary art form that has an extraordinary capacity to reveal the hidden soul. In a photograph you see things that pass by unnoticed in the flow of life. As you look closely at the images, fragments of stories come to mind—the past interrupts the present and is always the bearer of soul. You see the arc of your life, and for a moment you step out of time and visit the past. The camera's version of the past may be different from that of your current memory, and the jarring of a photograph can wake you up to a new interpretation of who you were and what you have become.

A photograph is especially suited to the cathartic process because it forces a meeting between the self you are now and the one you have forgotten. The image you have of your life becomes more complicated as you behold another version of yourself. I have in mind a faded photograph of my own from fourth grade. I see all the children in the classroom dressed in the style of the time. I recognize most of them, though I haven't exchanged a word with most of them in almost half a century. I see myself in the foreground, and I'm filled with fantasy.

Who is that boy with the slick hair and the outrageous tie and the coquettish smile? What has happened to all those relationships, many of which were so important at the time? Can I read my current self in that boyish grin and folded hands? What is the spirit of melancholy that comes along like a strong musky scent every time I look at this photograph? Why is it mildly embarrassing? What is the value of the nostalgia that floats all around that picture?

These are all soul questions. They seem especially acute when I look at the photograph during a time of turmoil. Then I wonder, more than ever, who I am and how I came to be here. The photograph empties me of agendas and worries and places me in the rare atmosphere of pure wonder. There it is that things happen, that life renews itself through a visit to the past. A photograph is a liminal space, neither real nor imaginary, a middle region where the soul comes to life. To the literal mind, a photograph may look like a record of the past, but to the poetic mind it is an uncanny presencing of self and world that is pure, deep, and revealing.

THE SELF IN SOLUTION

Tell your story to whoever will listen to it with respect. It is helpful if you have a friend who will respond to your story with good questions and observations. I have learned as a therapist not to succumb passively to the story a client tells me. A story is often rather rigidly formed and has its own will and ego. I usually ask for a dream as well, and I notice how the dream, in spite of its mysteriousness, will shed light where a story controls and conceals. The combination of stories and dreams works best for me. I treat them as in counterpoint, one correcting and complementing the other.

The search for a living story is so important that it would be worth any effort to find it. You may have to visit old places and talk to family members and friends with unusual honesty. Many people find pieces of themselves by visiting the country of their family origins. When I was twenty, I visited the ruins of the homestead where my great-grandparents lived in Ireland. The image of those stones and landscapes has stayed with me all these years, giving me a valuable sense of the soil from which my life has grown.

Jung discusses this process in the imagery of alchemy: "The selfish hardness of the heart is dissolved: the heart turns to water. The ascent to the higher stages can then begin."[20] Your story is a kind of water, making fluid the brittle events of your life. A story liquefies you, prepares you for more subtle transformations. The tales that emerge from your dark night deconstruct your existence and put you again in the flowing, clear, and cool river of life.

While "in solution" you may recover your innocence, which is an essential ingredient in every tranquil human life. Without innocence you are too burdened with the guilt of past mistakes. This is why many religions have rituals of forgiveness and absolution, to prepare people for the holy mysteries, which require a clean heart. If you want to proceed, you can't be full of guile and schemes. You need a certain purity of heart. As Jesus said, "Blessed are the pure of heart, for they shall see God." Incidentally, in Greek, for "purity" of heart the Gospel uses our word "catharsis."

In your innocence, you are fluid. In the water of a pond, Narcissus discovers that he is lovable and loving. He sees his own image there and is softened by the experience. He becomes water, and that way his hardness dissolves and his capacity to love is released. You need this "water" to soften the edges of your personality, those edges that keep the liquid soul contained and shielded. But there comes a time when the soul must be revealed and the encrustations washed away. The alchemists taught that there are two primary and indispensable processes: dissolve and congeal.

Dissolving your ideas, your habits, and your images is a way to cleanse and purify. All the many assumptions that keep your life fixed break apart as you take time to reflect and have serious talks with friends and maybe a therapist. The alchemists referred to this phase as *solutio*, putting all the hard stuff in the waters of reflection, where it breaks apart, shows itself for what it is, and gives you the opportunity for a fresh start.

This solution, which can be any method of dislodging the pieces of your life for reflection, is like baptismal water. It takes you out of a world of pragmatism and cynicism and restores a less jaded viewpoint. The cleansing reinstates a level of innocence and impressionability. Clearing away the debris allows life to flow, with all the grace of beginning.

I am speaking of water as a symbol. Any fluidity might do, but sometimes the symbol has to be close to the image. So, if you are in need of dissolving and cleansing, you might spend some time near actual water—at a river or by the sea. In that spirit, a psychic once said that my daughter should live near flowing water; it would serve her nature. It doesn't take a psychic to know that you need water of a particular kind. Whenever I return to Michigan's Lake Huron, the scene of my adolescent summers, I am flooded with feelings about my past. I recover something of myself that I can't find in the mountains or by salt water.

In religion, you wash your hands as a symbol of inner cleansing. In ordinary life, too, you can bathe at times of emotional blockage, whether your body needs it or not. You can look for special soaps and oils. I make a point of searching out lotions and shampoos that give me the inner sensations I need. When I take showers and baths, I often know that my soul needs the water and cleansing more than my body does. Ordinary bathing can be an effective ritual for clarifying your emotions and thoughts. You may sit in a tub or stand in the shower as your thoughts sort themselves out.

SOCIAL CATHARSIS

A society, too, needs catharsis. It can become log-jammed with ideas that have lost their liveliness. Ideas turn into prejudices, slogans, party lines, and mere opinions. People become conservative in a negative sense: self-protective, deadened, and unthinking. Deep conservatism is an honoring of eternal ideas and values supported by an intelligent appreciation for the past. A conservative view, in this sense, is essential, so that we don't all become futurists devoted only to the newest and latest.

Unwise wars and unenlightened political decisions can weigh heavily on a society. It may need strong catharsis as a way out of its dark nights, which may take the forms of economic depression and social conflict. Modern societies fail to appreciate the power of gestures, rituals, apologies, and formulas of forgiveness. But a society, like an individual, carries its own karma and requires serious rites of absolution and renewal. Ancient and traditional communities knew the importance of such rituals, and they paid close attention to their full, graphic enactment. We need the catharsis, but since we have forgotten that people have souls, the need for serious ritual rarely occurs to us.

A society that has lost its soul looks for security in the future and is willing to deny the reality of the present. But a society can't move ahead if its values and ideals are jammed behind failures and mistakes. It has to own up to its neglect and its atrocity, while at the same time proclaiming its highest values. It is possible for a society to deal with the moral pollution of its history. Gestures, language, acts of compensation, and rites of forgiveness can all be effective. But they have to be done sincerely, without guile and without mere formalism.

The United States, for example, has never really dealt with its guilt in handling its native people so savagely. It hasn't fully owned up to and sought forgiveness for slavery. We could, even now, show clear, sincere appreciation for the beauty and wisdom of our native ancestors. We could make strong, public resolutions to atone for slavery. Without strong, sincere, participatory expressions of remorse on our part, Native Americans carry the moral weight on themselves, and the society as a whole has little access to its original spirituality. African-Americans still struggle for their basic rights and dignity. Like a person burdened with guilt it may not be aware of, a country can be held back by its failure to deal with its past.

To some, dark periods in American history may indicate shame and negativity, but it mustn't stop here. The whole point of a dark night of the soul is the promise of new life. There is a crucial difference between manufacturing a high-tech, germ-free future and letting the future rise organically from a deeply felt and acknowledged past. The brave new world approach tends to be sterile and flat, while the embrace of history, its good and its bad elements, makes for a rich, colorful, and humane life.

Genuine catharsis requires the emotions of shame, dread, fear, puzzlement, and even hopelessness. Anything less is too superficial. The avoidance of these feelings, which beg for attention, makes people numb and foggy and therefore incapable of the necessary empathy. The poet Wallace Stevens said that the death of one god is the death of them all. This applies to emotions as well. Suppress the uncomfortable ones, and all the others will go into hiding, too.

Becoming a person or a nation with character doesn't happen without self-confrontation. It asks for strength exactly in those areas where you feel weak. It demands vision in those areas where we think we have everything figured out. It asks us to give up old pieties and sentimentalities and face the new challenges with tough vision. It demands that we live into life from where we are now, not from the comfortable place we achieved long ago. It asks for the surrender of the identity we won and now enjoy. It requires an emptiness of heart so that new life may enter.

The cleansing of society's soul is important for individuals as well, because often our dark nights are intimately connected with what is going on in the culture. At a time of international tension, throughout the world spirits sink and the light of hope goes dim. Downturns in the economy affect the moods of families and individuals. It does no good to give attention only to the individual, trying to make him comfortable in stressful times. We need ways to deal with the psyche of the society, to take its problems seriously at the level of the soul. Pragmatism can go only so far.

Look at the back of an American dollar bill. On the left side, just beneath the pyramid, an ancient image for the spiritual and the eternal, you will find the words *novus ordo saeculorum*—a new order of the ages. I hear catharsis in that statement that represents the Rosicrucian and Masonic sentiments of many of America's founders. America means catharsis: new beginning, freedom from the past, and purity of intention.

PURIFYING SOCIETY

Many societies in the past have used the ritual of a scapegoat to cleanse themselves of pollution, which the Greeks called *miasma*, a stain on the city or state caused by certain evil acts. Today it would seem impossible to employ any such rite with an actual animal, and yet in a way we still scapegoat by pinning the blame for society's ignorance on a particular person, usually a leader. An official at the United Nations once remarked that the letters S.G., referring to the Secretary General, usually mean Scape Goat. To adopt the scapegoat idea with more subtlety, we might realize, in a general way first, that the social disorder that surrounds us is not rational and can't be dealt with by rational means alone. We have to bring a deeper, more radical imagination to play in order to reach the irrational depths of our ignorance.

That is why marches, great gatherings, poetic and rousing speeches, slogans, and images of all kinds have been effective in many cases in turning society around. It is no accident that Martin Luther King, Jr. was a minister and a gifted speaker. His language and his comportment had more to do with changing attitudes toward race in America than the reasoning in his thought. These images have to speak to the people, and if they do, there is no limit to their power. Unfortunately, this power can also be manipulated for less noble purposes.

At a deeper level, a scapegoat in its original form was a figure— an animal or a person—who, in the imagination of the society, bore the guilt and could be removed from the culture. This idea makes sense in the context of a society in which images and rituals are still powerful. The Christian theology of redemption— Jesus suffering for the evil done by human beings—is not all that far from the idea of a scapegoat.

Religion teaches that, to be effective, a scapegoat can't be someone we rationally blame for our misfortune. It does no good ultimately to place responsibility entirely on political leaders. The miasma is a more subtle social infection. It can be found in every citizen. We all have to get the stain out of us. But how do I, an ordinary individual, respond creatively to society's imperfection?

The first task is to find a suitable image for the evil that afflicts us. We need the right language and the proper forms to identify the spirit that is now loose in us. Is it the spirit of greed?

Are we anxious about our power and identity? Is there some reason why we might feel inferior? Is the responsibility too great? Are we angry about past betrayals? Do we still feel the sting of the Vietnam War, of our own Civil War?

As I write this book, the whole world is anxious because of unbridled terrorism and international conflict. This is the darkest cultural night in my adult memory, and I admit to profound anxiety and dread. Every sentence I write here has special weight and bite because of the situation. I have to ask myself in the starkest terms, how do we rid society of this dangerous pollution?

The dark night offers us now a chance for real catharsis. Purity of heart is the goal. We have to recover, not naïvely and not in the usual terms, a vision of the divine. Our secular society isn't working, and in fact it is self-destructive. Perhaps the real evil is the spirit of this society—its self-interest, money, runaway desire, or ambition. Maybe these qualities are to be beaten and run out of town. Could we learn from our precious dark night to purify ourselves and turn self-interest into a broader, outgoing concern; the acquisition of wealth into the dispersal of money; ambition into a deep, positive vision for humanity?

One central theme in this book is to see a dark night as a cleansing of perception for the purpose of a deeper soul life and an increase in spirituality. A society is like an individual: in the face of a dark night it can either become defensive and avoid the challenge of new life, or it can reform itself and discover in the darkness where it has gone wrong. It takes a strong heart, a steady intelligence, and a visionary imagination to go in the direction of life. Sometimes society moves in the right direction; often it retrenches and gets worse. There appears to be no middle ground.

I have suggested an understanding of the scapegoat, not as finding someone to blame but uncovering the spirit in all of us that is the source of the evil in the world. That is the spirit we have to attack with a warrior's strength and tenacity. This moral battle can take the place of our literal wars and ultimately save us.

All of us need to be cleansed of those attitudes and urges that prompt us toward violence.

What we need is not a moralistic crusade but a spiritual awakening. When cities ban smoke-belching factories from their riverbanks and restore an important piece of nature to citizens, they are making not only a literal improvement in air quality and river access, but also a symbolic statement about the value of a purer life. Their decision makes for both clean air and clean souls. We need many such decisions, to clean our natural world, our politics, and our culture.

Society's dark nights may fill you with dread and depress your spirits, but you can keep in mind that the darkness is necessary for life to proceed. You may not avoid tragedy, but you have the opportunity for a recovery of soul. Everything depends on how the dark night is handled: Will you try to overcome it and run away from it, or will you let it transform you and, "in solution," give you new life?

CHAPTER FOUR

THE VIEW FROM THE MOON

I N YOUR DARK NIGHT of the soul you need not give up your intelligence, but you may have to change your idea of what it means to be wise in the conduct of your life. You may have to adopt a different kind of knowing, one that is suited to the darkness and not in conflict with it. Nicolas of Cusa, the fifteenth-century theologian, said you need the night-eyes of an owl.

You need special vision for your dark night because the ordinary ways of thinking may not work. You may become a darker person, changing in accordance with the mood that has come over you. Seeing in the emotional dark is a special talent that might draw out resources you never knew you had. You may allow your anger to come forth and your sadness to color your way of life. Ordinarily, you may be a quite rational person, but now you might start using your intuition and your psychic abilities more seriously.

When my mother first became ill, my father began making clear and firm announcements purely from his intuition. In the weeks before her stroke several times he told me, "One of us, me or your mother, is going to be in trouble soon." People would say, "It's wonderful how the two of you enjoy such good health." Uncharacteristically, he would warn against being optimistic. His dark night, which of course grew deeper and darker during my mother's illness, began before the facts appeared.

The Greeks and Romans worshipped a goddess of the dark, Hekate (Roman Hecate), who had night vision and is a perfect teacher for being in the dark. She is not well-known and is rather mysterious, but she is a strong figure that could educate us in this mysterious experience we are exploring. Let's allow her to show us what it means to be at home in the dark—what tools you need, how you need to think, and how to be.

THE DARK ANGEL

In the central Greek myth of Persephone, the young girl is enjoying the beauty of nature, picking beautiful, enticing flowers, when the Lord of the Underworld comes and carries her away to his deep and cold kingdom. She becomes his bride and queen of the dark. Her mother, Demeter, mistress of the earth's abundance, misses her and becomes alarmed at her disappearance. Only the night-goddess Hekate, who overheard the cries and the commotion, can tell her what happened. Then the mother goes off on adventures of her own as she desperately looks for her daughter. Finally, Hermes, guide of souls, brings the girl back from Hades. But the Underworld God is tricky. He slips the young girl the seed of a pomegranate, which works like magic. She would be able to spend two-thirds of the year with her mother in the upperworld of abundance, but for one-third would take her place as underworld queen.

Hekate embodies both the beauty and the terrors of the

night. She was the patroness of psychics and fortune-tellers. Her mood and atmosphere is the one you feel when you see a huge yellow moon on a dark night. She belongs in the dark places—alleys, corners, alcoves—and therefore is a perfect patroness for your dark night of the soul.

Imagine this Hekate spirit as something that lives quietly and deeply in you, a set of sensitivities and abilities. It is especially noticeable at night, when your senses might be keen and your imagination unusually active. It might show itself in ideas that come to you at night that are particularly useful, or frightening and disturbing. In our house, there is often considerable movement at night: getting up to write down ideas, dreams, or inspirations; the need to work for a while in the quiet hours; or just general sleeplessness. Children wander in the wake of their dreams and in search of physical closeness. Pets growl and shuffle. I know Hekate quite well.

James Hillman calls her "a dark angel," a consciousness that works in the darkness because it is at home there. He says that this "part of us is not dragged down but always lives there."[21] This is a point easily overlooked: in your darkness you may discover a part of you that is essential to your being, but unfamiliar. The darkness doesn't exactly come from outside, but is a revelation of something in your nature. In your black moods and dark fears you find an essential part of yourself.

However you present yourself to the world, on some level you are a dark person. You have thoughts you don't usually tell people. You are capable of things that your friends may know nothing about. You are probably more interesting sexually than the world realizes. You probably have some anger and fears that you don't tell people about. You may have secrets from your past that make you more intriguing than your persona would suggest. Certainly your potential for darker thoughts and behavior is rich.

People are often shocked to discover that their spiritual leader has uncontrollable sexual desires or perhaps a gambling habit. In the recent past many people of honor have broken down and revealed a dark side. The very idea of Catholic priests being pedophiles is scandalous and disturbing, but it also shows how naïve we have been or how willing to pretend that there is no underworld to human life. I remember as a young man, playing the organ for church services, being surprised and confused when a nun pushed me into the organ pipes and kissed me. It never occurred to me that the virginal nuns would have such ordinary human passions. I'm not pointing the finger at nuns but only expressing my surprise, perhaps my innocence.

We all have qualities that are opposed to the ones we want the world to see. Some are innocuous, some serious. This material we repress holds large quantities of vitality. We suppress it out of anxiety, fearful of what would happen if it ever got out. We are often afraid of the dark because it is so alive. I knew a man who was extremely quiet and unassuming in public, but I knew that at home he was a bull. There he would roar and shout and deal roughly with anybody and anything. Then he would go back to work like a mouse. Like him, many people divide the light and the dark in their lives, allowing the dark to show only where they feel safe.

Socially we usually try to present ourselves in the best light. We may have to pretend that we are brighter and more innocent than we actually are. We may do this so often that we come to believe it and feel cut off from the dark spirits in us we have hidden from the world. But all this dark material is extremely valuable, especially in times of tragedy and conflict, when an unsentimental, lunar attitude would be most helpful.

Again to use myself as an example, I have no doubt that my dark spirits could be named Venus and Mars. My wife is always expressing surprise that I am such an erotic person, so drawn to sensuality. My persona, carefully crafted in a pious Catholic context during the whole of my youth, is quite different. I was taught to appear more innocent than I feel. I admire men I know whose sexuality is right up front, but I could no more be like them than be a pirate at sea or a football quarterback. The other dark element is my anger. My children say that I don't get angry often, but when I do, the thunder rolls. I know that I am like many people who have a placid exterior but are capable of strong anger. I have no doubt that all of this is in part neurotic, and I do my best to transform the rage into creative expression and effective work. But it would take more than a lifetime to finish this bit of alchemy in which I mix my genuine innocence with my undeniable darkness.

And so I love this night goddess Hekate. I even love writing about her. She redeems many feelings and thoughts that might be undervalued if I didn't have her image to guide me. She validates many aspects of daily life that go into the garbage—we'll see the appropriateness of that image—because they aren't valued and approved. She sanctions a mysterious, socially challenging way of thinking and living that is ultimately liberating.

EMOTIONAL NIGHT

The strange gifts of Hekate are available to all, men and women. I have seen people in therapy begin in innocence, unconsciousness, and shallow thinking. They accepted all the superficial ideas of mental health and emotion that the popular culture pressed on them. If they were angry, they tried to overcome or control it. If they had unwanted sexual fantasies, they came looking for purity. If they were depressed, they wanted hope and cheer.

But it didn't take long for them to come to some painful realizations and give up their emotional and intellectual superficiality. They learned to be followers of the night spirit, and in that change of tone they found liberation. Their lives weren't solved, but they were no longer victims of a superficial outlook. One of the rewards of good therapy is to darken your personality and make you a child of Hekate. Even when it takes place during the day, therapy is a night business.

I recall a couple who were both extremely creative and accomplished, one a musician and the other an architect. They were each seriously devoted to their careers, but they hardly touched each other emotionally. They made a game out of marriage and came to me because they felt the emptiness between them. Hearing their story, I could almost predict some dark development that might serve as an initiation into deeper life. Sure enough, soon after we started therapy, the woman began an affair with a man of no education who was a drifter and a minor criminal. Her husband, of course, felt profoundly betrayed, not only because of his wife's unfaithfulness but because she chose someone, in his own mind, so far beneath him. He might have felt better if she went off with a movie star or a genius.

Now the conversations began in earnest. Old arguments came to the surface. They began to look at the underworld of their longstanding relationship, and in the process the woman grew darker and stronger. The man preferred to keep what he could of the virtue in being wronged and to play the innocent. I liked them both immensely and thought that the developments could help them individually, though I didn't know what it would do for the marriage.

The dark months of betrayal were fruitful, and the woman entered a period of remarkable creativity. The man continued to fade into self-pity. Eventually, they divorced, remarried, and divorced again. I remained in contact with the woman, whose career blossomed. I don't know whatever happened to her former husband. I trust that he found his own path into a much needed darkening of his own attitude.

TOOLS OF THE DARK

Hekate's symbols are the key, the whip, the dagger, and the torch. You may never have thought of the positive symbolic value of the last three on this list, because contemporary spiritual and religious language is almost all positive. But human life has a bitter side, and you have to be prepared to deal with it. Let's take a quick look at these symbols.

The Key

The key is Hekate's means of entrance to the underworld. She can come and go, a skill worth developing. Psychology sometimes defines psychosis as going down into the depths without coming back. Imagine if you didn't feel a stranger to your dark night and that you had the "key" to entering it and leaving it. This ability wouldn't be a matter of conquering or solving the mood, but it would allow an easier relationship with it.

At this very moment I'm using mythology as such a key. I also turn to poetry and music as a way to cultivate my relationship with the darkness. Some people enjoy scary movies or books about disasters. In my own career, studying the writings of the Marquis de Sade has helped me feel close to the shadow aspects of whatever I am writing or speaking about. They give me confidence in the dark. In recent years I have taken to reading mystery stories, yet another way to explore the dark.

You need a tool, a key in this case, so you don't succumb to the strange atmosphere and power of the dark night. I have often seen my role of therapist as standing at the doorway between ordinary life and the darkest emotions and fantasies. Ordinary people go through that door and find themselves confused and threatened by what they find there. My job is to use a whole set of keys that allow us to come and go, to keep a footing in the dayworld, while we explore the nightworld for its secrets.

You, too, could find keys that work for you. Jung found such a key in the imagery of alchemy. I use the Tarot cards. Psychoanalysis is still a highly developed key to the underworld, though it doesn't have the popular acceptance it once had. Most people are drawn to a symbolic system that speaks to their imagination, though in today's rationalistic atmosphere they may be embarrassed by it.

For many artists, dreams are a key to the underworld inspiration they need. Some would say that smoking, coffee, or hard drugs are essential. Some meditate or practice yoga or travel. Some artists and writers have to live in several places to feel ready for their art. I myself have an inordinate attachment to books, which I treat in every way as indispensable keys to the mysteries that surround human life. I also turn to films for an entrance to that otherworld of images and meanings.

An ordinary key that allows you to be both light and dark at the same time is the habit of honoring your darkness. You can speak from it and of it. Without falling into melodrama, you can show others your moods, instead of hiding behind false cheerfulness or emotional emptiness. You can find words for your night journey and, neither glorifying it nor criticizing it, you can invite it into your daily routine and even into your personality. As Persephone discovered, you are not a guest in the underworld; you're a citizen there.

Most of the keys I am describing get you into the underworld, but you need to get out, too. Jung recommended staying involved with your home and family. I have friends who transit off into the otherworld sometimes, exploring the highly charged realm of spirituality and fantasy. For them, being connected to someone who can ground them and yet allow them their "travels" is essential. I also encourage them to eat regularly and generally stay connected to ordinary life.

Everyone needs a special key, suited to their temperament, to help them move freely between ordinary life and the depths of their soul. You will find your keys if you come to appreciate the dark periods and at the same time understand the importance of your ordinary daily routine. These, too, are the yin and yang of a complete life.

The Whip

A dark night of the soul doesn't merely plunge you into darkness, it also batters you, so that you might well feel emotionally beaten and lacerated. The alchemists described this process as mortification, emotional suffering that leaves you feeling destroyed. As the word implies (*mors, mortis* means death), mortification entails dying to your will and ego. Ultimately it works in your favor, but during the process you may feel deeply discouraged.

This mortification, the feeling of being overwhelmed and torn apart, prepares you for new ideas and a fresh start. You can't be renewed unless past behavior and thinking are shredded and packed away. But this can't happen without torment. The ideas and styles that have become familiar to you are you. To give them up is to have your very identity ripped apart and disposed of. You try to hang on, and that's where the torture focuses. People say they want to change, but when it comes down to the heart of the process, they resist strongly, and there is a battle.

In your dark night you may feel as though you are being punished for mistakes you have made, or just for being your imperfect self. Images of whips and beatings found in painting and alchemy imply that the feelings of mortification are natural and play their necessary role. Knowing this doesn't mean you won't feel the sting, but it helps to realize that emotional pain is part of a larger, positive process.

Some people are fated to suffer physically. An outstanding example is the twentieth-century Mexican painter Frida Kahlo, who had polio and then was in a serious bus accident, in which her body was pierced by a long shaft of steel. She suffered extraordinary pain, especially in her early years, and managed somehow to transform all that suffering into powerful images on her canvases. Many of her paintings show her in a hospital bed and several picture her internal organs showing through her body. We see lacerations, blood, and plants growing in her body. One grisly painting is called "Without Hope," and another shows her as a deer with antlers, her body pierced and bloody with arrows. Kahlo has hopeful paintings as well, such as "The Love Embrace of the Universe," but pain is almost always present.

Some people are emotional masochists. They have a habit of seeking out rejection and suffering. In jealousy, a person might enjoy discovering some sign of betrayal—a letter, a phone message, a hotel key. Some enjoy deprivation and ill health, thinking them signs of spiritual sacrifice. There is considerable masochism in religion. Some, when they have been rejected, say, "See, I told you. I'm no good." They enjoy the supposed confirmation that they are inferior.

In each case there is a reward for the pain. The jealous person doesn't have to find it in himself to love without possessing. The spiritual person has found a way to be good and virtuous. The inferior one doesn't have to be somebody and enter the fray of life with strength. There may be other rewards involved, but these are a few possibilities.

We all get involved in minor sadomasochistic scenes every day. Medical people often expect us to submit passively to their authority, and teachers sometimes enjoy making their students suffer. Marriage can be full of control and submission. We sometimes submit too readily and too far. Or we use what power we have as a way of dealing with our own insecurities and passivities. All of this behavior is raw material for finding a more subtle approach to power.

Often it is exceedingly dark, as the film *Blue Velvet* demonstrates. In this story of graphic sadomasochism a woman character begs to be beaten and a young man, who thinks he is entirely virtuous, in a moment of forgetfulness unleashes his sadism. Both he and his spirited girlfriend feel compelled to investigate the strange happenings they have accidentally come upon, and as their curiosity deepens, they change. Gradually they slough off their childish innocence and discover the dark side of life.

The Secretary is another disturbing film that depicts two highly neurotic young people who come to love each other through symbolic acts of dominance and submission. The woman gets out of a psychiatric hospital and takes a job working for an equally disturbed lawyer. The boss plays into the woman's need for domination and punishment, and somehow, in the end, they discover that they can love each other.

The Dagger

Even though your dark night has much of positive value to give you, you shouldn't be completely passive in it. You have to be armed and ready for battle. You have to be a spiritual warrior and take on the emotional accoutrements of the knight and hero. You have to be a big person, which is not the same as being full of will and ego.

As I have been writing this book, a Tibetan dagger lies on my desk. It has three demon heads, frightening figures who are there to help deal with adversity. Traditionally in Tibet, the three sides of the blade represent charity, chastity, and patience. These don't sound like dark powers, but from the point of view of the demons of your dark night, they are potent adversaries.[22]

Your dark night may provide you with an opportunity to discover your toughness. This is not a place for sentimentality or squeamishness. You have to be alert and make difficult decisions when they are called for. Many sensitive people disown their capacity to criticize, to speak loudly for the truths they perceive, and to struggle against ignorance and prejudice. Many hide their dark desires and strange appetites. But to be at one with the dark is to be a dark fighter, willing to do the difficult thing.

On the surface you may be amiable and flexible, but in your dark night you may discover the very important ingredient of toughness. Oscar Wilde provides a good example. He was a brilliant man who played the role of society's fool and fop. He dressed as a dandy and had the reputation of being an expert on superficial style. But he was actually nothing of the sort. Wilde was a thoughtful and religious man, a man of principle who spent years in jail simply on account of his homosexuality. From prison he wrote one of the most remarkable testaments ever written, *De Profundis* (*Out of the Depths*), a letter a person suffering any kind of dark night might appreciate. The letter is apropos of our theme:

> I have lain in prison for nearly two years. Out of my nature has come wild despair; an abandonment to grief; . . . terrible and impotent rage; bitterness and scorn; anguish that wept aloud; misery that could find no voice; sorrow that was dumb. . . . Now I find hidden somewhere away in my nature something that tells me that nothing in the whole world is meaningless, and suffering least of all. That something hidden away in my nature, like a treasure in a field, is humility.[23]

You should read the entire passage and the whole letter. You might also consider writing your own "de profundis" when you are in the depths of a dark night. Take Wilde's letter as your model. Be honest with yourself. Write on a number of themes. Raise your scramble of emotions to a higher level of carefully chosen words. This is the alchemy of language, the transformation of life into simple art, the sublimation of experience into thought. If you don't like to write, then paint or sing, or at least talk frankly and openly to your friends.

Note that Wilde's great discovery is something as simple and unheroic as humility. It is the one virtue that stands out as Wilde's perfect shadow. In his other writing he never comes across as humble. You might follow him in this, too. What is your opposite quality? What is the last thing on earth you would expect people to see in you? Maybe that thing is your weapon, your dagger for the dark.

The Torch

Hekate is a lunar spirit, a soft source of strength when life is thick with feeling and there seems to be no way out of confusion.

This patroness of your darkness doesn't shed brilliant light on your problems. Instead, her torch gives you hints, intimations, and suggestions. After a while, you may feel comfortable with the wafer-thin intuitions you experience. You may not need explanations and solutions, but only indications that everything is essentially all right and that you can handle whatever comes along.

Hekate's torch illuminates the pervading darkness with a dim lunar light. In ancient classical literature she was known as one of the Daughters of the Night, and with her dogs she guards the gates of the underworld. If she is your angel, you have to learn how to think, speak, and act without countering the darkness that has hold of you. Hekate is at one with the dark. Your way of reasoning and understanding likewise has to be enlightening as the moon illuminates—soft, incomplete, obscure, romantic, slightly chilling, beautiful.

Psychology tends to be solar, wanting to bring all things to light, to overcome the darkness and make everything manageable. It wants to banish darkness with any means at its disposal. But no one needs such a harsh cleansing and brightening. It would be better to be deepened and darkened by an experience of the night. You would then become more complex, more interesting, less one-dimensional.

You can see that the point of staying in the dark is not to trick it into making you brilliant and germ-free, but to make you a more interesting person and to give you a more fascinating life. In therapeutic times like ours, these goals may seem odd. But they are ultimately more humane. Rather than giving you a spotless, well-adjusted personality, they give you substance. You become a person worth knowing, worth listening to, and worth loving, in all your dimensions.

PSYCHOLOGICAL NIGHT

The ancient medical book of Hippocrates, *Sacred Disease*, says that Hekate brings night disturbances. You wake up at night and worry about creaks and bangs in the house. You can't sleep because of some unnamed anxiety. You have a bad dream or even a nightmare. This is the work of the night-prowling spirit. She is the moon glowing faintly behind drifting clouds, and she can be felt in the haunting sounds of the night. With her spooky torch, she is all the light you can hope for, and so you should pay attention to disturbing dreams and night anxieties.

People sometimes say that a dark night of the soul offers no images, but the night is full of fantasy. It may not contain the imagery you consider valuable, but then, your sense of values may have to change. Night may give you a sense of alert, an unusual insomnia, a nightmare. These are the qualities of an ordinary actual night, and they also find their way into the moods and fantasies of a dark night of the soul.

Night, primordial and primitive, can be frightening, but even then it has its charms, as anyone who loves camping and hiking will tell you. Of course, Hekate is also fully present in the city late at night, in the alleyways and deserted streets and in the sounds and lights that evoke the ghosts of the place. Martin Scorsese's powerful film *After Hours* tells what happens to a man roaming city streets after his workday is finished. He meets odd and dangerous characters and finds himself in unexplainable straits. It's a time of heightened imagination and uncanny happenings.

You can expect similar unusual occurrences during your dark night of the soul. It is a time of special vulnerability, not only the kind that makes you feel weak, but also the kind that opens you to signals in the world around you. You may feel déjà vu and premonition. You may be unusually sensitive to sounds and sights. You may not know what it all means, but in general it is inviting you to exist in a bigger world, where magic happens and the mysterious is all that counts.

You can adapt to your dark night much the way you would deal with an actual night on dark city streets. You would be watchful and cautious and might expect odd things to happen. You would be quiet and observant. You would look differently in the dark, noticing movements in the shadows and hearing the slightest sounds. In your soul's dark night you have to be equally observant and discerning. It may be a time to stay still and be prepared for the unexpected.

THE GARBAGE OF A LIFE AND A DAY

In his writings on dreams James Hillman stresses the ancient association between Hekate and garbage. He equates this garbage with the day-residues Freud said were the stuff of dreams. But Hillman sees this garbage redeemed in dream and Hekate as "the Goddess who makes sacred the waste of life, so that it all counts, it all matters."[24]

You may think that the time spent in a dark night is a waste. You accomplish nothing. You feel worse about yourself and your life. In such a state, Thomas Aquinas referred to his life work as "straw," and Samuel Beckett, speaking through the voice of the title character in *Krapp's Last Tape* says, "Just been listening to that stupid bastard I took myself for thirty years ago, hard to believe I was ever as bad as that." Moments before he had sung a verse that places his play in the domain of Hekate:

> *Now the day is over,*
> *Night is drawing nigh-igh,*
> *Shadows—*

Such feelings are an important part of the creative life, of simply being a person. They don't undo all the positive thoughts, but they keep it all in perspective. Every life is full of garbage—wasted time, failed endeavors, broken relationships, bad decisions—to be offered at that strange altar of this night goddess, the place where three roads meet, an uncanny haunt of ghosts and magic. If you don't honor this night spirit, what do you do with all this trash? You probably just take it literally, associate it with your "self," and feel guilty. What people today call "losing self-esteem" might be nothing more than the highly visible waste material of a life that needs a home and that shouldn't be attached to the self.

When thoughts come to you deep in your dark night—that your life hasn't amounted to anything, that you've wasted a lot of time, or that you aren't as good as some friend or celebrity, thoughts of regret, bitterness and self-loathing—you might consider the necessity of these annoying preoccupations. They don't literally make *you* garbage, they merely allow you to see this all-important emptiness in your accomplishments. The fact is, we are all Charlie Chaplin tramps failing to fully realize our expectations. One of the most telling myths for my own life, a truth my family likes to remind me of, is Mr. Magoo, a man disastrously oblivious to the world around him. He climbs unknowingly into a passing bus, with his weak eyes confuses a mannequin for a friend, and constantly forgets what he was just about to do. I know him well. Thoughts like these, which you might well entertain late at night, help you rediscover your humanity and give you the great blessing of humility. Where but in darkness could you find this insight?

The work of Hekate moves in two directions: it ennobles what is often considered trash, and it reveals the great and virtuous to be not so wonderful. The process redeems the drudgery of a life and yet saves you from hubris. For when you identify with your trash, you also feed your egotism. Any material of the soul reduced to ego gets literalized, split, and taken to opposite extremes. The person who thinks he's humble is probably unconscious of his haughtiness. The person who feels powerless and cheated is probably controlling. You need to see the waste of your life as having a place in the nature of things, in the realm of Hekate.

HONORING HEKATE'S NEGATIVITY

Rituals in honor of Hekate involved unusual dinners given in her honor, where food scraps were given away to beggars and dogs prowled and nibbled. Every deity has its sacred food, its way of uniting spirit and devotee. Somehow in your dark nights you could incorporate, in a dark kind of communion, some of Hekate's negativity. You could acknowledge that this spirit has an important role in life, even though it is like trash littering the highway and of more interest to dogs than humans. When you scrape your plate after the evening meal and watch the scraps go into a bucket or garbage grinder, think of its symbolic value. Somehow your life is like that, and it is precious in the eyes of this spirit known for her sharp awareness.

At the dump—the recycling center—in our town, there is a large vat placed high on a cement pedestal where you can throw away food garbage. It isn't a pleasant sight. I often think of it as the lowest region of Dante's *Inferno*, but it could as well be the altar of Hekate. It not only displays the truth that we make a lot of actual garbage in our lives, but it is also a strong image for how we feel internally. We need an altar for this stuff; otherwise it weighs upon us and we begin to identify with it, thinking that our lives are a literal waste.

HEKATE'S ROLE IN DEEPENING MATERNAL FEELINGS

One day a woman may wake up and decide to stop being the nurturing mother. It's a significant realization, and she will need her anger and darkness to keep her resolve. Jungian psychologists describe this alternative to the nurturing figure as a "negative mother." Actual women may feel, when they enter this fantasy, that they have failed their children. But seeing the truth of Hekate might save them from the pain of judging themselves badly. It also saves men from blaming their own failures on the inadequacies of their mothers. It's part of being a mother to withhold affection and support, consciously or unconsciously as a way of encouraging independence for both mother and child.

Women can honor Hekate in a special way. When a woman's soul is set to blossom, she may feel at first that she needs to be released from the nurturing, sensitive identity she has known for many years. She may fall in love suddenly with a dark man and engage in dark activities—sexual, criminal, or simple mild rebellion. She may give up wifely and motherly duties that she feels have enslaved her long enough. She may become angry and hawkish.

Let's recall the ancient tale of Demeter and Persephone, where the daughter, at first innocent and preoccupied with the beauty of nature, becomes the mistress of the underworld. Hekate supports both daughter and mother, and in the history of mythology she is even sometimes identified with each of them. In the story, she tells Demeter that she overheard the daughter's cries. Later, she offers to assist Persephone in the underworld, because that is a place she knows intimately.

The young woman Persephone, once enjoying her mother's plants and flowers, now takes charge of the dark emptiness of Hades, where nothing grows. What she offers her followers then is nothing—void, lack, absence. This Persephone, this woman of the invisible and of fallow fields and loss and abduction, sometimes goes by the name Hekate, who in myth and drama became the patroness of Medea, who killed her children. Although the mothers devoted to Hekate, a women caught up in the Medea complex, may merely deny their children all the love and care they crave, some, of course, actually kill their children or at least abandon them.

It's important not to take care of and be taken care of all the time. But some people can't help themselves. They are always caring, always wanting care. They are stuck, fixated on the nurturing mother-child archetype. But you don't always need to be cared for. You don't have to justify your existence by caring for others. Instead of making mutual care an absolute principle, you could understand that need, absence, and ignorance allow wonder and new life. Children, husbands, wives, students, patients—at times everyone needs someone who will not give themselves in service. You need to feel your own essence—who you are when you are not acknowledged and supported by someone else. This empty underworld of your identity is an important ingredient in your reality, and when you are learning this lesson you may think you are in a dark night. Hekate is the spirit of this kind of dark night in which you discover your depth.

For many women, the shift from being the bountiful mother to being a person in search of her essence is a difficult period of change. Naturally, people admire the selflessness of the caring mother, but what's to admire in the search for a self? This effort will look narcissistic and far from virtuous. The dark values explored throughout this book are not the ones generally appreciated by society. When you make the important move to find your essence, you will probably have to go it alone. You may have to accept that you will be misread and underappreciated. Certainly your family will have to adjust.

Go to any supermarket or department store, and you will see mothers struggling with their children. Some of this struggle is nothing more than the normal difficulty of dealing with children's strong emotions and plain, vocal complaints. But often you see the struggle turn more vicious, and the child comes close to being abused. This is not Medea, the mother who honors Hekate, who was her priestess, but perhaps a sign of Hekate's absence. Hekate doesn't literally harm children; she saves the mother from one-sided virtue and kindliness. Paradoxically, her spirit ultimately protects children, because much violence comes

from the repression of dark mothering. She makes for a complicated expression of motherhood, in which the light and the dark
both have a creative place. Expect to see the Hekate spirit in a
subtle coolness and maternal reserve.

A woman may be a strong, positive mother, giving herself
happily to her family, when suddenly something shifts in her. She
is no longer content with this identity and isn't sure just how to
make the appropriate change in her life. There may be a period
when she is uncertain, between the giving mother and some
other focus altogether. Jungian analyst Patricia Berry describes
this difficult phase, using the Demeter/Persphone myth that we
have been tracking: "The upperworld became a Demeter realm
of concrete, daily life, devoid of the spiritual values, the sense
of essence and the dark (and beneath the dark) carried by her
underworld daughter, Persephone."[25]

Mothers can keep a sense of play and beauty in their role, but
eventually that satisfaction may go away. To use Berry's imagery,
that part, her Persephone, is now in the underworld, apart from
her and inaccessible. Now she has to identify more with the
transformed young self, who is now quite different. She has been
drawn into the depths, and there a bigger, more serious kind of
life comes into view. Many mothers suddenly want education,
more experiences, and friends who are not identified with the
bountiful, self-sacrificing mother. They seek a more serious and
more thoughtful dimension to their lives. Their husbands and
parents may misinterpret this development as being selfish, simply because the old self-sacrificing person is disappearing. The
bountiful mother is reuniting with her underworld daughter. As
she develops in this direction, she may feel that her former bountiful self was excessive. She may realize now that to be a mother
means to be both giving and withholding, both altruistic and
concerned about living a meaningful life herself.

This crisis in mothering is for many a highly disturbing dark
night. A woman's sense of self, her worth, her very meaning are
at stake. Sometimes she may feel the call to make the shift to a

more complex person, but resist. At this point her old giving self may return with a vengeance. She may say, or at least think, that her mothering days are over, but she returns to them with increased unconsciousness and fervor. Eventually she will find a route to the deep and dark, but the way down may be difficult.

I speak of this as a woman's passage, but it may play out in a man's life as well, for the archetype of the mother and child is also part of a man's experience. Some men in particular are defined by this myth and go through a similar development, in which the maternal feelings are initially very strong and then find their depth and maturity. The man may then tend his own life, his own child self, so to speak, and withdraw some of his excessive care for others, in whom he tends to see a child in need.

I have felt this particular pattern mainly late in life. I became a father at fifty-one. I can see traits of both my mother and father in me, and, like my mother, I feel the suffering of a child acutely. Once, while in New York for a business trip, I made an appointment to see the head of the United States UNICEF committee. I had hoped I might be able to do something for the organization, since I couldn't make a significant financial contribution. Nothing came of the meeting, but it represented for me an effort to express my maternal feelings more effectively. On another occasion I joined former U.N. ambassador Andrew Young on a program to raise money to help children caught in wars. It meant a great deal to me to participate in that event, though it was a small contribution. I keep trying to deepen the mother-child emotional pattern and give it more reality, but I don't feel as though I have made much progress.

As a therapist I found it a challenge to speak for the underworld mother. People expect therapists to be nurturing and supportive, and interested in their growth. But to represent the underworld mother faithfully, you have to honor the emptiness and the loss. The nature mother becomes underworld queen. You gain your depth at a price: specifically, you lose some of your obvious maternal attitudes and become more complex. You give yourself both to others and to the quest for meaning and identity.

Professional men and women have their own parallel dark night. They may spend their days and hours making a living, keeping the needs of their family in mind. Then they, too, find that this is simply not enough to make their lives worth living. They, too, have to discover a deeper dimension, their own underworld. Unfortunately, they may collapse into alcohol, affairs, or excessive work—underworlds that are too literal and concrete. Instead of completing the myth by finding first the void and then some purpose in themselves, they fall into various symptomatic states that disrupt their lives. Eventually they have to make their descent, like Persephone, into a deeper, more complex way of supporting their families, one in which their own needs and the needs of others overlap, or where they help their children find their own way in life.

DEEP AND DARK SPIRITUALITY

Hekate is a moon goddess, a witch and a shrew. She terrifies and deprives. She is at home in the dark and the empty. It isn't comfortable to discover her place and her necessity. And yet what she has to offer is nothing less than the entire deep spiritual realm of the soul, the invisible, unchanging core. She is a teacher of the invisible depths, and her tasks in that role are quite different from the ordinary concerns of the nurturing parent. Her job is to keep the way to your depth clear of debris and to inspire you to renew yourself eternally in the emptiness of your very being.

In other words, the dark night has an unusual guiding function in the soul's life. Berry says that when we arrive in the dark realm of the underworld—I am calling it Hekate—"One is, so to speak, deeper than one's emotion. One is beneath the depression, the black mood, by having gone down through it to the point where it no longer is." Sometimes you know the very minute you have passed beyond or beneath the emotion you have felt for a long time, now to focus on the matter of meaning. What does your experience imply? How can you look at yourself differently now?

In therapy we look for signs of this descent. At first there may be many complaints about the loss of meaning and the fear of being disconnected from life. But then we see stages in the descent. Fear turns to emptiness. There is nothing to talk about, nothing to understand. Silence becomes more familiar. Even dreams lose their liveliness. We discover that there is a place deeper than depression.

It can be helpful to distinguish between the feeling of depression and the sense of existential emptying. Here you are beyond emotion. You are sensing your reality and your personhood. The emptiness you sense may not be yours, not even personal. It may be the vacuum of life. You may be standing at the edge of your atmosphere, looking out on the empty space of your unknown world, as though you were in a space station looking out into the universe. This absolute, deep, highly personal religiousness is a gift of Hekate, the nocturnal spirit, a gift of your dark night.

BARDO: PREPARATION FOR NEW LIFE

The dark night of the soul may have a *bardo* quality. This is the state mentioned in the *Tibetan Book of the Dead* that is a liminal period between the old life and rebirth. One of the many instructions in the book for preparing for your new life reads: "Meditate for a long time on your special guiding spirit, as if it were a vision without any real inherent substance, an illusion. This is called pure illusory body. Then let this spirit disappear, from its edges inward, and rest for a while in the inconceivable state of emptiness-luminosity, which is nothing whatever."[26]

Admittedly, this is a strange instruction, but in light of our discussion of the emptiness of a dark night, it makes sense. It adds the intriguing idea of "empty luminosity," which is how I imagine the moonlike Hekate spirit to be. You arrive at the point where your sadness or sense of loss no longer dominate. They don't have the reality they used to have. You have finally fallen lower. You are now beneath all the emotion that has disturbed you for so long. Things are not better, but you are in a different state. Perhaps you are now where the dark night has been trying to take you. Now you are almost ready for new life, and that is the purpose of *bardo*. Slowly, a different kind of light begins to glow from inside you. Your friends may at first worry about it; it isn't sentimental, it isn't entirely rational, and it isn't always inspiring.

It's easy to talk about renewal and change, but profound shifts in the condition of your soul don't happen easily. They are always mysterious and happen in spite of your efforts. The dark night diminishes those efforts and in that way prepares you for the kind of change that is of the essence. This is why religious initiations are so strong emotionally and filled with such powerful images and ritual acts: they touch the very structures of your existence, the very vision you have of yourself and your world.

As we have seen in another context, in some primitive communities, the one being initiated will have his eyes covered with paste to signify the darkness of pre-birth. He may be naked, like a baby or embryo. He may be led into the forest blindfolded and then left disoriented and lost. All of these conditions mimic the child about to enter the world, because we humans are always entering new worlds of meaning.

When you have lost someone close to you, and friends try to comfort you in your grief, you know, but they don't, that what you are experiencing is beyond grief. You sense in your body and in the fullness of your emotion a great rupture in the world you have known, an irrevocable emptiness that is not just to be felt but completely absorbed if you are to go on. A genuine dark night of the soul takes you to this crossroad, this *bardo* place, where you have an opportunity, extremely hard won, to live in a different world.

LUNAR CONSCIOUSNESS

The dark underworld intelligence I am trying to describe is profound, but it begins in less dramatic ways. A man sits with me and says, "I really want to do therapy with you because I know you will take my spirituality into account." In the first few minutes of our conversation, I discover how much he wants to control what we do and say, even though his words say he wants to put himself in my hands. It's not at all unusual for words to contradict the message that is given in every other way. I say to him, "You don't look very comfortable."

"I don't know what I'm supposed to do here," he says, another comment I hear often. I wonder where this notion of having to do something in particular or well comes from. I am sitting there with an open mind, content to let almost anything happen. I wouldn't want violence, but I feel I could handle almost anything else.

The thought occurs to me that he is not going to stay with me long enough to get through his anxiety, and, sure enough, at the next session he tells me this is not what he expected. He wanted spiritual guidance, and he doesn't think that he's getting anything. I feel as though I have never glimpsed his soul, never got a hint of his dark night other than his defense against revealing it. I feel the let-down and disappointment. I would like to be with this good man as he explores his soul. I wonder if I have made mistakes, but in the end I don't blame myself for the failure. I try to be with the unhappy ending just as I would be with insight and the feeling of getting somewhere. The memory of this failure will stay with me for many years. I'll write about it, as I'm doing now. My door is still open to him, if he should ever want to continue. We have had no closure, because life's endings are more like cadences in music—endings that gracefully allow new beginnings.

My way is lunar. I want to sit in the dark and listen to the sounds of night. I don't want to be a solar hero battling monsters and racking up mighty accomplishments. I don't even want to convince you that my way is best. I don't think it is. I doubt that many would want to adopt my style. But I think it has value and may offer you an alternative for dealing with your dark nights.

For years I have studied the ancient and profound schools of magic. From the young and gifted Pico della Mirandola, who is known for his "Oration on the Dignity of the Human Being," I learned that the first principle in magic is to be in sympathy with nature. The magus doesn't try to overcome nature but to remain deeply in tune with it. To deal with the soul magically rather than heroically requires extreme sympathy with all that is taking place.

One couple who came to me for therapy argued loudly and fiercely during the sessions. I didn't try to tame them, though I personally prefer a quieter approach. Others have asked me: Could I go to sleep? Could I lie on the floor? Could I sing a song? Could I play the piano? Could I stand in your closet? Could I hide behind the furniture? I went along with all these things and many more. I wasn't trying to be clever and I tried not to overinterpret their actions. I didn't celebrate them or make much of them. I simply thought a magus should move with nature the way a tree bends when a strong wind blows.

I want to enter the darkness, because that is where the soul is. I feel at home when a client brings a dream, but I don't interpret it to death and turn to it for explanations about what is happening in life. I let the dream evoke the darkness. There is a kind of light in dreams, but it is moonlight. The dream glows but rarely shines.

You can bring a lunar consciousness to your own dark nights. You can look for hints of meaning and pieces of insight. You can allow yourself to be taken further into the dark and over time develop a lunar intelligence. You may learn to be patient in the darkness and see things not visible to heroic eyes. You may become less perfectionistic and judgmental. You may even discover ways to respond magically rather than rationally.

You may also become more adept at dealing with memories. The lunar way is to keep your significant memories in the dark. Give them the secrecy they require. But also give them your time and attention, because they are often the key to insight in the present situation.

Lately a certain group of memories keeps pressing on me. I'm remembering the situation twenty-two years ago when I was denied tenure at the university where I was teaching. Even now I feel the sadness of losing a way of life I loved. I wonder about people I thought were my friends and what they could have been thinking when, as colleagues, they voted against me. I wonder if they really judged my teaching as bad. I wonder if they objected to my close relationships with my students. I wonder if they thought I wasn't religious in ways they expected.

I suppose I could make inquiries and get some answers, but that isn't my desire. I hold the memories and let my disillusionment eat away at me. I'm finding out about myself as I consider them, and I see connections between them and my current situation. I have just been let go again. The publishing company I wanted all my life to work with has let me know that they have no more confidence in my work. They have forced a separation. I have been denied tenure once again. The losses pile up.

A psychic and an astrologer told me a year ago that losses would come. I'm watching things fall apart. I have a perspective on all that's happening, but it doesn't diminish the anxiety and other emotions. I'm as much in the dark as ever, and I'm trying to live my philosophy of staying cool, not looking for solutions and understanding, but being affected by each passing development.

Regularly I consult my well-worn Tarot cards, and I listen to the tapes of the psychics. I pray and meditate and go back to some old superstitious practices I learned from my family. I have faith that things will work out, but I have no certainties. After ten years of brilliant sunshine, night is arriving once again. It's a good time to write this book, which is a kind of sympathetic magic. I hope the words that come to me will give me some insight and heal me.

I play the piano every morning. These days I play some somber pieces. I improvise my emotions on the keyboard. I also turn to a poem or two about the dark. I'm drawn to one from Seamus Heaney's collection aptly titled *Door into the Dark*. The poem is called "The Forge" and makes me think of alchemy and the great smith of the Greek gods, Hephaistos. Both put the idea of forging metal in the realm of making soul. I have to quote it in full to get the entire image and because it expresses so well what often happens in periods of disillusionment.

> *All I know is a door into the dark.*
> *Outside, old axles and iron hoops rusting;*
> *Inside, the hammered anvil's short-pitched ring,*
> *The unpredictable fantail of sparks*
> *Or hiss when a new shoe toughens in water.*
> *The anvil must be somewhere in the centre,*
> *Horned as a unicorn, at one end square,*
> *Set there immovable: an altar*
> *Where he expends himself in shape and music.*
> *Sometimes, leather-aproned, hairs in his nose,*
> *He leans out on a jamb, recalls a clatter*
> *Of hoofs where traffic is flashing in rows;*
> *Then grunts and goes in, with a slam and flick*
> *To beat real iron out, to work the bellows.*

In the dark interior space of the forge, life is heated and beaten into soul. The anvil is its altar, because the sweaty work going on is a spiritual one, an alchemy by which the raw materials of life are shaped. The unicorn is a spiritual beast, an amalgam of the high and the low, just as the forge is a dark place where a tough smithy does his grimy work, hairs in his nose, a grunt in his throat. It's all very sensuous and very spiritual, and it all takes place in the dark, where the only light is made by sparks and fire.

This is the magic and creativity of the dark place. Here an alchemy of the elements transforms the raw stuff of a life into a thing of usefulness and beauty. The ring of hammer and anvil is music, and the iron anvil is an altar and a musical instrument. The work looks tough and basic, and yet it is full of beauty.

Some things are best done in the dark, including the transformation of raw material into tools and pieces of art. There is a smith in our soul who works the failures and successes of everyday life into eternal shapes that make us who we are. It's not extraordinary, this dark place of heat and hammering, but rather an unspectacular scene of hard work. You might think of your dark night as such a place and realize the importance of keeping it stocked and fired and dim. Your job is to provide the setting and let the divine smith do his work.

This night work is closely akin to the magic of Hekate. Both, hard work and enchantment, are proper to the dark night. In mythology, Hekate and the divine smith Hephaistos were lovers and had a son who was a smith as well. This bit of myth tells us that sheer emotional darkness and the forging of the soul, Hekate and Hephaistos, are connected and even overlap. There is much to be done during your dark night, which is full of mysteries. Your job is to take care not to interfere with the work being done by bringing your dayworld biases to it. Let night be night. It has its proper spirits, its tools, and its tough workers. It can do more for you than all your day work could ever accomplish.

A dark night can toughen you and steel you, helping you to be a real presence in your world. In the realm of the soul, most of us are wimps at first. We have to deepen and strengthen our outlook and style. Notice that the people I employ as models in this book felt the sting of their fate, but each also dared to live out the life that was given to them. They were defined by their willingness to be themselves and make something of their fate. The most precious gift of your dark night might be the sheer edge and heft of your soul, your presence as a person of real substance.

CHAPTER FIVE

LIFE'S IRONIES

DURING A DARK NIGHT of the soul, it helps to have your imagination wide open, both active and receptive. But we live in a world charmed by studies filled with numbers and charts, and machines full of blinking lights and a steady hum. We reduce most of life to factual and technical language and feel satisfied with talk of genes and DNA. In this environment, imagination, wit, and humor seem soft and nonessential. The problem is especially acute in North America, where we give more credence to the result of a poll than to a good idea. Many think of spirituality as a dour thing, and so they shy away from sharp humor, wit, and challenging ideas, which they consider irreverent. Permeating this whole scene is an intellectual sleepiness encouraged by passive media such as television, movies, and magazines that offer little intellectual challenge.

By wit I mean the ability to have an original response to

events or to see humor instead of tragedy everywhere. Wit allows you to take a large view of matters that might seem personal and small. In my practice of therapy, I always try to add some humor and intellectual spark to the often swampy and humorless experience of a life problem. Even in the dark you have to be awake and alert.

People often sense one emotion at a time, instead of appreciating the emotional complexity of the situations in which they find themselves. But it is possible to have "emotional wit," to see past the obvious feelings and appreciate the paradoxes and ambiguities that surround you. I have learned more about this important quality from Zen Buddhism and Sufism than from psychology books, which often deal with information in a heavy-handed way. Zen and Sufism use humor and intellectual zest as a way to convey complex mysteries.

The people I trust most to be my teachers and guides can laugh at the human situation and at themselves. They can see irony in the most serious matters. Their laughter seems to free up their compassion and liberate them from narcissistic worry about themselves. Tragedy tends toward self-pity, while a more subtle and complicated view allows you to go beyond any preoccupation with yourself.

In some dark nights, the heaviness and despair come from exaggerated seriousness. A person may collapse into the emotion instead of using his wits to see what is happening to him. Most of the people I cite in this book for having dealt effectively with their dark nights keep their humor and mental sparkle even in the worst of times.

The worst offenders of the virtue of irony, this talent for multiple emotional and intellectual points of view, are moralists. They think they know what is right and wrong, tell others how to live, and see themselves as models of virtuous living. Next in line are literalists, who anxiously take their every thought and belief as pure fact. They are incapable of appreciating the paradoxes in belief and need to feel that they possess the truth.

Irony keeps out both superficial sentimentality and intransigent moralism.

In many segments of culture today, having a lively intellectual life is considered "nerdy." It's "cool" not to know anything about history and not to have a thought in your head. The meaning of life is often reduced to cruising with the popular culture. It doesn't take a course in psychoanalysis to glimpse severe anxiety behind this posture of know-nothingness. If you had ideas and took yourself seriously, you would have to be constantly awake, educating yourself, and getting involved in your community. It's safer to hide out in a pretense of ignorance. For that is what "cool" mindlessness is, a way to sleep through life and not feel the sting and challenge of being engaged.

The media cooperate in this cultural narcosis by "dumbing down" discourse on world events and promoting a lifestyle that is passive. More now than ever, they appeal to the lowest common denominator of education and intellectual curiosity. I have met televison producers and station managers who believe that you have to be dumb in order to be entertaining. They assume that people want to be spoon-fed with lazy entertainment and that they don't want any intellectual challenge.

One of the most striking weaknesses of television is its lack of wit. Generally you have to go to independent films and out-of-the-way literature to find brilliant, imaginative alternatives to formulaic storytelling and low-brow entertainment. Yet the sentimentality and anti-intellectualism that has come to be expected in television educates, or "de-educates," masses of people on a daily basis.

The result of this culture of witlessness is a broad-based dark night of sleep. Our situation is like that of a fairy tale like *Sleeping Beauty*, in which the people of the castle have been enchanted and can't wake up until the right person comes along and dares to battle with the overgrown, thorny brush. Our soul is asleep, and the whole of life with it. No one seems to want to deal with the brambles that lie between us and our cultural sleep. Sleeping

Beauty is unconscious for one hundred years, a symbolic number that suggests a mental stupor deep in the society and its people.

IRONY: AWAKE AND CYNICAL

Some people complain about irony, confusing it, perhaps, with cynicism. They seem to think that too much irony keeps you aloof and insincere. But that isn't the kind of ironical sensitivity I am talking about. I'm decrying the collapse of a witty, comic understanding of the human condition. My personal preference is a subtle humor and wit, the kind I find in dry stand-up comics, in the writings of Samuel Beckett, and in stories told by Zen teachers and Sufi masters. But slapstick and gutter humor has its place, too.

Beckett's depressive humor runs through all his work and life. When asked to write the words for an opera, he wrote a single line of text: "I have no desire to sing tonight." And he once said to a friend, "There are two moments worthwhile in writing, the one when you start and the other when you throw it in the waste-paper basket."[27] Beckett would have made a good Zen master, or perhaps he was one.

It is the very nature of spirituality, which cultivates a more than human perspective on things, to be essentially humorous and ironical. It offers a different point of view, usually in sharp contrast with conventional wisdom, and so irony is of its essence. The teachings of Jesus, for instance, naturally flow thick with irony, as do most assertions and narratives of the religions. People asked Jesus who was the greatest in the Kingdom of Heaven. He brought a child over to him and said that unless you become like a child, you can't enter the kingdom. But this is an ironical teaching. Millions of people today are trying to become skilled at meditation and knowledgeable about spirituality, while Jesus says you have to be like a child.

To be religious is to be ironical, because you always see the bigger picture. The *Tao Te Ching* says, "He who speaks doesn't know; he who knows doesn't speak." This teaching, too, is ironical, since you would assume that all the many preachers and teachers know what they're talking about. Whenever I speak this line, which I often do in public lectures, I have already contradicted myself.

I have been saying all along that one way to get through a dark night is to become darker. Now I can add: A good way to become darker is to have a keen appreciation for the ironies all around you. You can develop a knowing sense of humor that allows you to see through the superficiality in your world and its false virtue. You don't become cynical—that would be going too far—but you lose your innocence. You notice that things are often the opposite of what they appear to be, and you use your wits to avoid being led along by naïve, one-dimensional interpretations of experience.

THE TRAGIC AND THE COMIC

One good road out of the "tragic" ego is a sense of the ironical and the comic. You may get to the point where you realize that if you want happiness, you have to accept profoundly and honestly the sadness that waits at every turn. Every decision for happiness will get you in trouble, and your occasional courageous forays into the dark will likely give you a taste of heaven. Opposites weave back and forth into each other, like a thousand yins and yangs interpenetrating.

Many theologians and religious people largely avoid irony and instead try to state their positions one-dimensionally, allowing no mystery, and therefore no real religion. They are often the most irreligious of people because they use the language of God to fortify their own human, one-dimensional ideas. Like all moralists, they speak from anxiety and therefore can't achieve the necessary humor. Humor is a sign of comfort with the unpredictable ways of God and nature.

This artful, subtle, paradoxical perception of the tragic/comic nature of our ordinary situations is the absolute rock bottom of any attempt to deal with a dark night of the soul. John of the Cross, like many mystics, appreciates irony and writes with quiet wit. Look at almost any line in his writing and you will immediately sense the irony with which he praises darkness. He is always turning the tables on the habit of spiritual people to praise the light. He begins one of his poems:

> *O dark night, my guide,*
> *more desirable than dawn.*

Brian Keenan, the Irish writer held captive in Beirut, was thoroughly ironical in relation to his captors. They had complete physical control over him. They deprived him of all basic human requirements and beat him regularly; yet, he never let them have the moral advantage. Reflecting on their brutality, he writes, "The more I was beaten the stronger I seemed to become. . . . To take what violence they meted out to me and stand and resist and not allow myself to be humiliated. In that resistance I would humiliate them." Of his friend and companion hostage he said, "I had seen John McCarthy turn from someone who was frightened, as we all were, into someone who was unafraid and totally committed to life." The shift from fear to vitality is a movement from literal collapse into the situation to getting a different, positive perspective on it.[28]

These strong-hearted men teach us how to deal with oppression and ignorance. You can't always beat your persecutors at their own game, but you can turn the tables on them morally. Literally you may be an out-and-out victim, without recourse. But in character you can turn everything upside down, making every small aspect of your dark night ironical. You can turn humiliation into courage, and fear into a love of whatever life is left to you.

CREATIVE AVOIDANCE

Brian Keenan's remarkable story teaches how not to catch the fever of the enemy. He used his wits constantly in an effort to avoid becoming who they wanted him to be. The same is true in all dark nights. There is always the temptation to take it all too literally and one-dimensionally, and become a mere victim. The loss of power through superficial victimization calls for a witty, ironical response. You can refuse to play victim, no matter how thick the layer of coercion that lies upon you.

One problem in much abuse is the tendency of the one who is hurt or oppressed to imagine himself as victim. I'm not saying that victims are responsible for the situation, but that they don't have to take oppression on its own terms. You can refuse to assume the role and, instead, find strength in yourself, no matter how private and internal, to keep from collapsing into victimhood. The problem is that by entering the field of victim you may constellate in others the role of aggressor. Life is full of such dramas and characters, and to a large extent they are unconcious. Brian Keenan's captors tried hard to play the roles of jailkeeper and oppressor, but throughout his captivity he was able to keep the balance imperfect, and through his various taunts and tricks prevent them from acting out smoothly and completely what they wanted.

In the most ordinary situations people want to bind you and give you orders, and often this attitude is entirely unconscious and on the surface kind. I run into the pattern as a lecturer. I'm asked in a polite way to arrive at the hall an hour early. By now I know that this lead time is for the comfort of the host. He wants to be sure I'm there for the event. But I tell him, "No, I'll be there ten minutes before the hour." Then the host wants me to see the arrangement of the lectern and go through a sound check. "No, I say, I trust everything is fine." I've learned that all these tests are a waste of time and keep me captive, when I'd rather be free to do something else. Almost always, everything runs smoothly, unless my Mr. Magoo kicks in and I forget about the event altogether.

In a similar way, as a psychotherapist, I thought it was my job not to get caught in the narrative and drama into which my patient wanted to put me. Sometimes I could be clever and slip away from their often unintentional manipulations, but at other times it was so difficult to avoid the patient's effort that my only recourse was to refuse to play the game altogether.

I developed a Houdini style of slipping out of the straitjackets my well-meaning clients prepared for me. I was not always successful, but year after year I learned how important it was not to join forces with the deep, daimonic powers that had possessed my patient and wanted to claim me. One of the chief ironies that characterized my entire career was the notion that the only way I could help someone heal was to avoid the intention of healing. I didn't make a grand case for not being conventional; rather, more often I simply avoided presenting myself as a healer. I found therapy to be full of traps in which people used the force of their imaginations to undo everything we were trying to accomplish.

An obvious example of such a trap is love and sex. Many women made themselves available to me, and sometimes I had to steer away from conversations that I knew were seductions. I knew I wasn't immune to such persuasions, and so I tried hard to remain in a different narrative altogether. This sometimes made for unusual conversations: one person speaking from one story, and the other operating in a different drama altogether. It was like having King Lear speak to Snow White.

Whatever the nature of your dark night, you might consider this basic principle about not being naïve in your response to it. Simply to play victim is to cave in to fear and make all the mistakes associated with literal-mindedness. You can always bring wit to your situation, actively reframing what is going on and how you are feeling. Emotions need not be taken on their own terms. The sharpness of your imagination can affect how you feel. You can always inquire into the origin of your fears and dread. You can ask yourself just what it is that bothers you, refusing to accept your situation exactly as it is presented. Irony promotes complexity, and it is simple-mindedness that usually gets us in trouble.

I have counseled men and women who were deeply disturbed and yet quite capable of seeing the irony in their situation. Maybe the disturbed are more likely to think more creatively than those blandly caught up in the thought-patterns of their families and the culture at large. A person threatening suicide, for example, may hope to lure you into the role of rescuer. I have always tried to refuse that manipulation. Of course, you have to come from somewhere. You have to act some sort of role, and you will doubtless be influenced by unconscious factors. Still, with imagination you can always find another option, a point of view that saves you from sailing into the unconscious hopes of the other.

Sometimes your small victories are symbolic. Keenan tells a story from prison of making a candle out of pieces of wax and a string fashioned from clothing fibers. He begins the story by remarking, "There is always something in us that will not submit." He and his colleague had been forced to spend hours every day in darkness, but this candle was a small, symbolic resistance. He concludes, "Quietly, calmly a sense of victory welled up in me and I thought to myself without saying it, 'They haven't beat us yet. We can blot out even their darkness.' "

A CREATIVE INVERSION OF VALUES

A woman of considerable wit who knew the underworld of emotion more than most is the poet Anne Sexton. I didn't know her personally, but her letters reveal a person who could be both intelligently ironical and naïvely susceptible. She once wrote to a friend, "Don't worry if they say you're crazy. They said that about me and yet I was saner than all of them. I KNEW. No matter. You know. Insane or sane, you know. It's a good thing to know—no matter what they call it." She knew that her constant struggle to live her emotionally ravaged life had its own validity and meaning. She was loyal to it in many ways, and yet she eventually committed suicide. Her sense of irony apparently didn't go deep enough to save her life.

Later she wrote in a very different tone to the same friend about her suicide demons: "I hope to hell my present shrink can help me work this out before it's too late." No irony here. No sense of her own strength. No distance on her situation. She has surrendered to the professionals, whereas before she could turn the tables on the supposedly sane public.

Compare this last plea of Sexton's with Brian Keenan's constant and faithful effort not to give in to his captors. Sexton wasn't as consistent and perhaps didn't realize how important it was for her survival to keep her wits at work. Brian Keenan may have had the advantage of a more literal captivity. The prison of Sexton's fantasies and professional care was not so apparent.

Still, Anne Sexton's ironical sense that she was better off than the public who considered her crazy offers a model for anyone dealing with a dark night of the soul. You have to *make* your own world, instead of succumbing to the one that presses on you. You have to turn the tables on what appears to be fate or the full weight of society. Against the greatest odds, you have to keep your wits about you and refuse to surrender to anyone or anything less than divine. You have to be faithful to the mystery taking place in your heart, rather than to any idea or system that would try, with the best of motives, to disempower you and make you theirs.

If the dark night is to be as beautiful and powerfully life-giving as John of the Cross says it is, then you have to grasp the special enlightenment offered by the dark. We saw this in the mythology of Hekate. You have to adopt a lunar style, one that is in tune with the dark, instead of succumbing to the bright intelligence of the world around you. But all of this requires an active reframing of your situation, turning it inside out, knowing that what appears to be defeat is actually survival.

A dark night of the soul need not be depressing. Today we tend to think of all emotional negativity as depression, and so we imagine ourselves sometimes to be depressed when in fact it is only the world that is pressing down on us. You can be bright, thoughtful, creative, and imaginative during a dark night. You can use all your power to imagine your situation in your own way. You can reverse expectations and refuse to be literally defeated. And none of this has to be a denial of your tragedy or the repression of your feelings.

SPIRITUAL WIT

The sense of irony I am describing is a spiritual attitude rather than a psychological technique. It requires a transcendence of your situation and a vision of things that is far more expansive than the circumstances imply. It asks for a degree of strength and imagination that can only come from a spiritual point of view.

The many Sufi stories about the mullah Nasrudin teach the importance of wit. Among my favorites: Nasrudin goes to a music teacher to take guitar lessons. "That will be ten dollars for the first lesson, and five dollars for each lesson after that," says the teacher. "Fine," says Nasrudin, "I'll start with lesson two."

You can always reframe the situation you are in and imagine it in a number of different ways. If you take it literally, only as it presents itself, you're lost. One year I was in a discussion group of highly successful business leaders. I was an assistant professor at the time, making a salary most of them would consider loose change. Someone posed the question: "If you suddenly came into possession of one hundred thousand dollars, how would you invest it?" For an hour they debated sophisticated issues of investment and stocks, a world I knew nothing about. I sat there with my Ph.D. and an empty head. When it came to my turn, I said, feeling quite inferior, that I would quit my job and live off the money, doing the writing I wanted to do and hoping that it might eventually start paying my bills.

The life and teachings of Zen master Shunryu Suzuki are rich with irony and a profoundly comic viewpoint. Suzuki's biographer and student David Chadwick tells a story of having trouble finding the proper balance between austerity and indulgence: "I told him I couldn't stop snacking in the kitchen. Sometimes I'd sneak into the kitchen at night, eat leftover guest desserts, and drink their half-and-half. Suzuki reached under his desk conspiratorially. 'Here, have some jelly beans,' he said."[29]

A little clean, honest wit can save you from the heavy seriousness that gives life a tragic tone. The odd thing is that your dark night need not be tragic. You can see through it and beyond it. You can avoid the temptation to be moralistic toward yourself or others, and also refuse to be the victim of someone else's moralism. Moralistic judgments are always based in anxiety. They sound high and righteous, but they come from a small, worried, and barely concealed desperation.

THE STRATEGY OF ECCENTRICITY

A good example of a life of paradox is the Canadian pianist Glenn Gould. He was known almost as much for his eccentricity as for his musical genius. Many thought he was insane, but most of those same critics celebrated and perhaps envied his celestial talents. One music critic said of him, "He was certainly neurotic, and definitely drugged in his later years, but the weird thing is that he was so much saner than most people, in a lot of ways. I mean, he was so much more thoughtful and funny and friendly and kind, on his own terms, on his own carefully controlled terms, than most people."[30] This most eccentric of performers wore gloves in warm weather and prepared for a concert by placing several radios around him tuned to different stations, conducted the roaring of elephants at a zoo and stopped performing publicly at the height of his career because he thought the audiences were voyeurs. And yet, paradoxically, "He was so much saner than most people."

Gould's way was to enter the eccentricity of his soul by playing the brilliant fool, and, like other artists, he made a great contribution to his society out of what many friends described as the torment of his personal life. The idea is not just to speak ironically but to live with such deep paradox, fashioned from your terror and strength, that despite its confusion and concerns, the world can't suppress you.

Gould was undoubtedly a highly neurotic person. His eccentricities, which blinded many critics to his talent, were not a problem for him. He thought his gifts far outweighed his mannerisms. His playing suffered only when he occasionally became sensitive to the criticisms. Generally, he transformed his anxieties through strong humor and imagination into parody and fun.

In therapy I have encountered people who were deeply disturbed and covered it over with their brilliance. What I saw in them was not irony at all, but a gulf between their emotions and their way of life. They didn't convert their conflicts into creativity but instead created a shield of aloof superiority that thinly covered the inferiority occasioned by their inner torment. Interestingly, their creative work fell short of the brilliance they feigned, as though it was necessary to reconcile with the pain in order to fire the imagination.

Gould seemed to convert his confusion (one friend said he had a "colossal" fear of sex) into eccentricity and creative adventurousness. He seemed to fear nothing aesthetically and professionally, but personally he was riddled with anxieties. Still, people liked him and enjoyed his company, in spite of his odd habits. It seems to me that Gould's eccentricity was a compromise between his inner torment and his talent. He could be the great musician in public life through the medium of his odd ways of seeing things and behaving.

Gould's example teaches a few key lessons:

1. If you are highly neurotic, or worse, you don't have to become normal and healthy to live a creative and loving life. You can learn to transform your insanity into eccentricity.
2. You can ask your family and friends to adjust to your dark night. If you are loving and reasonably creative, they will want to be with you.
3. You can shape a life around your insecurities and failures, giving them limited space as you go about your creative activities.

I once knew a young musician, an appealing and talented man, who thought he was Christ. He wasn't eccentric, he was highly neurotic, at best. There was no paradox in his personality. He appeared normal at first, but soon you discovered the extreme inflation in him. You couldn't be at ease with him because he hadn't found a way to give his grandiose vision any reality. You saw no dark night, so covered over was it by his exaggerated sense of himself. You knew he was suffering, but you weren't sure that he knew. Anne Sexton certainly knew. I think Glenn Gould knew himself very well, but he kept that knowledge strictly private.

That takes us back to Sexton's remarks about knowing. You have to know you are in a dark night and you have to live your life in consonance with that knowledge. To be in the dark and yet capable and forthright is itself rather ironical. The alternative is to pretend to be bright and carefree, when you know yourself to be solidly in the dark. What is needed is not pretense but complexity. You don't hide your suffering, you weave it tightly into the whole fabric of your life and personality.

CULTIVATING AN IRONICAL LIFE

How can you develop a constructive sense of irony in your life? A first step might be to reconsider basic ideas you have about human life. Many people live by sentimental notions that haven't matured into appropriately complex ideas. Life is complicated, usually more so than your understanding and philosophy of life. A sense of irony develops from deeper thought and a more educated imagination.

Don't be quick to accept the interpretations you find in the popular media. I know from years of experience many of the weaknesses in radio, television, and print media. Writers and editors are often in search of what is newsworthy rather than what is insightful. They are usually educated to be good at communications, but they often don't have much background in the material they are reporting on. In a day's time they may have to examine a host of topics and present intelligent reports on them. In my experience, they do their best but their ideas on the deepest questions are not any more sophisticated than the average person's. Still, they form opinions. Psychological interpretations of what I'm calling the dark nights tend to be based on research and lack fresh ideas. Religious interpretations are based on beliefs, and they tend to be highly slanted and moralistic. Political solutions are almost all ideological. You can't even trust your friends to give you an objective picture because they have your best interests in mind and may withhold their real opinions. They want to care for you, not show you your soul.

No, you yourself have to take your life seriously. Feel its weight. Admit its complexity. And as Jungians would say, honor its shadows. Irony can come only from an awareness of the good and the bad, the successes and the failures, the areas of intelligence and the zones of folly and ignorance.

Know that you are both intelligent and stupid, often in the same moment. Admit to what you desire and what you fear. If you did little more than these two things, you would be filled with irony and your actions would be infinitely more trustworthy for their honesty. It's all right to have grand and eccentric longings. It's all right to be afraid. Only by embracing these two emotional pillars will you glimpse the nature of your soul, which is the ground of your existence.

The soul is not the ego. The soul is made up of virtue and vice, neither of which need literal enactment. The ego craves acting-out, and it aims at being either singularly virtuous or vicious. It doesn't enjoy complexity, and that is why it is not a good base for companionship and community. Erasmus says that human community arises out of mutual foolishness. The only folly worth discussing is that made up of your desires and your fears.

A dark night of the soul takes you to Hell, where you not only feel withdrawn from life, you also discover your own perversity and dark inclinations. You find that you are a complex person, and that life itself can't easily be divided into good and evil. Maybe you stop identifying with the good and own up to your own tendencies toward the bad. Like Persephone, you give up your innocence and take some authority in and from your underworld.

IRONY AND THE DIVIDED SELF

You finally discover that it is not good to spend your life trying to be good and aligning yourself with the virtuous people of the world. It might be better to avoid that divided self altogether and instead simply live with compassion for yourself and others. You are not perfect, and you never will be.

Identifying with virtue only hides your tendencies to evil, it doesn't get rid of them. It makes it more difficult for you to see your own immorality, and if you can't see it, you can't deal with it. Evil people as such either have given up on the good and identified with evil, or they think of themselves as good and are blind to the evil they do.

You cannot be good by thinking of yourself as good. You have to sink into the complexities and go down far enough into life that you realize that it is not even good to be good. To do what other people may judge as bad may be the best you can do. Certainly you have to admit to your moral ignorance in many matters. Can anyone be certain in every decision that they are doing the right thing?

This is a point Mahatma Gandhi made frequently while encouraging his followers not to become too proud of their virtue. He wrote, "The impurity of my associates is but the manifestation of the hidden wrong within me. . . . The epithet of 'Mahatma' [a title of spiritual respect] has always galled me and now it almost sounds to me like a term of abuse."[31] An awareness of your imperfection does not have to be masochistic or exaggeratedly humble. It takes a deep sense of personal security to steer clear of the ego comforts of virtue. Apparently Gandhi enjoyed sufficient emotional security to examine his attachment to being good. The irony, of course, is that such a selfless person should worry so much about his moral failures.

In your dark night you may learn how to become darker. It isn't enough theoretically to believe in shadow. You have to live it in such a way that it is real but not literal. We honor Martin Luther King, Jr. today, but in his time many believed he was a danger to the society because of his civil disobedience. Even today, in a time of terrorism, it is considered wrong to criticize the government. Catholic priests have tried to purchase virtue through celibacy, and yet we are discovering that in many cases their virtue was merely repression, and the dark sexual shadow has been emerging as a loose, uncontrollable passion.

To do evil is not to manifest your shadow. The soul's shadow is itself ironical and paradoxical in that it has to be full and genuine, but it can't result in actual evil acts. It is a color of the personality that keeps you from excessive virtue and innocence. The darker hues of the shadow ground you and give your thoughts and actions substance. Compare the sentimental moral pieties of a superficial spiritual leader with the tough moral positions of those committing civil disobedience in the name of a great cause.

There is a kind of destruction that is necessary for the continuance of life. Religions praise this kind when they offer images of destroyer gods, such as Kali and Durga in India, and even Shiva, who dances the movements of death as well as life. Even the anger of the Old Testament God can be seen as a sign of necessary destruction, the kind that keeps life in motion. But there is a kind of human evil that is only malicious. It doesn't further the processes of life but only satisfies the emotions of the evildoer, and therefore it isn't real evil but only a pose.

The people who held Thomas More, Terry Waite, Dietrich Bonhoeffer, and Brian Keenan captive, and all their imitators up until the present, give a good impersonation of evil, but, though their acts are atrocious, they themselves are too simpleminded to be evil. Just as ordinary people can't seem to do all the good they would like to do, so evil people can't be intelligent enough about their concerns to evoke genuine evil. The same is true of those who oppose them in the name of virtue. Their well-meaning reactions are equally simpleminded. They end up responsible for actions that are as evil as those of their enemies. The entire drama of wars and terrorism gives not a hint of genuine virtue or genuine evil.

And so we are left with a great battle, not between good and evil, but between really living and just pretending. Both the righteous and the evil avoid life. They don't have the subtlety to understand that good and evil are the yin and yang of existence. Anyone passionate about life is neither all good nor all evil.

The great Hartford poet Wallace Stevens once wrote, "Realism is the corruption of reality." I take this paradoxical adage to

mean that whenever you get caught in realism—taking everything factually and on its own terms—you miss the chance to
really live. The really real is made up of both fact and the human
imagination. If you can't think, reflect, and actively imagine your
life into existence, you are condemned to a half-life of unconsciousness. You are mired in facts and information and opinions
and slogans. In effect, you are imprisoned in the stale notions of
a dead society.

Wallace Stevens also wrote, "Things seen are things as seen."
Another mind-twister. Imagination is everything, because we
can't know or experience anything outside our imagination of it.
But the imagination can be old, tired, and irrelevant. It needs to
be revived continually. You need to reform yourself at regular periods. Otherwise you become soul-dead, and you live and act as
though you were not alive. How many contemporary people feel
that way?

Perhaps the dark night comes upon you from inside or outside to wake you up, to stir you and steer you toward a new life. I
believe this is the message of most religions, and certainly it is
the gist of Christianity and Buddhism. Your dark night may be a
bardo, a period of apparent lifelessness that precedes a new birth
of meaning. Maybe your dark night is a gestation, a coming into
being of a level of existence you have never dreamed of. Maybe
your dark night is one big ironical challenge, just the opposite of
what it appears to be—not a dying, but a birthing.

PART TWO
DISTURBANCES

A man must wrestle till the dark centre,
that is shut up close, break open,
and the spark lying therein kindle.

—JACOB BOEHME, *ON TRUE RESIGNATION*[32]

CHAPTER SIX

LOVESICKNESS

ANYONE WHO HAS BEEN THROUGH A DIVORCE, lived with a jealous lover, or suffered domestic abuse knows that one of the primary sources of a dark night is love. Love may begin in darkness, as in the image of Cupid blindfolded when he shoots his flaming arrow. You are suddenly taken by another person and possessed by passion. Then come periods of confusion, longing, and, perhaps, thoughts of ending. What begins full of hope and promise turns into serious questioning and emotional ambivalence. While a lover may interpret these ups and downs as a personal problem in making a commitment, it might be more accurate to understand that love itself is inconsistent and has a kind of inherent hysteria.

People in love may be threatened by or possessed by jealousy, find themselves the victim of another's need to control, get stuck in a cold and maybe abusive relationship, or fall into an impasse in which their love gets nowhere. They may feel they are with the wrong person, at the wrong time, in the wrong place, and for the wrong reasons. Frequently love doesn't work out or it gets stale. People dream of passionate love, thrilling sex, and a tranquil life, but their dream often turns into a nightmare.

The ancient Greek poet Sappho, one of the great love poets of all time, was the first to call love bittersweet, though she reversed the words to sweetbitter. The philosopher and poet Anne Carson says this is because love is usually sweet at first and then turns bitter.[33] My impression is that love alternates between sweet and bitter or is perpetually bittersweet. People often talk about love's sweetness and keep its bitterness private.

Love is also a kind of madness. It seals you in a bubble of fantasy where emotions are intense. You feel unbalanced. You do silly things. Your sense of responsibility disappears. You are deaf to the reasonable advice of friends and family. In your delirium you may get married or pregnant. Then you spend years in the aftermath trying to make a reasonable life. At any point you may fall into a dark night of the soul created by the profound unsettling that love leaves in its wake.

WALKING ON COALS

One curious aspect of lovesickness is its tendency to last long beyond its period of ripeness. People know that they are in a situation that is not good for them, and yet they let it go on and on, often for years. Even if they don't do anything actively, they expect the relationship to improve. Many cling to the security they have rather than risk it for a more vital but unpredictable relationship with someone else. But often people are just reluctant to end a relationship until it sheds its last drop of promise.

Some people put off the inevitable until they can stand it no longer. Then their resolve is clear and forceful. I had a client once who one morning was sitting at the breakfast table waiting for his wife to join him. Eventually she came down from the bedroom with her bags packed. That was the last he saw of her. Apparently, the decisive moment had arrived for her, but he was devastated. Talking with him, I was surprised to see a huge blind spot in him. He had no idea what his wife was going through. He assumed life was as simple and pleasing for her as it was for him.

It takes time for the soul, so deep and complex, to sort itself out and arrange itself for a decision. My own way is to wait and wait until the apple of decision is about to fall on its own. No doubt, I am extreme in my patience or temporizing. When I counsel others, I feel no rush. I think it's important to gather oneself together before making a move. Many people make decisions just on the principle that you should do something. I'm afraid it may take a while for the soul to catch up with them.

LURED INTO DARKNESS

After years of practicing psychotherapy with men and women of all ages, I am convinced that love is the most common source of our dark nights. It may be romantic love, it may be the love for a child. The lure is strong, but the darkness is intense. It is as though love always has two parts, or two sides, like the moon, a light one and a dark one. In all our loves we have little idea of what is going on and what is demanded of us. Love has little to do with the ego and is beyond understanding and control. It has its own reasons and its own indirect ways of getting what it wants.

Robert Burton, who lived in the time of Shakespeare, diagnoses love as a sickness and at one point suggests that it might be better to avoid it if you can. But to choose not to love is to decide not to live. Everyone needs to love and to be loved. You surrender, and then the spell descends, and you get swept away into days and nights of fantasy, memory, longing, and a strange sensation of loss, perhaps the end of freedom and of a comfortable life. Even if you have had many experiences of painful and unsuccessful love, you don't give up on it. The soul so hungers for love that you go after it, even if there is only the slightest chance of succeeding.

Some people appear to give up on love, and you see the lifelessness in their faces. The soul craves love, and if you give up on love because it is so difficult, the life will seep out of you like air out of a punctured tire. You will go flat. You may wonder why life has no meaning. You may not realize that meaning is love, and it is love that gives life its shape and purpose.

Clearly, love is not about making you happy. It is a form of initiation that may radically transform you, making you more of who you are but less of who you have been. If you don't realize that you are walking on coals and running the gauntlet and surviving the wilderness in quest of a vision—all within the confines of a simple human relationship—you could be undone by it. Love gives you a sense of meaning, but it asks a price. It will make you into the person you are called to be, but only if you endure its pains and allow it to empty you as much as it fills you.

AN AFFAIR OF THE SOUL

Love is an affair of the soul and is intimately tied to your destiny. It comes when you least expect it or when it isn't convenient. It may disappear at exactly the wrong moment. It may come and go and return again, with no apparent reason for its volatility. Ancient artists pictured love as an adolescent with wings, a sign of its flightiness, a quality that may afflict a person of any age. For love itself is young and can make you feel younger than your years. It can also age you, especially at those times when it suddenly departs, or when the object of your love is no longer there for you.

The dark night aspect of love is shocking in its contrast to the bright airy quality of love's beginnings. How then do you get from adolescent wings to the adult doldrums? The answer may be again that love is in service of the soul, and so its natural direction is down into the depths. You may want to remain at the level where love feels like play, but it takes you quickly far into the seriousness of life. The couple who thought they could experiment with sex, and later find themselves pregnant, know well this quick descent into reality.

Adult friends and family might try to warn a young couple about the dark side of love, but, of course, the warnings can hardly penetrate the tough yet thin bubble of fantasy. It seems somehow important that love be free of the encumbrances of wisdom and practicality. It can't burn itself into a life if it is held back by practical wisdom.

Some people find love's darkness within the context of marriage and partnership. Others go through a long period of distress because for one reason or another they can't achieve a lasting relationship. Whether you are looking for love or trying to make it work, it can be the most difficult challenge in life and at times may seem absolutely impossible. The impossibility slowly cracks you open, teaches you the limits of human understanding, and gives you a bridge from the human to the divine.

WHY IS LOVE SO FRUSTRATING?

A woman named Amy told me recently of a man she has loved for many years at a considerable distance. He is the meaning of her life, and yet, she says, he can't express his emotions and can't satisfy her need for a real lover. She goes on with her active life, but all the love in her stays focused on him. Friends tell her that he will never be available to her, but she hangs on.

Amy remains stuck because she believes that her man is capable of opening up and he never does. As so often happens, there is a magnetic pull toward impasse. It's as though the soul wants to be stuck. It doesn't want success, and it doesn't want life to flow and move on. Friends and family don't understand this situation, because they are concerned about life, not soul. They want their children and their friends to be happy and to show signs of success in everything—family, work, and love. If they could look into the soul of their friend and child, they might understand that it's not time yet for happy conclusions. The soul has its own timetable and its own needs. If those needs are not met, the stalemate may stretch out for a long while.

Amy talks about her frustrations in love as though they were completely external. She firmly believes that if the man she adores ever shows his love to her, everything will be fine. But I doubt that's the case. When love is stuck or frustrated, you have to look at yourself and your own part in it. Yes, it's very likely that your loved one is also stuck and has a problem with love. But your impasse indicates that your imagination may have to broaden. You may have to look closely at the way you are living, because it is this life of yours that you are bringing to the unhappy relationship. You have to look at yourself, not just at the other, and you have to consider the whole of your life. Your love life is not disconnected from all other dimensions of your daily experience.

Although it may seem obvious that love is all about getting people together to share a life, it is also, if not primarily, an introduction to further depths of the soul. You may never have meditated or contemplated before, but now you are forced to brood and think. You may never have felt so affected by your emotions, and now your emotions crowd out most other considerations. You may never have given yourself much to fantasy and daydream, but now that is your preoccupation. All of these developments show an increase in the activity of the deep soul.

Now, as the relationship develops, it can become, as Jung says, a container for the soul. As you change and as the relationship goes through many stages, you are introduced even further into the soul. If the relationship doesn't get far or has an unexpected ending, even then you may feel compelled to feel your emotions and rehearse your story again and again in a process that may sculpt out the space you need just to have a soul. At this point, some couples reconnect, but often it takes a new relationship to build a mature form of love.

As the religious traditions say, love is the creative force, making out of your life and experience an articulated world, a life of meaning and sophistication. People who are experienced in love are at a different stage in development compared to those who have yet to go through this particular kind of initiation. Love fuels every dimension of life, and what looks like romance or relationship may be the development of a more widespread passion for life. That is why our love initiations are crucial. If we can work them out, all of life can have an erotic quality.

HALF IN AND HALF OUT OF LOVE

I received a letter recently describing yet another kind of impasse. A man wrote to say that he is completely devoted to his wife and family and yet is in love with a fellow worker. They have had a "relationship" for years, but, he complains, she won't make love with him because he's married. He waits and pines, shifting between seeing his passion as an expression of soul and as an invitation to change his life. He doesn't know whether to stay in the impasse, give up his family, or let go of the passion. None of these options is acceptable to him, and so he stays where he is.

Reading the letter, I was reminded of the words of James Joyce: "In the muddle is the soundance." In this impossible impasse, something of importance is happening. Most of the alchemical work of C. G. Jung goes back to his idea that the process of becoming a person begins with a mess. If you don't have the mess, you might have to look for one. Most of us, of course, don't have to look far.

Therefore, I was not entirely dismayed by this man's muddle, but I was surprised to see his focus on sex rather than the desire to be with the one he loved. If they have a sexual relationship, he will still be in a triangle, and, as far as I can see, nothing will be resolved. He might feel less conflict than I would, being in a sexual triangle, but I suspect that something else is going on. Often in love it isn't clear what you're looking for. Wild enthusiasm for a new person might be love for sheer wild enthusiasm.

These two people have established a form that works for them at the moment—both married, with an asexual relationship on the side—that satisfies the minimum of their passion and answers their need to be responsible to their spouses and children. They feel frustrated in relation to their love, but satisfied enough to remain where they are. Still, a triangle usually wants to expand, and my correspondent feels an urgency for change.

I encouraged this man to look at the larger role of eros in his life. When passion gets so focused outside the normal structures, it can be a sign that something is wrong with the status quo—at work, at home, with friends and family. I suggested that he use his frustration to fuel his imagination and reconsider the whole shape of his life. With our modern mind-set, we tend to separate meaning from emotion. We don't understand that our passions have something to do with life making sense. We also tend to focus on the problem at hand, as though it were a mechanical issue in need of engineering. We often fail to see how all parts of life are connected, and how difficulty in one area may indicate change in another.

One possibility in this case is that, considering that the "other" woman is a coworker, she shares the man's professional life more than his wife does. This is a common situation. One spouse, man or woman, is completely connected to the children and household, or perhaps to another profession altogether, and there just isn't enough life for the couple to share. It's a simple point: Love invites us to share not only our persons, but our lives. In the creation of a life together, it might help to realize that love needs to expand, including friends, families, work, ideas, and cultures. People often wait for life to take shape unconsciously, instead of cultivating the various areas as parts of a whole. They may become aware of these needs too late, or they never understand the root of their dissatisfaction. So they start over with a new person.

I don't know if this is the issue with the man who wrote me, but my guess is that it is something similar. His image of relationship seems too small, and as a result he is caught between two different loves that offer him the kind of life he wants. Marsilio Ficino frequently said that if you are faced with the choice of two or more things, always choose all of them. In some way it would be good if this man could choose both loves. It isn't obvious how this could be, but I'm sure that eventually he could find a way out of his impasse and dilemma.

LOVE EXPANDING

Jungian psychologists, such as Adolph Guggenbühl-Craig, see marriage as a means of individuation. Through the trials of marriage, you forge yourself into a person. I would add that marriage is not only about the psychology of each individual, but the making of a creative partnership that might issue in good work, effective parenting, a strong family, a vital circle of friends and neighbors, and, ultimately, even a more mature nation. Our personal efforts at love affect the world in which we live, not just sentimentally but by building character and giving depth to the personalities that make culture.

I recently heard a former president of the United States make a crude, sexist comment about a woman who had been debating with him. Immediately I thought of ways in which this man's anxiety about women and sex, transmuted into a crude way of speaking to and about women, showed in his national and international policies. Marriage and other intimate partnerships are the crucible in which your soul matures and allows you to be a creative, ethical, and thoughtful person in other areas.

With this understanding of love, you don't try to resolve

love's dark nights by engineering a better relationship. Your focus is on the soul and its deepening and strengthening. In therapy I have seen many people go through fierce torments of love and emerge from them not with some sentimental ideal of harmony and compatibility, but with eagerness to live and work and contribute to society. Perhaps it is appropriate for love to incubate for a while in a cocoon that keeps life at bay, but eventually this long-incubated love can extend outward to a world in desperate need of mature relatedness.

MASOCHISTIC ENTANGLEMENTS

Love's dark night is often painful because one person feels completely dependent on another's willingness to foster the relationship. Waiting for the dam of another's love to break is yet another example of masochism. You have to be endlessly patient while the one you love decides to respond. The masochism may continue even if you end up living with the one you love. There may always be something else that is promised but not given. The masochism may be the way of the relationship and not a single issue.

Many people find this pattern excruciating. Of course, it can be a way for one partner to have power over the other, and it does seem that the powerful and the meek often find each other. The solution is not for the powerless one to build up enough anger and resolve to switch roles, but rather to surrender to something greater, to life itself. The power play of the couple may be a stand-off that serves as a defense against either partner really living. Such couples may fruitlessly focus on themselves and avoid a creative life in the world.

James Hillman has criticized a pattern of personalism in contemporary culture, explaining everything psychologically and focusing on self-improvement. I would add my own complaint about "couple-ism," the tendency to reduce the meaning of life to romantic love. One of many problems in such an emphasis is the disappointment that follows marriage or some other kind of partnership. People are left without excitement and purpose. Their lives become dull because they see the resolution of romance as an end-point, instead of the beginning of a life in which they contribute to society.

I once knew a young man who hated the job he had in the financial world. He had the potential to do well in it, but he felt little desire for it and gave it little energy. At the same time, he was completely dependent on his wife. He never felt secure with her and constantly imagined her being with other men. As so often happens, he never made a connection between his problems at work and his misery at home. He seemed to know nothing about the ways of life. He was like a child expecting the world to always comfort him and ease his worries. His childlikeness made him an appealing person in some ways, but soon you saw his inner torment and then his tendency, a common problem of masochists, to try to control you.

Here was someone in need of a serious rite of passage from childhood to adulthood. He came to me mainly for help in dealing with his feelings of insecurity in his marriage. But to me it appeared that he was ripe for a fundamental change in being. His marital problems were only the surface of a fundamental weakness of spirit.

It wasn't easy talking to him, because a masochist often believes rigidly in his virtue. He thinks he is all good and the world is giving him a bad time. We had to break through that protective illusion and see who he really was. I don't mean that I knew everything and had his whole system figured out. But I could see the contradictions. It seemed to me that he had yet to enter a real dark night of the soul. He was keeping it at a distance by acting out a false kind of surrender.

Here is another interesting dynamic that you may find in all kinds of dark night. You have to distinguish resistance against the dark night from the dark night itself. People trying to avoid the pain remain in an empty, defensive, and fallow period precisely because they won't let the dark night happen. The real dark night is not as bad as the resistance to it; a dark night has more life in it and less ego.

Recently, I had a conversation with a friend who is often victimized by the person she loves. An unusually intelligent and sensitive woman in her forties, she complained to me that her partner refused to get married because, he said to her, she was only after his money. She was deeply hurt by the remark but didn't want to upset the delicate balance they had in their relationship. After all, he was generally a kind and attentive man. She had it in her mind that either he would suddenly be enlightened, and change, or she would finally learn how to be in a relationship. I didn't have much hope for either of these solutions.

I thought she might need to deal with her passivity in other areas of life. Her romantic relationships were too explosive and complex. She didn't have the vision or the strength to change her ways there, but she might make changes at work and in relation to her family, both of which were in need of attention. It is often the case that destructive patterns in romantic relationships reflect a larger habit of giving away too much or identifying with powerlessness. Often, it's more effective to deal with these issues at work or some other place than in the highly sensitive arena of a sexual relationship.

Masochism is disguised control. My friend's life had been on hold for years because she considered it important to keep all her relationships calm and ordered. This highly controlled suffering is full of ego and essentially blocks the natural flow of life. When that flow is finally released, a deeper source of strength becomes available, shattering the masochism and establishing the paradoxical condition of strength in yielding. Finally being able to let life flow through you, you discover a calm and courage you may never have felt before.

The only effective way to deal with masochism is to let it gradually corrode your willfulness. If you are in love with someone you know will never be available, you may have to admit your passion to yourself and to a few others, maybe even cautiously to the person in question. You may have to be humbled by the emotions until they release you. Eventually you may have to give in to the conditions life has imposed: the love you want may not be available. It's that simple.

The relaxing of your will, however desperate, allows life to proceed. It may not go according to your plan, but whatever it makes will be more secure and ultimately more satisfying that anything you could force into existence. Such are the lessons of a dark night.

STUCK

To the man waiting for his triangulated love to burst into sex and life, I would say, "Live more generously in every area. Your lover's obstinate resistance to your love mirrors your own resistance to life." The final resolution of a love triangle may not be a new marriage, but a new way of participating in life. Love is not interested in calming your storms. It wants life to flourish—in couples, families, and communities. Ultimately it wants to connect you with the source of life itself. Your being stuck may signal the limits of your imagination. You may have to understand, finally, that love is not about you, but about the world.

As a therapist, I am careful not to offer false means of escape from impasses and relationship binds. I am in the business of caring for the soul, not engineering a person's life. It's tempting to become the hero and savior, but getting life in apparent order is not the same as giving the soul what it needs. It may need more chaos, deeper impasse, and increased darkness.

To the woman stuck in her devotion to a heartless man who seems ever at a distance, emotionally and physically, I would say, "Love your life unreservedly. His detachment from you mirrors your own failure to love the stuff of your person and your life. You have to go down into your inferno and discover what is really going on. Waiting for another person to love you is not living. Once you allow your own life to flow, you have the best chance of attracting the lover you should have."

To the man who can't get his professional life moving and is obsessed with his wife's supposed infidelity, I would say: "Grow up. Discover the joy of good hard work. Learn that if you don't force or trick people into loving you, they will give you honest and secure affection. The more you try to control it all, the less you will have of what you so strongly desire. No one gives you a sense of security. You have to get it for yourself, mainly by living your own life with enthusiasm and by learning to love yourself. How will you get to this point of feeling secure and loved? Probably through a real dark night of the soul."

THE MIRE OF LOVE

In the summer of 1974, the poet Anne Sexton wrote about her feelings about her divorce to the writer Erica Jong. "There are many times when I wish I had not left my husband or that at least I had left him for somebody, and although that would have engendered guilt on my part, it might be easier than this madness. . . . My brain waves keep telling me that this is simply disgusting and debasing, but there it is, and I am sunk into a mire this past week of utter despair."[34]

People often think that once they have solved the immediate problem in the relationship—in Sexton's case, divorce—they can get on with life and forget the past. But the soul holds these intimacies eternally. On the surface, divorce is an ending, but in the depths it is only a beginning. Memories will persist, and remorse might make an appearance time after time over many years. You might wish you had made a different decision, and your regret may pull you off balance. You may have to look beyond the relationship as a life structure and come to appreciate the profound level to which love, complete with its difficult endings, takes you.

Romantic love has a purpose, an enormous purpose. Its task is to free you from the bubble of practicality and ordinary busyness, to reveal the fact that you have a soul and that life is far more mysterious than you imagined it to be. Once you make the shift from pragmatism and literalism to soul life, in which imagination and emotion are far more significant than mere action and analysis, your dark night will have done its job. It may lift. You may see light again and feel lightness. But you will not be the same. Part of you, like Persephone, naïve girl and queen of the underworld, will live in this realm of shadows even as you act and react in the sunshine. Never again will you be quite so innocent in matters of love.

In some instances love may ask near impossible patience. You may have to wait for circumstances to change, for the loved one to wake up to the possibility of real love. Often people meet and begin their connection in circumstances that would seem to preclude any serious, lasting relationship, but over time the obstacles melt and life takes new shape. It's often impossible to know if the passion invites a shared life with the other person or if it will remain impossible. Either way, the soul is involved, and you have no choice but to stay close to the emotions and the fantasies. You can trust them, not to arrange life the way you want it, but to arrange the elements of your soul in a way that will offer rich life in the future.

THE LOVE TRIANGLE

We have discussed triangles in passing; let's now focus on this, one of the most common complaints of people coming to therapy. I have often listened to a man or woman seemingly dedicated to their marriage and family, confess to being stricken with a new and threatening love. Most didn't want new passion in their lives, but they savored it. Before they knew it, they were in the very eye of a storm, a triangle that offered no satisfying exit.

You may be married, with children, relatively comfortable and even happy. And yet a new love appears to shake up your entire existence. You spend hours and days trying to sort out your emotions, searching for a solution. With some insight and guidance, you may discover that it isn't a problem but a mystery. You may realize that you have to enter it more fully in order to get out of it. If you try a quick and easy exit, you will soon find yourself back in it. These romantic triangles don't come out of the blue. They have a purpose.

The love triangle is one of the most common forms of impossible love. It may take you through several stages of struggle. At first you may be deluded into thinking you can will the unwanted love away or maybe weave it into the smooth fabric of your life. But soon you discover that neither option is workable. Then you reach for your moral principles and try to shame yourself into a solution. You think you should be loyal to your marriage and protect your children. You should stick to your principles and uphold the values that you learned as a child.

The second phase is the shocking realization that the moral route doesn't completely work. The passion remains, and for all the contortions to embarrass yourself toward a solution, your longing increases and you go a step further into the darkness of desire. As the Greeks pictured it unsentimentally, the goddess of love is Aphrodite, a spirit that adds immense grace and pleasure to life, brings sexual joy to marriages and to lasting partnerships, but also disregards established structures to cause jealousy and separations. A modern reading of the ancient Orphic hymn to Aphrodite addresses her as a goddess of the sea and says:

> *You are beautiful necessity*
> *Even in the frenzy of the shark*[35]

In his famous painting *The Birth of Venus*, Botticelli showed us the alluring side of the love goddess being born from the waves, but he didn't give any sign of the shark. In your innocence you may first envision your love with Botticelli eyes. Only later will you smell the presence of the beast.

What is the purpose of illicit and inappropriate love? Why do we fall hard for someone just when life is making sense and coming together? In some cases a new passion may signal problems with your partner. It may also be part of that long and challenging process of finally feeling in the right place and with the right person. On the other hand, you may realize that the new person wouldn't make as good a partner as your spouse or lover, and yet the passion continues to flare up.

The great poetry of the ancients consistently says that love is fundamentally mysterious—not just difficult to understand, but vast in its implications. Why, you might say, did this person come into my life just as my marriage was settling down or just as my first child was born or just when I finally felt in control of my life? You may ask the "why" question, but it doesn't go far enough and allow that there is another will or design involved. "Why" doesn't take you into the mystery.

In his extraordinary book on the soul and love, *The Myth of Analysis*, James Hillman writes that impossible love tortures the soul into a new level of awakening. "Before connection is possible, psyche goes through the dark night of the soul, that mortification in which it feels the paradoxical agony of a pregnant potential within itself and a sense of guilty, cut-off separateness." [36] I have seen this explosive confrontation of desire and guilt in many people suffering the confusion of an impossible love. They shift back and forth, from one halting decision to another, from one loyalty to the other. The very instability of their thinking and feeling is a sign of the dark night and the failure to achieve the attitude necessary for resolution.

The love triangle forces you out of the fusion, as Hillman calls it, to recover your individuality, whether or not you want it. As psychiatrist Robert Stein put it, love always involves a desire to couple and to uncouple. The desire for fusion paradoxically breeds an immediate or eventual desire to disconnect, and this separateness is confusing, especially when fusion has led to a home and family. Besides, everyone talks about the power of love to build relationships; they say nothing about its capacity to destroy them.

COMPETING DESIRES

Robert Stein's insight into the coupling/uncoupling paradox is crucial. You might realize, when you feel a strong desire for union, that an opposite desire lies in the background. The more you press for connection, the more you may be setting yourself up for disconnection. It isn't enough just to be aware of the paradox. You have to give something to both sides. If you get married or live with someone, you might also give serious attention to your need for separation. You don't hold back on your love and involvement, but you understand that you need your solitariness and individuality as well. You have to be subtle, loving your partner and loving yourself, or very soon you may find yourself in a dark night.

The very impossibility of some loves brings you close to the mystery, allowing the soul to be initiated by your strong emotions and even your confusion. You are brought to a new level of loving where it is possible to work out the paradox of being a person and being a partner. In Hillman's version, the pain of love is the discomfort of psychic pregnancy. Love's impossibility forces you to become a different person. You are forced to think and consider what love is all about. You believe you have to make hard choices, but, more important, in your deliberations you are educating yourself.

You can't love deeply until you are a deep person in the first place, and the torture of difficult love is the very ordeal that makes you a person capable of strong love. Your love for another, especially when it is difficult or impossible, works on you and prepares you for a different way of loving.

Theologian David L. Miller says that the presence of a third love keeps the soul engaged. "The eros by triangulation seems to signify the constant refusal to substantialize the third, to keep it in talk, in fantasy, in story; it is not a thing or actual person, but the interplay between two persons."[37] You may be convinced that the problem in the triangle is the other person, but Professor Miller suggests that the real problem is the situation, the triangle as a whole. You have to envision where this dynamic triangle is taking you.

Many of the love triangles I dealt with in therapy involved parents. The question often asked is, will it hurt the children if their parents separate or divorce? You can't give a universal answer to this question, but you can safely say that if one of the parents is stifling himself or herself for the sake of the children, chances are that the children will suffer. They need a parent who is boldly and caringly embracing life, and it's unusual for life to be both strong and neatly ordered. Chaos is one way in which life renews itself, and if a parent avoids chaos, the children will not have the energetic care and modeling they need.

I remember a woman caught not in a triangle, but in a pentangle of new lover, old husband, children, her parents, and herself. They were all implicated in her love life, and each of them added pressure to the muddle. After a few years of struggle, she resolved the emotional geometry by discovering that she hadn't been giving enough love to her own interests and abilities. Once her career blossomed, the other loves all took their highly original, unconventional places. It was a resolution she never could have imagined in the early days of her despair.

THE UNKNOWN LOVER

In a triangle the third "person" represents the soul. Being out of reach, this soul figure keeps you in a perpetual state of wonder. This is when you may seek out a therapist to give attention to your deeper life. This is when soul shows itself and becomes an unavoidable factor. The impossible love sublimates in argument, self-analysis, and wonder. Through the very difficulty it presents, you become a person of enlarged understanding.

Artist Joan Hanley calls the third figure in the triangle "the unknown lover," the secret fantasy lover of the soul who lies behind every lover in the flesh. Part of the pain of love is that no person, however suitable and satisfying, completes the desire for love. There is always a remainder, because love takes us beyond the human sphere. It puts you in touch with the ultimate object of desire. It invites you to transcend yourself, to be more than you ever have been.

Once you see that love is more than a human emotion, that it is a passion whose work is to keep life going, you may not expect it to suddenly turn off when it has accomplished the human goal of making a marriage and a family. It has larger purposes, because love is the fuel of life. You can't get too settled, or you will stop living. On the other hand, you can't act out on all your passions. You might continually ask, what is it that I hope to receive from this new, third person, and can I get that in some other way? This is a crude, initial question, but it points in the right direction.

David L. Miller says that the third takes shape as fantasy and story. You have to learn how to live more symbolically and poetically to let the "unknown lover" do its work. The third lover is not real, in the sense that he or she doesn't quite fit neatly into your life. His very distance makes the love impossible and, at the same time, creative. In the restructuring of life it forces you to consider, you may come up with a fresh idea of how life could be. If the love made sense in the context of your life, the new lover wouldn't be a third. You have to think and talk it through, and even if you never arrive at a solution, you will have gained much from the process.

INSIDE, OUTSIDE, IN BETWEEN

People who are caught in triangles talk about their "side" relationship as though it were not an integral part of life. The illicit romance often sounds like an excursion into playland, not that it isn't serious or real, but that it lies outside the boundaries of normal life. That trespass of the ordinary may be part of the attraction, and indeed, people speak as though the adventure were as important as the other person. French philosopher Georges Bataille says that real love always involves a transgression.

In a broader context, we spoke of a dark night of the soul as being in a liminal place, somewhere between normal and completely otherworldly. A love triangle has its own style of liminality. Couples meet in transient places—restaurants, hotels, automobiles, out in nature. They don't want to be seen by friends and family, and they soon realize that their shared passion is somehow set apart from life. This liminal quality may be disturbing, but it is also creative. Sometimes married people, in an effort to renew their life together, try to recover the liminality of illicit lovers. With that same intuition that transgression gives love an edge, rather than rush into a staid marriage with a conventional wedding, some couples elope.

Still, the question remains for many people: What do I do when I'm caught in a triangle? Is there a fix for this problem, a cure for its suffering? Some people are especially sensitive to the pain they cause their partner or their children. Children sometimes disown the mother or father, depending on which one is seen as the destroyer of the family.

The couple may feel pulled both toward respectability and toward adventure. Both are desirable and both require equal attention. The impossibility of it all leaves you in a profound impasse. You may even suspect that once the adventure—the transgressions and the liminality—is over, you may be left with the familiar problems of the respectable relationship. You may enjoy the liminality, no matter how much you complain about it.

THE TRIANGULATED SOUL

One woman I knew, who was in a relatively happy but dull marriage, was powerfully attracted to a man who had a serious problem with alcohol. It seemed that her desire for an affair had nothing to do with wanting to be free of her husband, but instead represented breaking out of a too conventional life. She needed some new and adventurous experiences. She resisted the affair for a long time, because, she said, she would upset her conventional extended family. I certainly didn't encourage the affair, but we did explore her habit of suppressing her passion because of her upbringing. I thought that perhaps if she could work that issue through, she might be spared the confusion of an affair. But, in fact, she had a brief relationship with the other man and then returned, considerably changed, to her familiar situation. Her friends were surprised that she expressed no regret or remorse.

People often make the decision to separate or remarry, but I don't take even these developments literally. I try to keep the state of the soul in mind. A practical solution doesn't necessarily mean that the crisis is over. Tensions may ease, but the soul may not be satisfied. You have to dig deep, realizing that a triangle is indeed a spiritual invitation for radical reevaluation of the whole of life. It is not a problem to be managed and engineered, but a mystery that most people have to deal with at least once in their lives.

Life is full of triangles, not only in romantic relationships, but at work, in the family, and in politics. Whenever you try to harmonize two factions, a third appears. For years I have tried to keep my work and my family connected. I work at home, and I sometimes co-teach with my wife. My daughter has grown up in adult seminars and book signings. What I didn't count on was a powerful third factor—the world asking me to travel frequently. In many ways, the enticements of a big world are like the seductions of a third person. So far, we live in the tension of this triangle, working it out the best we can, frequently trying new arrangements.

Once the triangle settles, you have to move on to the next challenge. Initiation is not education, and a dark night of the soul is not a learning experience. After it, you may not be wiser. You may still fall into complicated and painful situations. You may not emerge an insightful, together, experienced person, able now to handle life's complexity with ease. But you will be more familiar with love and perhaps more open to its own kind of creativity. You may be able to let go and delve into the mysteries of love. These may not be the lessons you want to learn, but they may be more valuable than anything you could concoct, because to be undefended against love is to live life more fully. The lesson in countless tales and paintings is that the torture of love ripens the soul.

DARK RELATIONS

Love's dark nights of the soul don't end, of course, with romance. Many people endure years and even lifetimes in marriages and other intimate partnerships that drain the life from them and destroy all signs of tranquillity. In the extreme, both men and women enter abusive situations and find it difficult to leave them. The dark night of the soul finds its mirror in literal nights of fear and disgust.

You may wonder how you ever got into such a mess and why you can't get out. Some people seem drawn toward abuse, finding it everywhere. You could imagine literal abuse as a substitute for the alchemical mortification, the lacerating and suffering of the soul. And yet the shift from love to loathing is often part of love, keeping marriage mysterious and dynamic. The hygienic fantasy of marriage may seem positive and beneficial, but it locks relationship into a static expectation of success and happiness that has no life in it.

People often talk and write about marriage as though it were a surface arrangement full of life problems and interpersonal emotions, but it goes far deeper. It is a mystery that engages the deepest memories, fantasies, and feelings. When people marry, their souls, as John Donne said, intermingle, but not always for the good. Being married is to enter into the morass that is another's web of past and present experience and to allow the other to enter yours. It isn't so surprising that over time it feels like a dark night, so jungle-like is the terrain of the soul. Furthermore, it is primitive stuff, reaching far into childhood and also into the primitive depths of human culture.

In intimate relationships the family saga is played out, as are the archetypal, mythic dramas that are the foundation of all human life. The loved one is a body of persons, some from memory and some from myth, and it isn't always easy to know the figure you are struggling with or the one with whom you are in love. Not that the love isn't real. The loved person is genuine and the emotion is genuine, but it is complex, involving the whole field of personal history, character, and fate, much of it irrevocably mysterious.

Lovers sometimes say that each brings half of life to make a whole. It might be more accurate to say that two parts of a story draw each other together. An aggressive person might attract someone who habitually plays victim, so they can play out their unfinished patterns of power. A nurturing, maternal person, man or woman, finds a helpless, vulnerable child to care for.

These patterns are many and varied, and usually they're subtle and largely unconscious. Once in a while a relationship seems a complete and total myth. When the myths are simple and lived out without much reflection, they can become difficult and even dangerous. The work of a relationship is to bring out the complexity in each person and create a fresh story, in which the common motifs weave together like subtle colors in a fabric.

LOVE'S OWN UNDERWORLD

Love has its own underworld. If you glimpse that deep interiority in the most mundane of situations, you may have a chance of finding your way through love's maze. If you don't appreciate the deep soul, you may find yourself spinning in confusion and wondering why you keep repeating the same "mistakes." You have to become initiated into love's mysteries rather than its techniques. You have to be swept away by it and yet intelligent about it, taken further into your spiritual destiny, rather than lost in the mirrored sphere of sheer romance.

Love is a dark night. Dark nights are largely about love. Once you give up the bright light of consciousness and understanding, you may discover that you can be in this world in a darker way, living by love and desire rather than by rationality and control. You don't give up your intellect, but you allow love its natural dominance.

A dark night of love forces you to reassess the place of love in your life. Eventually you may discover that the most ordinary loves among your friends and family and with your partner may lead to a more mysterious kind of love that is essentially religious. Your love expands to include the world and beyond. The Sufis, those passionate mystics of the Islamic tradition, say that our human loves form a ladder to the divine.

CHAPTER SEVEN

WEDDING NIGHTS

M ARRIAGE, too, is a kind of madness. People often enter it thinking they have a glorious, trouble-free future in front of them but later feel betrayed by their desire and stuck in a nightmare. Even happy marriages have their moments of stress when thoughts of ending it snake their way into consciousness. Many opt out of the difficult marriage and head for divorce, only to repeat the same patterns in a new relationship. The biggest mistake people make is to think that marriage is a rational arrangement rather than an insane attempt to give life form and stability.

You may think of marriage as a choice based on a feeling of love for your spouse and the desire to be together. But this image of marriage doesn't recognize the madness of it all. One day you may be shocked to discover how difficult living together can be. You probably didn't know how deep your feelings were and how radical the change was when you took your vows. You also probably don't realize how your past relationships, going all the way back to childhood, play a prominent role in your current marriage, complicating it with an invisible underlayer of memory and habit.

Marriage is a rite of passage wrongly understood as a rational life choice. It is not a surface change in living arrangements, but rather a shift in being, in your identity, and entire outlook. Marriage is a shock to the system of each partner; that is its promise and its pain. It can mature you like few other experiences can, but the process is neither easy nor entirely pleasurable.

In counseling couples, I discovered, first, how often people link up with the wrong partners. Maybe most marriages are odd, as two unlikely people bind themselves to each other. People also marry for the strangest reasons. They are charmed by a single quality in a person and never think about what it would take to live a full and long life together. They imagine eternal courtship and confuse the fusion of their fantasies with a creative linking of lives. The wedding is part of, and often the end of, a period of romance, in which the main factor is a thick and dreamy unconsciousness.

AN ALTERNATIVE TO COMMITMENT

I never like to speak against romantic love, because it is one of those illusions that forces you out of practical thinking and allows the soul to come into the foreground. The problem is the life decision made from that place. Marriage appears to be an intensification of romance. Or it may offer the security of commitment and social approval. You may marry out of your jealousy or a desire to possess and limit. A basic question in deciding to marry concerns deep motivation: Is this an affirmation of life, or is it an attempt to constrain it?

This word "commitment" is one I often question. I know

that it is considered sacred by some and healthy by others, but I see it as little more than a sentimental euphemism. Often it has a moralistic tone—"What is wrong with you that you can't make a commitment?" So, men and women feel bound to commit themselves and guilty if they fail to honor their commitment. I don't sense much soul in the idea. In fact, I'm not sure you can be committed and at the same time actually love someone.

An alternative is to offer your love and companionship freely, refreshing your attachment every day. You may love in a hundred different ways without feeling "committed." Many people go through deep and dark torment either because they can't commit themselves to another, or because the one they love won't "make a commitment." Maybe the lesson from all the pain is to give up the idea of commitment altogether. It isn't rich, free, and genuine enough to be worth all the attention.

Without the moralistic obligation, you may be able to love from a deeper place. Love is like life itself: You can't restrain and control it too much without losing its vitality. You have to trust it and enjoy its gift for the moment. That doesn't mean your love won't last, but what use is a love that is long-lasting, but bitter and forced? I suspect that the many dark nights associated with marriage offer the possibility of a maturing of the very idea of love. Through your dark nights, your marriage might become more subtle, more deep-seated, and truly secure. Forced and controlled security is quite ungrounded and easily lost. Real security comes from open-hearted loving, not from resolutions and promises.

The soul of a marriage needs the elaborate rituals, parties, food, music, dress, and family gatherings that help people weave their lives together. Promises and vows can be soulful, but they can also be rooted in fear and empty principle. The extraordinary expense of a wedding is a payment made to the spirits hard at work in the great mysteries of romance, marriage, and homemaking. You don't need an expensive wedding just to live together, but you do need a strong acknowledgment of the depth to which marriage takes both the lovers and their families. Marriage is a creative, disturbing, long-lasting, pleasure-filled and sometimes tormenting upheaval in the soul. You need all the help you can get, including a powerful ritual.

THE UNDERWORLD OF MARRIAGE

No one, of course, fully knows the person he marries. All lovers are mystery partners. The person you are married to now may be quite different from the one you married years ago. Is this the person you dated? Were you blind when you made the decision to marry? Cupid causes people to fall in love, but he himself is blindfolded. It isn't so much that you were blind when you got married, but more that love is supposed to be blind. It might be better for you not to make a rational choice of a partner. On the other hand, your intelligence does have to come into play as you design your life. You have to consider carefully whether this person, this one that fills you with emotion, is also destined to be your mate for life.

When you got married, your families were married, too. Marriage is as much about families going through a rite of passage as it is about new life for a couple. Parents lose the child they have raised for many years, while brothers, sisters, and other relatives sense the change to the organic whole they have known the family to be. Marriage is a rite of passage for everyone involved. Part of its darkness comes from a limited understanding of what it entails.

Jung says that many of the conflicts in marriage are spiritual in nature and are only disguised as matters of love.[38] Why else would the religions of the world give so much attention to matrimony and use powerful and precious symbols—rings, goblets, rice, canopies, diamonds, gold? It is not just a matter of saying, "I am going to love and live with this person for the rest of my life."

It is a dedication to a form of existence based on sharing rather than self-interest, perhaps on raising children, which is a vocation and not just a consequence of being married. Maybe we shouldn't be terribly conscious of all this when getting married—it might be too daunting—but eventually we have to deal with the spiritual challenges as well as the personal relationship.

Marriage might mean different things to different people, even to the two who are married to each other. Some people imagine marriage as the very meaning of life, while others see it as a way to feel secure with someone they love and need. In many ways you may repeat the life you knew as a child in your marriage, even if you try hard to be as unlike your parents as possible. More likely, you will be both the same and different. The marriage of families is concrete and particular, relating to the house in which you live, the food you eat, the way you spend your time, and your degree of neatness. It isn't easy to marry two families, especially when the couple thinks they are starting all over.

Jung observes that one of the partners may feel completely embraced by the marriage, while the other partner focuses on life outside the marriage. This alone can cause pain for the person who feels too attached, or codependent, as we say today. The roles may shift back and forth. At one time you feel the tension of the marriage and at another time your partner has similar feelings. At first, you might crave closeness but later feel that same intimacy as a stranglehold. Marriage is made up of many opposite feelings, confusing reversals in attitude, and the constant challenges of developing personalities and ongoing life.

The affable Charles Dickens is an example of a highly creative person who experienced matrimony as a painful limitation. "The domestic unhappiness remains so strong upon me that I can't write, and (waking) can't rest, one minute. . . . I must do something or I shall wear my heart away."[39] His wife Catherine had given birth to ten children with him, but he felt no love with her, and for years he felt his marriage was a trap. Catherine was a friendly, loving, and involved woman, and Charles was attached to the children, but apparently the marriage felt too restrictive for him.

His friend, the philosopher Thomas Carlyle, had an even more devastating marriage to Jane Welsh Carlyle. Jane supported her husband throughout their long life together and at the same time tried to live an independent life. She was an original thinker and gifted writer, but she couldn't deal with her husband's obsession with work and his dark outlook on life. Late in life, she spent a good deal of her time in bed, suffering from headaches and depression. The letters of the two Carlyles reveal two thoughtful but tortured souls, and yet show how their marital conflicts spawned ideas and insights that were among the greatest achievements of their age. You sense the tragedy of Jane—she didn't give herself the chance to fully realize her immense talent—and the tragedy of Thomas—he never allowed himself the joys of intimacy.

Carlyle's biographer describes his forty-year marriage to Jane as a painful, depressive, sexless combination of innocence and repression. The husband appears to have been for the most part impotent and joyless, while his wife suffered her own innocence and sense of obligation. It was a case of individual lives being successful and of a marriage condemned to frustration.

Both Dickens and Carlyle represent a failure in imagination. Neither of them could picture marriage in a positive light, equal in satisfaction to the solitary life of the writer. Marriage took them into despair and made of their marriages long dark nights of the soul, for them and their spouses.

We might learn from the examples of these otherwise brilliant and productive men the importance of what we might call "internal diversity," the capacity to hold opposite desires in creative tension. Isn't it possible to be both solitary and wedded, hardworking and relaxed in companionship? Carlyle's root problem seems to have been a bitter religious suspicion of sexuality on the whole, and Dickens was highly articulate about social problems and largely unconscious about the demands of marriage and home life.

Even today, the Carlyle and the Dickens syndromes continue to make marriages difficult. People still don't know how to do several things at once or understand the importance of imagination in relationship. They suffer their unions because they think of them as unconscious, surface acts instead of deep developments of the soul. Many people aim for surface compatibility instead of deep, nonrational connection.

Alchemical pictures show the king and queen embracing in a retort or pear-shaped vessel. They are contained in a vessel and in solution. This is marriage, a sealed place where the soul ripens and a watery solution in which the two chief figures can unite, like chemicals separating and coagulating. The process is dark. You don't know what is going on and often confuse the deep alchemy for surface personality issues.

We come back to John of the Cross and his praise of the dark. You don't do well in marriage by avoiding pain and challenge but by learning to focus on issues that matter most. If your work is satisfying, your children thriving, your contributions to society solid, your marriage may have its place at the core of your life. Its purpose is to give you a vessel in which you and your partner come apart and grow together in a rhythm that is fundamentally human.

In therapy, I often felt obliged to create a vessel in my consulting room. The marriage was springing leaks and coming apart. It needed containment, because that is what marriage is—a vessel of transformation. It is a small version—a retort and not the ocean—of the night sea journey. It all takes place between two people and in a single home. The issues are similar. Will you rise to the occasion and become a real partner? Or will you look for an escape and sneak out through the holes in your vessel?

THE PERSEPHONE MYSTERY

In mythology, as we have seen, we meet Persephone first as a young woman charmed by flowers and close to her mother, Demeter. But then she loses her innocence when Hades, God of the Underworld, seizes her and makes her his bride in the dark place invisible to ordinary eyes. As queen of that place of death, Persephone is a very different figure, now full of power and, in some stories, in possession of a deeper beauty. She is married to the confusing, sometimes painful, and always mysterious ways of the deepest and darkest spheres of the soul.

The story suggests that there is an eternal, archetypal, and underworld matrimony, that the tortures and struggles, the ups and downs, the longings and the bondages are proper to marriage, elements of its underworld, and not aberrations and failures. The Greeks honored the fractious but loving marriage of Zeus and Hera, but they also acknowledged this strange underworld wedding. We understand the surface union that we call marriage, but generally we avoid the underworld partnership until we are forced into psychotherapy to deal with jealousies and conflicts. It might be better to have a full notion of marriage from the beginning.

The Swiss psychoanalyst Adolf Guggenbühl-Craig says that the purpose of marriage is individuation, a Jungian term for the work of transmuting the raw materials of your common humanity into a creative, individual person. He observes that many people approach marriage narcissistically, expecting it to give them all they want without asking much in return. On the contrary, he says, marriage is a form of sacrifice, a surrender of self to a greater life and will.[40]

Sacrifice is a spiritual act. You get it wrong when you sacrifice yourself to your partner. Marriage is not just for the couple, but for all couples. Think of Noah's Ark, on which every kind of animal found refuge in pairs. When you get married, you are walking onto that ark, representing all of humanity. Think of all the males and females of the animal and plant world, all the opposites in every aspect of life. They all need to be "married" in some fashion to promote life. Your marriage participates in this cosmic pattern and has a wealth of meaning that you will never grasp.

When you make a sacrifice, you don't just give something up, you acknowledge a realm greater than yourself. "Sacrifice" means "to make sacred." You go beyond self. You make room for a greater mystery. You may experience this larger sense of sacrifice in ordinary deprivations, as you give up many freedoms and soften your willfulness. You listen to your partner's opinions and plans. Your whole life may take a different direction because you're willing to share your vision.

Such sacrifices serve the marriage. They represent a deeper and more substantial surrender of self to a spiritual process that has drawn you to love this particular person and share your life. Together you become "mingled souls." Nothing is more important in a person's life than to gain soul by expanding the limits of what defines him. This is transcendence, and it is an essential part of religion.

The story of Persephone centers on a mother's sadness at the loss of a daughter, and marriage has some of that same sadness. Parents and families, too, give up something precious when a son or daughter gets married. There is good reason for the tears shed at a wedding and for the mixed feelings of everyone involved. Sometimes you get the impression that the good cheer is somewhat overdone, perhaps hiding the deeper feelings of loss and change.

If marriage were simply a matter of getting people to agree on a lifestyle, it would be relatively easy. But, according to the Greek story of Persephone, marriage takes place in Hell. This is not to say that marriage is impossible or inadvisable, but to point to the reality of this mystery often obscured by sentimental defenses against darkness. Marriage is an ordeal in which two souls, at least, mature and blossom. I say "at least," because children and relatives also benefit from the couple's generosity.

Sometimes marriage is an alchemical acid pouring over your life and personality, reshaping it and deepening it. It makes you a better person, though not necessarily a happier one. One hopes it offers moments of bliss, but you can be sure it will entail unexpected ordeals. Together, moments of bliss and periods of struggle make it a humanizing force, a way toward personal fulfillment that paradoxically involves an immediate, concrete, and felt transcendence of self. You are forced to move beyond self-regard and seriously consider another person.

The acid emotions of matrimony etch a new face. You now look at life not as an entitlement for yourself, but as a precious gift that you share. You don't become one with the other person, but you melt into the marriage, which is a merging of lives and the connecting of personalities. Your inner divisions are "married," you are deeply connected to your spouse, and you have a new relationship with your world.

NAVIGATING MARITAL NIGHTS

When you get married, you want the joy of deep companionship and love, but you are asked to give up some of your individuality, much of your freedom, and any desire you may have to be intimate with someone else. It's no wonder that some people, like Dickens, feel imprisoned. How can you keep your joy, a necessary degree of freedom, and your individuality, and yet still be involved in the marriage?

One way might be to give some attention to all your felt needs. It may be impossible to fully satisfy each of them, but often even some little offering spares you the feeling of being deprived and imprisoned. In Ireland men have their local pubs and women more varied social groups. The pub acknowledges the need for same-gender socializing and an approved relief from the marriage. In America, for men, the game of golf might be the closest parallel. Women today often gather in formal or informal discussion groups. For years a group of women has gathered with my wife in our home for dancing, talking, and mutual support. These may not be perfect solutions, but they aim at keeping marriage from completely dominating a life.

It also helps to submit to the marriage but not to the other person. Marriage is the proper vessel, not your partner. Giving yourself too much to another person can be masochistic. You suffer it, and it doesn't give you much in return. But if both partners surrender to the marriage, they may escape feelings of masochism and even enjoy the limitations of being with one other person. Building a marriage can be a joyful experience, but surrendering to another person is never a happy choice.

For many, marriage means living with your partner's insanity. Poet Donald Hall writes openly and revealingly about his interactions with his wife Jane Kenyon's bouts of depression. He mentions a particularly significant insight that came to him during a manic episode, a rare break in her depression, in which Jane was bossy, energetic, and full of desire. "Then I understood, with shame, that for years I had used her depression to think well of myself: I was the rock, unchanging in all weathers; I was the protector. Now her manic elation and her certainty cast me down."[41]

This is an incisive observation; his energy was a response to his wife's lethargy. Even after her death, he says he still acted out her strong emotions, shifting from being manic to depressive the way she had done. "Maybe I perpetuated Jane by imitating her," he says.

A poet, Hall is an exceptionally reflective man. He doesn't explain away his challenging marriage; instead, he considers many possible interpretations of the couple's interaction. As he writes of his marriage, he tries to find meaning, but he never gives up his love and wonder. The marriage is the source of his struggle, his self-discovery, and his poetry. His pain and confusion don't diminish, but they are beautifully sublimated in his reflections and his poetry. Donald Hall is a good model of a dark night purifying the soul and opening up into insight.

As a first step in navigating a marital dark night, I suggested imagining marriage less simplistically and allowing it its mystery. As a corollary, I would also recommend seeing your partner as a mysterious concoction of memory, emotion, and history, who doesn't even know herself well, and who, on top of everything, changes significantly at different times in life.

It is futile to try to simplify your partner and make her fit your expectations. Without real, complicated people as partners, there is no marriage anyway. Marriage means the coming together of differences. Still, we delude ourselves into thinking of it as a rational construction, in which we live effortlessly with people much like ourselves. As Jung puts it, "One person presupposes in the other a psychological structure similar to his own."

To honor the underworld of marriage, you have to appreciate the irrationality and mystery in both you and your partner. This is a simple rule, but it may help as you sink further into the swampy regions of marital life. From the beginning you are in the underworld, with some consciousness and maybe even some willingness. The minister or rabbi, as representative of mystery, should probably tell you at the wedding that you are saying yes to Hades and Persephone, the real models of successful human marriages. You have to have your eyes on the promise of bliss, but you also have to be prepared for the dark. The upperworld of marriage offers a degree of happiness and fulfillment, and civility and tranquillity at that level help immeasurably. But the underworld is not a place of peace and harmony. There, you can expect conflict and confusion.

It isn't advisable to try to make an idealistic model of married life out of a union blessed in both Heaven and Hell. Don't expect to solve all your problems. Don't imagine that one day everything will settle down into harmony. Don't expect perpetual sunshine. Know that marriage, for all its beauty and pleasure, is also a dark night of the soul.

SACRED MARRIAGE

On the surface, marriage is the coming together of two people to share a life. But to the soul, this arrangement has such deep implications that it touches on the spiritual and the sacred. When two individuals decide to share their lives, the opposites in all of life come closer to each other. Human marriage is part of a larger process of reconciling differences. It has social and cosmic implications, and, when entered deeply, can even contribute to world peace.

Marriage is a long process of reconciling differences in family, background, experiences, and values. Two people find themselves attracted to each other and immediately begin telling each other stories about their childhood, their families, and their experiences. These stories are by no means superficial or insignificant, for they give a taste of a complex union yet to come.

The couple may not realize the full meaning of their attraction, but they have to explore the basic question, can we and should we wed our differences? But this is the fundamental social question as well. Is it possible to blend Catholic and non-Catholic, Jewish and non-Jewish, black and white, liberal and conservative, sensitive and brash? The love of the two people for each other doesn't seem to be about these issues. Their love seems more personal, but the images surrounding weddings suggest that the union being celebrated is far greater than that of two people.

Most sacred literature suggests that the opposites that make life so interesting and painful cannot be resolved intellectually. You have to find some other means of getting differences in one place and letting them coexist or blend. Alchemy implies that it is a long and painful process, full of lacerations and dismember-ments and deaths. It has its moments of glory and its nights of pleasure, but these are empty without the other processes in which differences link up and coexist.

Even the mysterious story in John's Gospel of the wedding party at Cana suggests that in marriage, and by implication in so-ciety, water has to be changed, through an alchemy one finds in a dark night, to wine. Some kind of unnatural and uncanny trans-mutation has to take place. In the Cana story, the change of wa-ter to wine lies in the background to a marriage, implying that marriage is like transmuting water into wine, or, as Jung says, or-dinary life into spirit. When two people are truly married, their plain lives go through a transformation that makes them more complex, refined people.

The beauty of this alchemy lies in its positive use of darken-ing, separating, dismembering, and dissolving, processes ordi-narily considered negative, but here creative. Marriage's dark night is integral to its work of changing ordinary lives into a vital process sustained by love. Marriage, imperfect, trying, and per-haps failed, educates the soul, draws it out of hiding, and gives life its substance.

I place my mother and father's sixty-four-year marriage next to the three-hundred-year honeymoon of Zeus and Hera and see both as marvels of relationship. In my parents' marriage, two ordinary people were transmuted into two sensitive and hon-est sons, three outstanding grandchildren, a happy home, memo-ries of good times and close friendships, and even a little money in the bank. It is Cana all over again. Water has become wine. Simple practicality has turned into the most precious qualities of human life.

Today people assume that the goal of their work on them-selves, whatever it is—therapy, religion, fitness, education—is health and success. But Cana suggests that the result of such magic is even more precious—family, friendship, and a heart at peace. Culturally we might benefit from a shift in values, from focusing on health and success to pursuing the education of the heart, which would result in real community, intimacy, and social concord.

The grape has to be harvested and crushed. Then it ferments, as it disintegrates even further. On the way to becoming wine, the grape has its own dark night. Its bite and flavor are reminders of its journey from the vine to the vat to the carafe. You can taste its history of vegetal tragedy. You can delight in the effervescence of its maturity.

The image of Cana shows that marriage is a similar process. Not every marriage makes it to the wine cellar—there may be false starts and dead ends, but marriage has the potential to help you become a person of intellectual, moral, and emotional sophistication. But you have to participate in the process of fermentation, which may sometimes appear as a dark night of the soul.

The marriage of Thomas Carlyle and Jane Welsh Carlyle seems tragic on the surface, and yet the story of this remarkable union shows that the love survived and sustained it. Charles Dickens left Catherine and went on to a more satisfying, though much less socially acceptable, relationship. He resolved his surface tensions and fulfilled some of his wounded desires, but the deep marriage mystery went on. Donald Hall's reflections on his life with Jane Kenyon are poignant and more insightful than many a psychologist's discourse on relationship.

In some ways the dark night defines a marriage, and the way you deal with it determines whether or not the marriage has a soul. If you insist on happiness, good communication, harmony, compatibility, and steady and uniform love, you might well be disappointed eventually, not because your partner is inadequate, but because you have focused on the wrong items. The raw material of the relationship may not be pleasing. Jung describes it in alchemical imagery as vinegar, urine, excrement, and chaos. You come to marriage with the pleasant scent of naïve ideas and undeveloped emotions, with perhaps infantile and adolescent ways of relating, and then you behold the arguments and differences of opinion and style. This unlikable primal stuff can be transformed by the marriage process into something beautifully complex and subtle.

ENDINGS DEFINE A MARRIAGE

Marriages and significant relationships end in many different ways. You may separate and divorce. Your partner may die. You may go through a major change that marks the finale of an era in your relationship. How you navigate the ending is crucial.

You can remain within the complexity of your feelings and resist the temptation to numb yourself through explanation and resolution. If you follow worldly wisdom and start over fresh without a thought to the past, you may not be bothered by remorse or memory, but you will have gone nowhere. Then you might well repeat the same mistakes. The common wisdom about getting on with life can backfire, because the only way to move ahead is not to deny or repress the past. Escaping the past makes you a slave to it; you are not free to be freely in the present.

Compared to surface life, the mysteries of the heart unfold within a different time scheme. The soul reveals itself in cycles and timeless circles of experience. In your dark night, time may seem to crawl or even stop, giving you an opportunity to connect differently with your past. You can reconsider old relationships that shift in memory with the changes in your life and character. You may reassess how you acted and thought and, perhaps for the first time, feel genuine remorse. You may even be freed of guilt that has hampered you for a long time.

There are ways, certainly, that you may be stuck fruitlessly in the past, but these may be symptomatic forms, signals that you have failed to make the necessary deep connections. Someone who keeps repeating the same mistakes hasn't taken his past experience to heart. The person who can't move ahead in life may need the grounding that past experience offers. Moving ahead too quickly may be intelligent but not wise, a strong effort of will without the wisdom of a well-considered past.

The mystery of marriage is eternal, and if you have been married several times, those marriages are eternal. If you have had many relationships, not necessarily marriages, they, too, have an eternal quality and contribute, positively and negatively, to your present struggle to be related. Those dark nights of the past continue to feed the soul, provided they are not gutted by current judgments about them. People say, I know better now. I've learned from my mistakes. I won't make the same mistakes again. I've grown; I'm wiser. But these attitudes keep the past at bay and in that way try to relieve former nights of their darkness. But this well-intentioned denial of the past doesn't work, because the soul is fed by the darkness at least as much as it is by the light.

Occasionally one meets people who remain in difficult marriages for many years. Their friends try to persuade them to separate or get a divorce, but they stay where they are. It's difficult to make judgments about these situations. Sometimes it appears that the love is deep and somehow sustains life in spite of the surface problems. Sometimes the person is in danger and seems insanely stuck in a relationship that is threatening. I've also seen cases where a person has such a strong inherited sense of virtue that they think it is wrong or weak to give up. I've counseled people who finally overcame their inhibitions and were forever grateful for finally getting out of a marriage that was not threatening but inhibiting.

There are countless ways to end a relationship. Some depend on the person's temperament and time of life. It helps to know yourself, so that you find some certitude for your decision deep within your heart. You can be secure in your position, even if the situation isn't black and white. Then you have to act from your values, trusting yourself and knowing that you can handle any repercussions. The person who habitually mistrusts intuitions and inner guidance will likely have a big problem ending an important relationship.

Even the strongest people, however, may need time to sort things out, and that time may well be experienced as yet another kind of dark night. A marital dark night, in other words, may be quite different from the empty, black mood of despair that is sometimes taken as the only definition of the soul's darkness. On the contrary, it may be full of decisions and analyses and false starts. Profound unhappiness may lie far down in the soul, piled high with explanations, personal histories, and ideas. Your task is to live from that deeper place, where decisions are brewed.

THE MARRIAGE WITHIN YOU

A mysterious kind of marriage takes place entirely within the individual. The ancient Greeks called it *hieros gamos*, the sacred marriage. It is the reconciliation of the many contraries that exist in your makeup and that, reconnected over time, may leave you free to be creative and vibrant.

The Greek deities Zeus and Hera, honored for their eternal, outrageously volatile love, represent this holy matrimony of the soul. It is said that when they enjoy their love in a soft cloud of light, the great god's semen fills the universe in a spasm of creative energy.[42] Sacred stories from India similarly state that from the lovemaking of Shiva and Shakti the world comes into being. The Upanishads tell the same story about Atman creating a woman partner from whose love the world takes form. In Christianity, Joseph and Mary represent a special sacred union from which a new kind of kingdom arises.

These stories from mythology and religion can be read in relation to the cosmos, human culture, or the individual person. At the personal level, there has to be an inner partnering, an intimate connection among the various elements of the self, which often show themselves as opposites; emotional/rational;

warm/cold; youthful/old; happy/sad; intimate/distant. The ideal is not wholeness or integration, but marriage and love, not an overcoming of differences but creative coexistence and mutual influence.

It's difficult to discern these secrets in someone else, so I'll try to describe them as I experience them. All my life, for example, I have felt called to teach and have something of a public life, and yet at the same time I am unusually shy and awkward, especially in certain social settings. Most people seem comfortable speaking in small groups, but I easily become embarrassed. I feel that this is a highly neurotic aspect of my character, and as much as I have tried to overcome it, it stays with me. So I try to "marry" my sense of public calling with my extreme sensitivity. These opposites can take something from each other without one overcoming the other. Though the sensitivity is still uncomfortable, I try to love it, even as I wish it would disappear. I let it influence my writing and my ideas and even my public work. The result is not a perfect marriage, but then, I have never seen a perfect marriage anywhere in life.

In this light, I find the goddess Hera a comforting image. Her role was to bring the creative power of her mate into human life. She was passionate—jealous, angry, and loving—but she was also the epitome of long-lasting, supportive companionship. The ancient *Orphic Hymn to Hera*, like a psalm of praise, says that without her there is neither life nor growth.

The Greeks believed that every human marriage imitates the creative union of Zeus and Hera. They also represent the individual's desire to reconcile with himself. The ideal here is not the integration of those things in yourself that are in conflict, but their effective linking. In marriage differences continue to exist, but they are brought into fruitful connection through love. We have to love our own complexities and contradictions, encouraging an interior marriage and eroticism of the soul.

You live this mystery not by literally dividing the soul chores between the man and the woman but by being both in yourself.

You can offer support to your spouse, letting the Hera grace move through you. Man or woman, you can be Zeus temporarily, taking charge and feeling your deep-seated authority. You can be both at once, for yourself, for your partner, and for your marriage.

Alchemy pictures a king and queen embracing in a bath or a vessel. The result of this chemical wedding, Jung says, is the *unus mundus*, a unified world, the conscious and the unconscious, in his language, reconciled. I might express it as a creative contact between the spiritual and the worldly, or the sacred and the secular. Ideas, values, aspirations, the transcendent self (Zeus) married to ordinary days, material life, the body, and human emotions (Hera). When our ideas are grounded, our values lived out, and our highest selves at work in ordinary life, the holy marriage of the individual has been achieved, and that is worth celebrating.

We are back at Cana, at a wedding. The mother of Jesus, according to the story, points out that the wine, apparently an essential element in the celebration of marriage, has run out. Jesus responds immediately, not so much by performing a marvelous feat, a stunning miracle, but by exhibiting a profound mystery, the Dionysian mystery of holy intoxication. A divine and human mediator, he allows this wedding of the soul to go forward by maintaining the supply of wine. He is the adept, the magus, and the holy teacher who can link the spiritual with the ordinary, just as these are linked in his own human/divine nature.

This marital dark night of the soul is a fermentation, a process Jesus accomplishes in mere minutes, but that usually takes years in a human relationship. Opposites blend to bring out the effervescence of each life and the third thing that is the couple. It is a sometimes painful alchemy, but the result is worth the wait, like a good wine that can't be rushed but needs to rest in the cool, dark cellar before it matures.

It is a blessing to have a long and complex marriage. The state of marriage promotes a special kind of incubation, creating a vessel that allows fermentation of the individuals and the couple to take place. It may look simple and ordinary on the surface, but always the juice is gaining its tang. In marriage, a mere personal love between two people turns cosmic. Like the night and day of nature, a long marriage enjoys both fruitful days of relative bliss and dark nights of the soul.

CHAPTER EIGHT

NIGHT EROS

I was brought up in an Irish-Catholic family in which sex didn't exist. No one talked about it, and, indeed, the word had such a charge to it that you couldn't use it without setting off a silent emotional explosion. I could sense the intense discomfort around sex, though no one said anything. I attended a Catholic grade school taught entirely by nuns who pretended to be sexless. I was in the eighth grade before I held a girl's waist at a dance. Then, at thirteen, I went off to a seminary where I was taught the virtues of celibacy. I didn't have my first sexual experience until I met the woman I married when I was twenty-seven.

The current generation could never understand my early experiences. And yet, in spite of this highly reserved upbringing, or maybe because of it, I love sex and consider it a gift of life. I love the sensuality, the vision, and the exploration. I believe strongly that a marriage could be based on the sensual experience of the couple. I enjoy sensitive experimentation, and I believe that if everyone could maintain a degree of innocence while fully enjoying sex, peace might become a reality on the planet. Most violence is closely related to sexual repression.

But I also know from my own experience and from being a therapist that people often go through genuine dark nights of the soul because of their sexuality. Many different kinds of frustration hang like a dark cloud over otherwise happy people. They search for the right partner, they battle with the repressive teachings they learned while growing up, they are naturally shy, they fall in with violent people, they have abortions, for unknown reasons they feel uncomfortable with sex, they become impotent, they have too many partners, they don't have enough partners, they feel used, they find themselves stuck with a person who doesn't enjoy sex. They abuse and are abused, they are victim to compulsions that seem to overpower their wills, and they make mistakes and live with profound remorse.

The wish for good sex can drive you nearly insane, because sex reaches deep into your soul, and the desires and anxieties connected to it touch your very foundations. Sex represents life. When sex is good, you may feel that life itself is good and positive. When sex is bad, everything feels off-center. If you are preoccupied with some sexual issue over a long period, that dark night may be trying to give you back your sexuality. Remember that a dark night is not a purposeless pain but a specific work going on far beneath the level of your awareness.

Sex often becomes an issue when you are about to shift to a new level in your life. Couples are often thrown off by this tendency of sex to rise up out of its calm and cause embarrassment and conflict. You may confuse a sudden surge of vitality with the need for a change of partner or with sexual experimentation for its own sake. You may be confused about your feelings, knowing well that eros has stirred, but at the same time feeling that you don't want to threaten your relationship.

If you do attempt a sexual connection with someone else, you may not feel fully satisfied, because this new attraction may point to another kind of change altogether. I've seen people struggle over the temptation to go off on an erotic adventure, and in the end discover that what was asked for was a change of career. It's easy to confuse the objects of your desire, because sex is often more about desire itself than about a particular object of need.

Even casual sex is full of significance and may have many layers of meaning. The very wish for uncomplicated, uninvolved sex is a significant fantasy, maybe as meaningful as the desire for a long and involved relationship of love. Some people need to discover love; others need to learn that love is not all. If you have thought of sex only as the expression of emotion, you may be surprised at fantasies and desires that have no relation to love. You may be shocked to find fantasies floating in your head about new partners and new kinds of sexual expression. People sometimes say that only men have such desires, but I have heard them from women as much as from men.

THE BODY OF THE WORLD

Before we can understand what its particular dark nights are about, we have to explore the deeper dimensions of human sexuality. It's safe to say that it always has a purpose beyond its own pleasures and passions. Sex initiates a new level of living and provides a couple with a powerful means to be intimate and share their deepest emotions and fantasies. But sex can do much more. By bringing out your sensuality and vitality, at its best sex can connect you to society and to the natural world. It can be the vehicle by which you surrender to life and can restore a sense of your body. Sex accomplishes a great deal for the human soul through the emotional relationship and through sensuality.

Sex involves precisely those things that are most important to the soul: love, curiosity, fantasy, desire, pleasure, intimacy, and sensation. In sex, there is no obvious work to be done and no particular outcome, unless, of course, you are trying to get pregnant. Sex can be repeated, the way you listen to a song or look at a painting again and again. The goal in sex, if there is one, is so deep-seated that it is difficult to pinpoint and explain.

Sex is more like a ritual, an act done for deep and mysterious purposes, a highly symbolic act with its own special language and gestures. It addresses the soul and stirs emotions. In sex, the body is a world to be explored. Just as you might know your garden for all its particular plants and flowers, so you might explore your lover's body. Just as you may want to travel to see a coastline not entirely different from one near home, you may have the desire to appreciate slight variations in the human body or in the expression of love.

Margaret Atwood captures this idea in a poem:

> *My hands*
> *where they touch you, create*
> *small inhabited islands*
>
> *Soon you will be*
> *all earth: a known*
> *land, a country.*[43]

Sandor Ferenczi, the early follower of Freud, said that sex is a return to the oceanic sensation of the infant in the womb. I imagine this as the dreamy, mesmerizing fog that descends when you are swept away into the bubble of lovemaking. This altered state is essential to sex, because in it the soul comes into the foreground and practicality recedes. What happens then is of great significance to your sense of meaning, to feelings of relatedness, and to a sense of self. We saw the importance of this kind of "regression" when considering the night sea journey. The bubble of lovemaking is similar to the belly of the whale and can be a place of rebirth and transformation. It is the alchemical vessel in which changes take place, the stage on which dramas work themselves out, or a dream where the soul sorts itself in utmost purity.

SEX, THE OPUS

Sex, then, is an important "work" that time after time makes a soul. Alchemists call this subtle work of soul-making *opus*, the art of becoming a human being. Any particular experience of love-making may not make a baby, but it does continue the work of making your soul. At its best, sex is this kind of opus. Of course, the sex may be inadequate, forced, wounded, and completely un-conscious, and so its effect may be diminished, but it has the po-tential to do nothing less than make you into a person and to create a world that is sensuous and alive.

This helps explain why many people like to look at the hu-man body. We are compelled by a strong desire and the promise of intense pleasure to know our world, our life, our bodies, and ourselves. Just as the pleasure of eating inspires us to nourish our bodies regularly, so the pleasure in sex leads us to nurture our souls. Lovemaking and all experiences of an erotic nature, when relatively free of neurosis and ego, nourish the soul the way food nourishes the body. To look at and feel the naked human body is to behold, perhaps without much understanding, the mysteries of life.

The important soul work of exploration is best accomplished with a partner who so loves you that he generously overcomes any inhibition about lovemaking to be fully present. But love doesn't guarantee good sex. In addition to love, a partner has to be comfortable with her sexuality, at least moderately sensual, and unencumbered by serious inhibitions. In a society so con-fused about eros and love, it isn't easy to find such a partner. You may have to take the initiative and lead your partner, and maybe someday he or she will learn to trust enough to be eagerly in-volved in sex.

THE SEARCH FOR A PARTNER

Your search for a partner may be nothing less than a mythic adventure. It may go on for years, and there may be false discoveries and continued longing. You may believe that the very meaning of life is at stake, that if only you could find the right person, you would experience happiness. But you may find a good partner and still long for more. This is because the ultimate object of all desire is life itself, or, as mystics say, God.

If you can't find a suitable partner for sex, you may spend months or years in a dark night of the soul. You wait, you search, and you experiment. You get discouraged but keep your little hope alive. You may crave a new partner but eventually give up and resign yourself to not having someone to share these intimacies. There are many lonely and depressed people who simply don't know how to be sexual in a satisfying manner.

Some people never find the right person. Some don't want an active sex life. Some lose their partner to death, illness, or some other kind of separation. In these cases, all is not lost, because sex is not limited to human loving. Qualities of sex can be found in other ways. You can have intimate friendships, actively enjoy the beauty of your world and home, live sensuously as much as possible, and seek out deep pleasures of another kind. In other words, you may live a celibate life and still be sexual.

When I was living in a Catholic religious community under the vow of celibacy, I didn't have an active sex life at all. Yet I never felt repressed or deprived. Since then—this took place in my youth—I have wondered why I almost always felt relaxed and happy under those conditions. There were perhaps two brief periods when my desire rose up and I felt some frustration, but these moments never caused me to question my way of life. I wonder now if the strong sense of community and the dedication to a special way of life made up for the absence of sex. In any case, my experience leads me to believe that it is possible to "sublimate" plain, physical sexuality into other forms equally satisfying.

POTHOS, DEEP LONGING

Many people, however, painfully long for the right person to come into their lives, and their loneliness can reach a level of despair. They can't get away from it, no matter how many people love them. They feel the aching emptiness, as though some necessary organ in their body were missing. They see their friends, to their eyes, deliriously happy in their marriages and partnerships, while their own lives shrink to this one issue: Will I ever be happily united with my beloved? And, like any dark night of the soul, the condition can last for months and years.

The ancient Greeks honored this devastating feeling with a god, Pothos—longing personified and deified. One wonders why we don't the have the word "pothology," like "pathology," in our language, so widespread and severe is the craving for the right sexual partner. Sometimes you may have the right person in your life, but something stands in the way of full sexual satisfaction. He may be married, anxious about sex, or perhaps just not interested.

Some people make light of this longing because they have a negative or superficial understanding of sex. But if sex is as deep and significant as I have described it, it's no wonder that people fall into such pits of despair when it is lacking. They know intuitively what they are missing, and they feel the absence. Sexual emptiness is a form of depression, a collapse of the fantasies and emotions that make you feel alive.

This discovery of the importance of sex lies at the heart of the poet Kathleen Raine's memoirs. Reflecting on the dry years with her husband Charles and her rediscovery of sex with another man, she confesses: "Having left Charles, I waited in vain for word or sign from my demon lover; yet I knew I would rather thus suffer than return to the painless state in which I had formerly been; for now, after long years, I was alive."[44] The demon-lover was for her the life-force, sex in all its low, primitive power, that rescued her from her lifeless marriage and incidentally woke her power of making poetry.

For some people, a dark night of the soul is a long period of painless expectancy, a life that has not yet got under way, even though external appearances suggest the opposite. Raine had a husband and children, and yet she longed for a real mate, not understanding at first the importance of her sexual desire. It's tempting to dismiss such longing as unworthy of desperate attention. Somehow it doesn't feel virtuous.

Kathleen Raine, now an extraordinarily articulate, subtle poet and literary critic, plainly confesses in her autobiography to the divine/demonic power of sex. About the man who finally set her afire after leaving her husband she writes, "What Alastair was like, as a person, I neither knew nor cared. I was not interested in him; a fact which does me no credit. I never noticed what kind of human personality he had; to have done so would have dimmed and obscured the image of the god he for me embodied. . . . For his immortal soul I did not care, only for his mortal beauty."

Sometimes, perhaps to preserve their sense of innocence, people cover over their soul's sexual needs with the language of love. Of course, love can have a central role in the sexual life, but sexual desire also has its own inherent value. You may have to admit to your need for another's body and intimacy, and your attraction may have nothing or little to do with love. Raine's honesty is a good model, especially for the person who has not sorted out love and passion.

She relates with extraordinary insight and language how the daimon of sex saved her and gave her the urge toward poetry that would make her famous. Coming from such a high-minded expert on William Blake and W. B. Yeats, her appreciation for the power of sex is compelling. She was waiting for the right sexual partner and suffered many years of lifelessness, while living with a man she admitted she married wrongly because she felt no sexual attraction.

Raine's situation is yet another version of waiting in darkness for someone who could evoke the depths of sexuality. During her time of dry expectation, she was married to a man she neither loved nor desired. This is a common story: a man or woman marries for the wrong reasons, chiefly because of a failure to appreciate the importance of sex to the soul.

I met Kathleen Raine in her old age and heard her tell some of the stories of her youthful romances. What struck me was the way you could see her passion—maybe it was her sexuality—in her subtle, loving, and intelligent way with words and ideas. Modern Americans generally don't understand how passion and artistic ideas are a continuation, perhaps a refinement, of the same emotions that drive us toward satisfying and complete sexual expression.

Raine's marriage to Charles was her long, painful dark night that incubated the poet and the woman in her. It gave her the impetus throughout a long life never to surrender to the minimum of passion again. This is a gift of sex and its particular dark night. Until you honor the spirit of sex and are blessed to have it animating your life, you may feel its absence as the withdrawal of vitality.

To be fully alive is to be sexual in some way, maybe not actually involved in a sexual relationship, but living an active, engaged, sensuous, and colorful life. The qualities of lovemaking spread out over the whole of life, giving it vitality and spice.

LOVER DEMON

For Kathleen Raine, the demon-lover was the spirit of sex she desperately needed and found only after years of longing. Some have quite a different experience: They have a lover and the sex is electric, but it is dangerous and perhaps violent. The dark night of the soul is now not a longing for sex, but a dangerous and threatening union with a demonic person.

What could attract you into this kind of danger? Has your view of life been one-sidedly good? Have you no experience of darkness? Are you stretching yourself now to embrace a more

complex world? Do you need to be in touch with the evil potential in you? In discussing irony, we considered how every person
needs to sense the evil in them not as literal destructiveness but
as a necessary and ultimately beneficial capacity for the dark. Actual evil deeds are merely a sign that this evil hasn't been taken to
heart in a refined way, and therefore has to be acted out. In the
arena of sex, you may feel drawn to a person who invites or lures
you into a world of unknown intrigue and darkness.

No matter what the benefits may be, linking up with a demonic person ensures a dark night of the soul. This person puts
you in touch with evil, but precisely because he is an evil person,
the evil in him is impure to some degree and may be dangerous.
You will learn something about the dark from him, but you may
put your safety and happiness in peril.

I have worked in therapy with several people, for the most
part women, but a few men as well, who went through this particular dark night. I have witnessed the abuse and the excuses,
the beatings and the long-suffering. These connections to dark
partners suggest a need for that special spirit. One always hopes
the initiation will not take long, but there is no absolute
timetable.

I worked with a woman in her thirties, Carrie, who had
grown up trying hard to be a "good" girl. As she talked about her
lifestyle, she attributed it all to her father, who had big dreams
for her and tried to save her from various kinds of disaster that
he imagined—drugs, unwanted pregnancy, a bad partner. Naturally, she was fascinated by everything her father labeled "forbidden." But she married properly and had children and was
involved in her church. Suddenly, her husband died. After a brief
period of mourning, she began to date. She looked for suitable
men who would appreciate her religion and her motherhood.
But none of the men she met satisfied her. They wanted her, but
she quickly grew tired of them.

One day she met a man who excited her. She told me that
he was the most sexually alive man she had ever known. She felt

that finally she was entering the life she had been looking for. In her own mind, she was a changed person, but I felt that she was experiencing change only vicariously, through this dangerous man who was leading her in directions that might give her only trouble.

The man moved in with her, into her old house, and suggested expensive trips. Carrie had never traveled much, and she was thrilled with the interesting places her lover introduced her to. He was also investing some of her money and selling some things he found in the house. All the while, she kept praising his sexual prowess.

When he started hitting her, she was surprised but explained it as the result of years of frustration at his not having a good chance at life. In the classic lines, she said to me, "I know that I can change him, because I understand him and he trusts me." I told her how familiar her words were and warned her of the danger she was in.

People always try to be too smart for themselves. "You don't know Harvey," she said. "I'm not so stupid as to get involved with an abuser."

Of course, over time the situation worsened. She stopped coming to therapy. Months later I received a call from her telling me that she had just got out of the hospital, after having been beaten badly, and Harvey had run off with another woman and with all her money. She was ready to reconsider and to reflect on how she could have been so blind.

Carrie's sexual dark night consisted of months of physical and emotional abuse. It's difficult to understand how someone would subject herself to such treatment, until you realize how powerful is the need of the soul for sexual fulfillment. That satisfaction may require an acquaintance with the depths, the underworld, which should be subtle and not nearly as literal. But life is never that perfect.

Sexual desire also cuts a wide swath. It takes up into itself other fantasies that are difficult to separate out. In Carrie's case, it may have been a habit of saving people, or maybe she got so far into the shadow world of her lover that she mistrusted reflection of any kind. She sounded defensive when she talked to me about him. Something in her knew that she had made a bad decision in linking up with him, but in another way she desperately needed what he represented.

I knew of another situation where the man was fascinated by a woman who was a "call girl," an expensive prostitute. Rather inexperienced and naïve himself, he loved to brag to his male friends about his lover's sexual professionalism. But she was also involved in criminal activity that she dismissed as safe and insignificant. Eventually, he began to assist her and got caught in an invisible web of money laundering that got him a year in jail. When I saw him, he felt remorse for his stupidity, but he was still confused about sex, craving a partner who would lead him out of his innocence. I suspected that, if he could, he would do it all over again.

THE JUSTINE IN EVERYONE

People talk lightly about personal growth, as if they know what it means and that it is a positive, progressive development. They don't realize that the soul's progress is both deep and dark and requires a descent as well as an ascent. "Growth" is entirely the wrong word for what ripens and matures us into people of substance and gives us a soul. Sex is integrally involved in that process, and it isn't always "nice," clean, uncomplicated.

Carrie need not have gone through the literal abuse. She might have found a less brutal way of learning the dark necessities of life and shedding the naïveté she had acquired in her family. She might have learned to express her sexuality in all its colors, instead of waiting for a brutal man to show her the extremes of what she was looking for.

The Marquis de Sade portrayed this pattern in his novel

Justine, in which a naïve young girl finds herself again and again taken advantage of by brutal men. It is also hinted at in the classic tale of Eros and Psyche, in which the innocent young girl, banished to a remote forest, is told that the lover she finds there, Love himself, is a beast, a dragon in fact. Prompted by her jealous sisters, she breaks the rule by which she is forbidden to see her nighttime companion, and, once revealed, he runs away. Most of the story deals with her various initiations in the ways of life that prepare her to restore her connection with Eros and have his child. In this story, Psyche is so desperate that several times she attempts suicide. Sex takes us into situations that mature us, but sometimes the maturing fails and we merely suffer.

Your first sexual experience may take away a certain kind of childish innocence, but after that you may have a desire to experiment, so that other sexual experiences can continue the process of loss of innocence. There is a difference, however, between becoming more mature through dark sexuality and literalizing that darkness in actual violence. There, you have gone over the line, out of the ritual of sex, in which symbolically you visit the underworld of fantasy, and into actuality, which is not an initiation but victimization.

In the best of circumstances, you have a lover who enjoys stretching the limits of the sexual imagination in very small increments and still within the play of sex. There is always another step to take. You are always, man or woman, Persephone becoming the underworld queen. If you don't have the opportunity to go deeper sexually, you may enter a dark night that can be emotionally and physically painful. You may be with someone who doesn't enjoy sexual play or who too easily crosses the line into actual pain. I've seen instances when both partners experiment with bondage and pain, at first playfully and then more seriously. Sometimes the play bleeds over into life, where mutual dominance and violence become a way of life.

Some people are like de Sade's *Justine*; they never stop acting out. They suffer literally, perhaps in one relationship after another.

Their dark night is unending. Others make the shift from mere brutality to initiation. They become sophisticated persons, understanding the fictions and theaters of sexuality. The transition from one state to the other may entail a long dark night of pain and confusion.

SEXUAL CONFUSION

Sexual dark nights can take many different forms. Some people discover that their fantasies and urges move in directions not approved by society. They may discover their homosexuality, their bisexuality, their need to be of the opposite sex, their strange desire for pain and submission, their incurable promiscuity, their fear of sex, or, like Havelock Ellis, the great sexologist, their kinky loves and attractions—he had a fascination for urine. These are not just problems but also occasions for long periods of risky confusion.

These conundrums may preoccupy a person for years or even a lifetime and may cast a dark tone on the whole of a life. For the time that they are in play, they are the meaning of life. They claim the emotions and dominate the imagination. Working them out is working out the centrality of life. They epitomize the whole effort of making sense of one's time on earth and shaping it accordingly.

Jan Morris, a gifted writer, tells the story of her transformation through a sex change operation and hormone treatment from a man, married to a woman he loved and the father of five children, to a woman. In luminous prose and disarming honesty she describes a particular moment when, sitting under a piano her mother was playing, she first felt like a woman in a man's body. She was four years old. She relates a childhood free of tensions and conflicts and dismisses all the many medical and psychological explanations for her condition. Referring to her long quest for a female body she says, "I equate it with the idea of soul, or self, and I think of it not just as a sexual enigma, but as a quest for unity." [45] Yet, she underwent her own dark night, referring to her situation as her terrible "entombment within the male physique." She describes the darkest period of her life: "Rather than go mad, or kill myself, or worst of all perhaps infect everyone around me with my profoundest melancholy, I would . . . have my body altered." She did indeed have her body altered, receiving the femininity she craved all her life, and her soul was healed.

Like many people desperately trying to find their way into life sexually, Jan Morris could talk about her situation to very few people, notably her wife at the time. People are simply too anxious about their own sexuality to offer an open mind to someone else in trouble. But Morris had a spiritual understanding of her situation, and the loftiness of her imagination helped her maintain her dignity and calm during years of yearning. She always thought she was the right gender but the wrong sex.

Morris offers us a graphic and articulate example of how human sexuality may force us into our eccentricity. I see this tendency as a grace. It is a revelation of how eros is working our individual soul. Of course, we may object to our desires, simply because they don't conform to standard notions of normalcy. But those objections are rooted in anxiety and become for us the obstacles we have to surmount on our way toward the embrace of our soul.

I have great admiration for someone like Jan Morris, whose clear devotion to her deepest reality allowed her to work out the necessities of her life. That she writes so beautifully and insightfully about her unusual dilemma is an added gift. She explicitly understands her challenge as an issue of soul, and not just body. She says, "I interpreted my journey from the start as a quest, sacramental or visionary, and in retrospect it has assumed for me a quality of epic, its purpose unyielding, its conclusion inevitable. . . . I have collated it with the medieval idea of soul." [46]

Morris shows remarkable insight into her strange experience

of gender mistake. She understands that for all its apparent physicality, the real struggle took place in her soul. She could see past
the literalism of physical gender to her nature as a person. She is
an inspiration to anyone experiencing deep sexual confusion with
no apparent hope of resolution.

Few people have the extreme discomfort of a Jan Morris, but
many long for a change in situation. They have little deep understanding of their sexuality and find it difficult to feel good about
themselves. They experience sex as a compulsion that gives them
little freedom of choice, rather than as a passion they can fashion
for themselves. Morris was bravely loyal to her ultimate desire
and patiently found her way to an unusual solution that solved
the problem of her sexuality. Others, too, could respect their
sexual needs and make their long dark nights of confusion ultimately worthwhile.

FEAR AND ANXIETY

The act of love, for all its promise of pleasure, fills many people
with anxiety. Lovemaking is not great performance, but it is an
art and requires a degree of craft. Essentially it is the unmediated
expression of desire and the enactment of fantasies associated
with the most intense longings. You may not understand or be
conscious of the roots of your wishes in lovemaking. Some acts
may be important to you—a kiss, a touch, a sight, a sound—and
you don't know why. You may never ask the reason for your particular tastes, and yet they may be yours alone. You may not find
them described in a sex manual, or you may worry that they may
be perverted. Fear appears naturally once your wishes are given
some play, because it isn't easy to trust desire.

The unveiling of the body is also the unveiling of the soul,
because the body is the soul. To allow the body to be seen in its
nakedness, to say nothing of being touched and embraced, is to
show soul in all its glory and complexity. But it isn't always easy

to be so thoroughly exposed. Who wants to be seen so completely by another person, no matter how much you love them? Who can you trust that much?

Eventually you might meet someone with whom you would like to experiment with that ultimate degree of self-disclosure. You may be compelled by his attractiveness or by what she represents to you. You may simply crave physical comfort and touch, or you may feel sexually hungry. You have sex, and you may try to be vulnerable with your partner. It may be very pleasing, satisfying your attraction and your craving. But at the same time it may be worrisome. You may discover, even subliminally, in the signals of lovemaking, that there are limits to your trust, either in general or with this particular partner. The inhibitions in sex are as significant as the freedoms.

LIMITS ON SEX

In your sexual dark night you may learn to appreciate your virginal qualities, your hesitancies and inhibitions. The daimon of caution is as important as the daimon of desire. Lovemaking has its yin and yang, wish and fear, coiling around each other like lovers, both equally valid. Having no inhibition about sex would be like having no limits on your pursuit of money. Your single-minded passion could ruin you.

But anxiety is different from inhibition. Your reticence to make love with a particular person may have some wisdom in it. On the other hand, your anxiety about sex could be due to your failure to grow up sexually. You may not yet have resolved some of the conflicts you picked up in childhood or through painful experiences. You may need, finally, to decide that you are a sexual being and need to give yourself permission to be so.

You may come to lovemaking full of old anxieties. Many people in modern life have been brought up to feel guilty about their sexuality. Or they may have had rules laid on them early in life.

Many carry the burden of moralistic religious teachings, which make them feel inferior and inhibited. They may feel great desire and the wish for sexual liberation on the one hand, and a deep, unconscious guilt on the other.

For many, sexual desire clashes with teachings that warn against pleasure. This conflict is so hidden and set so back in the tunnel of memory that most attempts at healing it don't touch it. Somehow you have to find your way into that area of extreme sensitivity and bring some calm. You have to work out a compromise between your urge toward life and your guilt for not suppressing yourself. Even those people who seem unusually free and uninhibited may have to find their way to that same place of comfort, because acting out freedom is not the same as feeling it.

The dark night may also contain memories of bad experiences. It is not just a case of realizing that not all partners are selfish or too aggressive or distant. The memories contain lessons that have been absorbed. Whether these lessons are good or bad, helpful or not, they remain stuck in the impermeable and immovable memory that is active subliminally in sexual situations. It helps to discuss those memories openly, to the extent that it is possible. But they also call for a fundamental change in perspective, a washing away of the roots of the conflict.

It might help to realize that your sexuality is unique. You have your own fantasies and desires, your own past, and your own inhibitions. These all go together to make up your sexuality, complete with its good parts and its challenges. Over time you have to make this erotic material work well for you. You may have to forgive yourself for past mistakes, deal with the neurotic elements, and allow yourself certain desires that you and others may not understand. You may also have to ripen to the point where you appreciate how your sexuality, in the form of sensuality, an appreciation for beauty, and intimacy, may reach out into the whole of your life. You may use it as a resource for making a personal contribution to society, which is an important element in making sense of your life. Sex is not only personal; it is an aspect of cultural life, and your sexuality can be a means of connecting you to the world.

SOCIETY'S SEXUAL DARK NIGHT

Historians tell us that during the Dionysian festivals the ancient Greeks would carry in procession huge phallic images, sometimes made of wood and decorated with garlands. Such a practice would seem inconceivable today, and yet our movies and magazines are filled with peek-a-boo sexual scenes. Today, many young people won't go to a movie that doesn't promise extreme quantities of sexual thrill. We have our own phallic images, too, in missiles and guns and tall buildings. But at the same time we have a reserve that seems to be rooted in anxiety about sex.

The solution to an excessively sexualized society is not to moralize against it, which merely pushes sex further into extremes, but to be more sexual in a mature and subtle way, to acknowledge forthrightly the prominent place of sexuality in life, and to allow great variation as we try to work out our sexuality throughout our lives. Some would interpret my suggestion as permissive and amoral, but I am simply recommending not making sex bigger than it needs to be. The bigger it becomes in our daily experience, the less substance it has, and the more confused everyone is.

The extremes of sex that we see in the media and in the preoccupations of ordinary people indicate that we are sexually bereft. In a deep way we lack the pleasure and vitality that a more genuine sexuality would give us. When deep-seated sexuality disappears, the result is not emptiness but anger. Aggression and violence often enter to take its place. Or people become depressed because eros is not present to grant life its energy and passion. At a deep level, society's challenge at the moment is to convert its infantile sexuality into a thorough life of sensual pleasure, beauty, intimacy, and community. We have to transform our materialism into soulful physicality. We work too hard and too long just to have the pleasures we might better attain through a simpler way of life. Without that subtle strain of sexuality in our daily activities, we will force eroticism into the darkest and least constructive forms, like an Internet full of crude sexual sites. We will be depressed and angry—not a good basis for peace and fulfillment.

We have seen that many kinds of dark nights can be transformative and renewing. The same is true of sexual periods of stress and emptiness. They provide an opportunity to reassess the many biased ideas about sex you picked up along the way, from childhood on. They can cleanse your mind and your feelings so that you can start fresh, reclaim your passions, and discover the qualities of your particular kind of sexuality. It may take courage and imagination to overcome the moralism of your family or society, but you may learn how important it is for the whole of your life to sort out your sexuality and dedicate yourself to it. It is your life and a great part of your meaning. It is yours to cultivate in ways consistent with your values and your life purpose. It is your joy and your pleasure.

CHAPTER NINE

CREATIVITY, THE CHILD,
AND THE SURE-FOOTED GOAT

EVERYONE, without exception, has what Jung calls "an instinct for creativity." You must find a way to put yourself out into the world and be present as a unique person. You don't have to be an artist, but you do have to shape this world, at least in a small way, according to your own talent and vision. If you don't exercise this creativity, you might well feel depressed and unfulfilled. On the other hand, even as you try to be creative, you may find yourself in yet another tunnel of frustration and disillusionment.

It is said that artists are born "under Saturn." That means that the source of their creativity is also the root of their suffering. In the Middle Ages and Renaissance, Saturn was believed to be the patron of both melancholy and artistic inspiration. The creative life is not all positive. If you are going to risk creative expression, you may have to deal with Saturn—his melancholy, his coldness, and his constriction.

The connection between the creative life and emotional torment has been discussed for centuries, and artists still ask themselves, in light of so many examples of suicide and difficult lives, if there is a link between creativity and suffering. The answer is not simple, and it applies to all of us as we try to add something to our world.

Certainly, creative activity is often full of frustration, simply because you can't always make the life or creative work that you imagine. You may be just shy of the required knowledge or talent, or you may have unreasonable expectations of yourself. In either case, the self is usually implicated in creative work, and you might well get so much ego into the work that any flaw will make you insanely frustrated. Narcissism, which is sometimes rooted in the failure to give yourself enough approval, is more painful than it looks, and narcissism creeps into creative work among the most inspired and altruistic people.

But the old tradition about Saturn suggests that within any creative act or creative life, there is not only expansion of vision but a contraction of life and person. We get it wrong when we think of creativity only in inspiring and expansive terms. As the painter Craig Stockwell has put it so well, a painter enters a monogamous relationship with his painting and his art. It is like a marriage, both the opportunity for expression and the necessity for restraint.

INFLATED CREATORS

Creative people often obsess over their failures and blocks and desperately search for acceptance and success. As a writer and a musician and having an artist for a partner, I am forever running into highly creative men and women, and I'm astonished at the level of their desperation. The people I meet are usually full of ideas and happy with the books, music, and plays they have produced, but they crave success and rarely find it. They take criticism to heart to such a degree that blow by blow they feel beaten and unappreciated.

I notice two issues that torture these people. First, is the quality of their work. Generally they overvalue what they have done and are reluctant to edit, change, and educate themselves in their art. They tend to be inflated and self-important. I can understand that to be creative in the first place, you have to have a large sense of self. But an unrealistic assessment of the work can make you uncertain. You don't know if your efforts are good or bad and you may question yourself constantly. But at the same time you may think of yourself as a genius.

The second problem is that you may judge yourself by the kind of commercial and financial success you read about. You may not be satisfied with the rewards of doing good work but crave high levels of recognition and financial compensation. Since it is only the few who make large amounts of money from creative expression, you may feel deflated and hungry for success. This hunger, unrelenting and bitter, lies in the category of envy and jealousy. Among the many creative people I have known, very few seem immune to the need for enormous acceptance and adulation.

For many people, not becoming a star is a tragedy, and they become dissatisfied with life in general over their failure to achieve great success. Eventually, most learn to live in a realistic world and settle down to their work. A few achieve their dreams and even then run into problems. Creative people live on the edge, where wonderful gifts lie in wait for them and where the fall into failure and disillusionment is always a possibility.

I have had my own experience of the peaks and valleys of success. For years I collected rejection slips. Occasionally publishers would make tantalizing remarks, such as: "We are very interested in your manuscript, but it is not quite right. Send us your next one." I keep those letters in a file to remind me what it was like trying to get started as a writer. Once, some time ago, I was invited to give a workshop at a large, prestigious adult education center. I needed the money badly and the chance to get a career going. At the last minute, they called to say they found someone else who was "more appropriate." Today, that same organization calls me frequently to give a lecture for them. Their staff is too young to remember my earlier trials with them, but I don't forget.

The very successful creative people I know are happy with their lives, but even then you can see how the need to be habitually inventive makes them eccentric. You wonder how comfortable they are. They have money and adulation, but they never fit in with "normal" people. The well-known have to struggle to get some privacy, and the lesser known are always looking for recognition.

To create usually means to make or do something for public consumption. If the public accepts you, life is exciting. If it ignores you, your spirits may slump. This ambivalence is depicted in the traditional astrological Capricorn image for Saturn: the goat on the mountain peak. The ascent and sure-footing are inspiring, but the ravine is steep, deep, and always at hand. A creative person has to be like a Capricorn goat, able to climb high and yet nimble enough to deal with a slide and a fall.

QUIET DESPERATION

By its very nature, creativity requires a high level of individuality, and yet, it isn't easy to be a true individual in a world that loves conformity. With groups, hierarchies, and organizations everywhere you look, to be a true individual you have to be assertive and imaginative. You have to make an effort to live an original life and to avoid being carried along on a wave of cultural unconsciousness. In an insecure world, everyone wants to tell everyone else how to think and live.

Millions of people today feel lost because culture, full of

mass media, chain stores, and anonymous jobs, makes them feel anonymous. It's typical today to get excited about a new job that pays well, but then quickly discover how dehumanizing the work is. At home, most sit in front of a television set and receive the same digest of news and the same entertainment. They also eat the same fast and processed food and wear the same clothes. The sameness may be comforting and easy, but day after day it creates a feeling of ennui and erodes vitality.

Society romanticizes creativity, exiling it in a limited group of celebrities and "stars." This extreme idealizing of the creative type is a form of defense—you don't have to be an exceptional person yourself if you idolize high achievers at a distance. By allowing these few to be the creators, you become uncreative and unexceptional. The world gets divided into the highly paid and highly visible creative types and the ordinary majority filled with envy and longing. The vague feeling of being nobody is not exactly a dark night, but more a hazy evening of the soul.

For many, a dull sense of ordinariness crushes the spirit. You know that no matter how hard you try, it is difficult to have your creativity accepted and admired. Sheer numbers can be discouraging. The proportion of writers, painters, and musicians to publishers, good galleries, and hit recordings is overwhelming. Creative people who are not artists run up against employers who don't want to take any risks on creative ideas. You may sit at home in your simplicity and wonder why the days pass without excitement.

Society seems confused about this issue of individuality and creativity. The assembly line, the many anonymous and low-paying jobs, the enormous financial and political power of the elite—these qualities of a stratified society leave the ordinary person feeling frustrated. He longs for a feeling of worth. He imagines winning the lottery. The degree of his need gets in the way of the quality of his work, and he finds himself squeezed between grand ideals and disappointing realities. It's no wonder people today have dreams of being stuck on elevators and escalators, maddeningly going up and down without pause—they are continually contemplating high ideals and heroes, and feeling mired in the more mundane realities of their own uninspiring lives.

Henry David Thoreau said the same about his society over one hundred years ago in his famous words: "The mass of men lead lives of quiet desperation. . . . A stereotyped but unconscious despair is concealed even under what are called the games and amusements of mankind."[47] This "quiet desperation" is part of society's dark night, in which most participate in varying degrees. A few are saved from the soul-dampening toil that keeps the machine of society working, and fewer, like the main character in the play *A Thousand Clowns*, decide not to participate. He quit his job unexpectedly and started living the life he wanted. I recently heard the story of a classical pianist who decided to opt out of the "boring" concerts he gave many times a year. As a symbol of his protest, he hurled his piano out of a window, smashing it in the street below. Then he went from town to town on a piano-bicycle he had invented and played for ordinary people. I felt much in common with this man and applauded his gesture. We could all toss our machines, our brooms, our paper, and our computers out a window and start over. As we'll see in a later chapter, a good way to deal with a dark night is to do something quite out of the ordinary and richly symbolic.

You can use your desperation as a guide and barometer. Precisely where you are desperate, you can take back some of the adulation you give to others. Making it your own, you find value in the simple things that give you meaning. Gradually, you find entertainment closer to home, more individual than collective. It might be something as simple as playing a local game of basketball instead of paying a considerable sum to see a star. You could become a musician, instead of giving all your musical attention to star performers.

There is nothing at all wrong with spectator sports and arts. It's thrilling to see a gifted athlete or musician perform. But a little spectating goes a long way. It could season your life, while you find many ordinary ways to be creative. You could look for adulation among your family members and neighbors instead of to the world as a whole. Small is beautiful!

CELEBRITY FOR ALL

The exaggerated attention we pay to celebrities is part of the contemporary decadence. It is unreal and excessive. No doubt, celebrity will always be part of life, because it expresses a need for myth, for a level of experience far beyond the normal and literal. We "look up" to people, as though they were stars in a galaxy. There is something celestial going on in this idol worship. But it isn't serious. It's more symptomatic than sincere. Centuries ago people could go to a temple and see images and realities that were truly celestial. They honored actual stars in the sky, not metaphorical stars in Hollywood.

Ask celebrities what they most wish for, and they may admit that they enjoy the limelight but would love some privacy and ordinary life. Both celebrities and noncelebrities, from different ends of the spectrum, need a certain kind of simplicity. Real creativity is to be found not exactly at the middle but in a mixture of the ordinary and the special. The proportions may be different for each person, but extremes serve no one.

People ask, "How can I become a writer?" My answer is simple: "Write." It's more important to create than to be a creator, in any inflated sense of the word. Creativity means to create, to add something worthwhile to the world. A theologian would say that a creative person participates in the Creator's work. The creation of the world is an ongoing project, and part of the divinity of the human being—an idea cherished by Renaissance philosophers—is to add to that process. If you approach your efforts insecure and uncertain, your ego may get in the way, and you will focus more on being a creator than on creating. But that is backwards. Start with some ordinary creative work and then discover what it feels like to be a creative person. The idea is not to make you a star, but to give your work the shine and sparkle that are the signs of divinity.

CREATIVITY AND
THE SPIRIT OF THE CHILD

It is useless to try to define creativity. Whenever we speak of it, our words are shaped by an archetypal image that gets hold of us. Whenever we speak of ourselves as being creative, we are expressing a myth, perhaps an image of supreme genius, grand success, or mad talent. It might also include fantasies of being an uninhibited child. We may think of creativity as originality, spontaneity, or mere beginnings, and beneath those ideas lie memories of childhood.

To create from scratch, it may help to be free of excessive influences and habits. You could be like a child, fresh on the earth, full of wonder and questions, relatively untamed and uninhibited, willing to experiment, and above all, driven to play. You could have what the Zen master calls "beginner's mind," the spirit of the child who is relatively free of cultural contamination.

Often we think of this child in purely positive terms and emphasize its spontaneity and vitality. But the child is also demanding, clumsy, uninformed, and maladapted. If you are going to tap into the deep child, you have to take both the good and the bad. Some creative people like the play aspect, but at the prospect of hard work they act like spoiled children. They like the pose of being a creative person but don't enjoy the doing of it.

In modern life we generally suppress the child, because childishness is an affront to the particular kind of ego we admire. We prefer an educated, controlled, adapted, and largely uniform person, someone who has learned how to fit in with our social purposes, which are largely shaped by our belief in capitalism. We define maturity in these terms and support an educational system that sustains the philosophy. Our lack of civility is largely due to the repressed child, who reacts against society's harsh demand for conformity. People are angry and depressed by the joyless life they are forced to lead, and they manifest their frustration by repudiating manners and neighborliness, as though they were children who never learned how to be social. Part of our contemporary social dark night is due to the suppression of the child.

We repress and we idealize. We repress the child by forcing children into religious and character-building camps, by excluding them from social life, by containing them in poorly equipped and dispiriting schools, and by demanding that they grow up quickly through extra lessons and limits on play, and by surrendering them to too many au pairs and babysitters. In repressing the child, we keep the troubling human soul and specifically its child qualities away from adult pursuits. We also suppress the child soul by idealizing and romanticizing children's virtues, which we see as a far-off goal in adult life. But idealizing is a strategy of defense and self-protection. Everyone wants to be spontaneous and playful, but few do it seriously.

If your efforts to be creative lie behind your dark night of the soul, I would suggest looking at your childhood. Your child spirit may be lost in memories of your past, and it may come to life if you reconnect with it. I have known several men and women who complained about a loss of creativity and the resulting disorientation and sadness. They recovered their creativity in concrete ways—by moving back to their hometowns, by returning to involvement with their families, by cooking foods they remembered from childhood, and by resolving conflicts with family members. The gap between your adult self and the spirit of the child can be overcome in simple, concrete ways. You have to remember that the child qualities you need as an adult are connected with your own childhood. You have to redeem that childhood and come to peace with it.

JUNG'S BREAKDOWN AND
DISCOVERY OF CHILDHOOD

In his late thirties, C. G. Jung went through a major transition in his life, which sheds light on our theme of restoring the child. In his memoirs he calls it his "confrontation with the unconscious." He felt compelled to resign his professorship and focus on the images and emotions coming to him in both night and day dreams. The crisis took place at the start of World War I, a time of widespread and intense anxiety. Whether it was a dark night is difficult to say, but there is no doubt that it was a period of extreme confusion. Jung's biographer Gerhard Wehr refers to it as his night sea journey.

Jung felt the ground falling from under him, and he waited for some sign of inner help. Finally he had a memory from his eleventh year of making things out of blocks and stones. The memory was full of emotion, and he thought he should take it seriously. So he began to play again with wood blocks and stones, making a model village. He did this "work" during his lunch hour and then after his patients had all gone for the day. He felt squeamish about reconnecting with his childhood by acting childishly, but the practice was of great importance to him.

Later, he described the experience: "The small boy is still around, and possesses a creative life which I lack. . . . This moment was a turning point in my fate, but I gave in only after endless resistances and with a sense of resignation. For it was a painfully humiliating experience to realize that there was nothing to be done except play childish games."[48]

Jung spent three years in this uncertainty and fallowness. He said it was most important during that time to maintain strong connections with his family and his profession to keep him stable and grounded. He recorded his dreams and fantasies, made sculptures and drawings, and paid close attention to odd and sometimes spooky events around his home. He describes the process

as one of unfolding urges and inspirations and not a precon-
ceived therapeutic program.

Jung later felt that this difficult period was the richest time in
his life, giving him the raw material from which the rest of his
life work was made. His efforts at that time taught him how to
deal with the soul. He quoted an alchemical text that uses familiar words, "Cleanse the darknesses of our mind." Catharsis. He
was clearing out his troubled mind with the things of childhood.

This strong example from Jung's life exemplifies our theme,
staying close in touch with childhood as a means of tapping its
spirit. Creativity is not just about making fascinating inventions
or great works of art. It has to do with shaping your life and cultivating your very soul. The child spirit has a role to play in this
creativity, not only as an image of spontaneity but as a slice of life
that may not have been happy or successful.

James Hillman says that we have to find a way neither to romanticize nor reject this child quality of the soul, to sense both
its promise and its shame. This is an important point: If you
don't feel some shame, as Jung did, in the child's inferiority, you
are probably caught up more in your idealized notion of the
child than in the child spirit itself. The feeling of inferiority that
often accompanies the child archetype is not necessarily negative. It can keep you humble and let your creativity flow without
interference from an ego desperate for fame and accomplishment.

THE LOST CHILD

In the early Christian period and in the late Renaissance era a
story was told of human "development" that differs from our idea
of evolution. In their story, the human soul descends through the
seven planets and receives an imprint from each. The closer it
gets to earth, the more human it becomes. I imagine the fate
of the soul similarly in our lifetime. The various stages we pass

through stay with us, imprint themselves on us, and, as we progressively incarnate, we become more and more complicated.

You are the sum of your phases and experiences, and therefore childhood is not something you leave behind. It is a piece of you that weaves itself ever more tightly into the fabric of who you are becoming. Jung discovered the importance of acknowledging one small segment of childhood and finding in it the secret to his entire life as an adult. Perhaps the very purpose of his dark night was to find that eleven-year-old child.

If you don't reconnect with certain phases of your childhood, you may find yourself living out that segment of your personal myth in your adult life. Many people seem stuck in a specific phase of their personal history, and it is that intruding piece of personal narrative that gets in the way of their leading a creative existence. Their long dark night is due to being stuck at a certain level of development.

I had a relative who was dominated by his mother. She didn't want him to grow up. Any time he would decide to move away, in an effort to get some distance from her, she would suddenly get sick. He would always change his plans and stay with her. As far as I know, this pattern never ended, and there was an air of tragedy about his life. He was never quite delivered into his maturity. He didn't let his mother completely dominate him, and he seemed to have good times in the midst of his darkness, but you would hardly say that he lived a creative life.

It's difficult to know when you're stuck in a particular phase of development. One hint is to notice if you are being childish or parental, especially in the extreme. You may notice, as I do, a problem dealing with parental figures. You may act the child to their parent. But patterns like this usually reverse themselves. You may also be quite judgmental of yourself and others. When you finally get past the struggle with the parent-and-child phase, these themes will become more subtle. Then you can both receive criticism and enjoy the playfulness of your creativity.

Regularly you are given a choice, as these stories show, to

live or to retreat from life. The retreat is often a decision to live in the past, to remain in the comfort of a familiar pattern. If you were to choose the new opportunities—which is a kind of creativity all its own—you might not get stuck in the past. The past can be a resource, like a spring of water bubbling up to refresh and nurture. But it can also be a box that keeps you shut away from life.

Still, there is a big difference between being stuck in the past and being connected to it. Paradoxically, to be fixated in the past is to deny it. Earlier, I gave examples of people recovering their creativity by returning intelligently and freely to people and events of their past. The two actions, being creative and being related to your past, support each other. If you can stop fighting your history and find workable ways of staying connected to it, you might be free to respond to new opportunities. But if you're busy struggling with the past, you won't be available to the present.

Like many people, you may have been coerced too soon into adulthood. You may have been the oldest child in a large family and were expected to do the job of the parents. When you got older, you may have felt a gap where your childhood should be. You never lived certain important ages, and now you feel incomplete. This pattern often leads to a particular kind of chronic sadness: You don't have your eternal childhood to bring you vitality and joy.

I had an experience like this myself. By shipping off to a seminary at the beginning of my teenage years, I skipped normal adolescence. I had to become an adult overnight, and the pressures were extreme. Now I believe that this treatment set me back, and I've been longing for childhood ever since. Fortunately, I find some of it in life with my own children, but for years I have sensed a sad child wandering around on the lonely streets of my soul.

I haven't had many dreams of lost children, but I have had recurring dreams of airplanes flying low, trying to avoid city buildings and taxiing on roads and streets. In the past I have interpreted these dreams as successful ways of keeping my soaring spirit grounded, but lately I have wondered if they represent a child spirit that needs to soar. Children's stories are full of magic carpets, hot air balloons, flying broomsticks, and delightful beings living on other planets. I could use some of that airy magic.

You may be like me, confused about whether you are too much a child or not enough of one. In myself I sense both strong idealism and the need to follow the rules and keep people happy. Usually I consider myself a *puer*, to use Jung's term for the spirit of youth. But clearly, parent and child are still split apart in me, and I need to be more childlike in my adult pursuits and more serious about my child qualities.

You might look closely into your ways of being and see how the child fares. Once you embrace the child more openly and intelligently, your creativity may be released. The child is by no means the only route to the creative life, but for most people it plays an important role. It is especially crucial in dark nights related to creative expression. You may be searching in the dark for your lost child.

RESURRECTING THE CHILD

Many people live in emotional darkness because they have never fully enjoyed a child spirit in their overly serious lives. The child wanders homeless in the lives of many adults, who are captivated by psychologies of the "inner child" and books and films of childlike fantasy, such as the stories of Harry Potter and the Disney movies. Modern society, so adult and sophisticated, so busy at work and serious about knowing everything, has lost much of its childhood. Instead of playing actively and seriously, we let other people entertain us, and instead of enjoying a strong feeling of community, we are highly dependent on our electronic connections.

You have to find your own way to your childhood. It may be something quite simple and meaningful only to you. One of my clients revived her childhood by making an old family recipe for soup. Another found it in forgiving her mother for betraying her. I mysteriously find the child stirring in me whenever I am in Italy or Ireland. In some mysterious way, the "old world" is home to my deepest childhood and allows it to come forth. Others find it in allowing themselves to be irresponsible in certain areas of their lives, such as stealing time for themselves, eating "forbidden" foods, and reading for the fun of it.

With his wooden blocks, Jung shows how to reinvent the world in which you live by playing creator with toys and simple objects. In making a village, he took the role of divine creator, and this playacting jump-started his own creative life. Sometimes young people make their homes and raise their children in ways their parents would never have imagined. In that way they re-create their universe. Some live in exotic places or make a living in ways opposed to their family's values. There are many ways to create your cosmos symbolically.

Heraclitus said, "Life is a child playing checkers. Life is ruled by the child." The child Jesus lying in manger, visited by kings and proclaimed by angels is yet another great image for this insight. At Christmas, much of the world honors the archetype of the child, who is seen as a light appearing at the end of a long dark night. In India, the great god Krishna is worshipped as a divine child, and people celebrate his pranks and his runaway eroticism. In ancient Greece, stories of the infant god Hermes were always entertaining and enlivening. This god became the guide of souls; he pointed the way to go in life.

Somehow you have to resurrect the child spirit in a way that it is fully compatible with a mature, adult life. It should enhance maturity, not get in the way of it. This beneficial child spirit is extremely subtle, far from literal childishness and anti-intellectual emotionalism, which are symptomatic forms of it. It gives a color and tone to the whole of life, but it doesn't dominate it. It is the difference between an old person trying too hard to look young and one who ages gracefully with a youthful spirit.

Glenn Gould was often ridiculed because his style of playing the piano didn't conform to expectations. After a concert in his hometown of Toronto, a newspaper reacted, "During the entire work, his left leg was carelessly draped over his right knee." You can imagine a child being told the same thing during a lesson. After a performance in Pittsburgh, a reviewer noted, "The discovery of new drugs and vitamins can cure such contortions, much as the witches exorcised them centuries ago." There was a child spirit in Gould that became clear when he began to put on elaborate and public musical skits, dressing up as outrageous figures like Sir Humphrey Pryce-Davies, a pompous musicologist. As so often happens, Gould's outrageous humor balanced out a heavy pedanticism and depression.

Psychology sometimes gives the impression that you should somehow find a *blend* of child and adult in your personality. But Gould's example shows that a better idea might be to give full attention to both, but maybe not at the same time. In different contexts, Gould could be either the heavily opinionated artist or the comic child.

James Hillman once commented during a public discussion that the contemporary Western ego is not just a function, not just a way to maneuver through life. It has its own underlying myth and image, and it is Saturnine. That means that it is capable of vast imagination, intricate skills, and profound art. But it is also depressive and restrictive. It is the ego of an old man that finds it difficult to appreciate the style of the child. It has its own brand of creativity, but it is not the spirit of the child.

So you might expect some difficulty being creative in this way and being accepted for it. Playfulness is not deeply ingrained in this attitude toward life. It seems more important to work hard and spend your time wisely. From another viewpoint altogether you could reverse that advice: Spend your time playfully and don't waste too much time trying to be wise.

BEING THE CHILD

Whenever you try to bring to life a creative spirit, like that of the child, you can never do it perfectly. Occasionally you slip from the spirit of the child to childishness. As Jungian psychologists say, you can never have anything good without its shadow. But there is another slip, from the happy child to the hurt, depressed child. There is a kind of dark night proper to the child who can't get what he wants or whose spirit has been corralled and dampened.

The English composer Peter Warlock, whose real name was Philip Heseltine, is an example of this problem. He combined his interest in the occult with a passion for English folk music to create a small amount of imaginative and appealing music. But he fought his muse all the way, doubting his talent and overvaluing the work of his contemporaries. His friend D. H. Lawrence put his finger on Warlock's main issue: "He seems empty, uncreated, not yet born, as if he consisted only of echoes of the past." Warlock himself said, "The inner developments of the soul are alone of real importance. . . . I have been on a hopelessly wrong track for years, completely fuddled, *groping blindly in the dark* for something of whose very nature I was quite ignorant."[49] At thirty-six Warlock committed suicide by leaving the gas on in his flat.

His statement about his ignorance and groping in the dark shows how the child in him was not supporting his adult life. He was an intelligent and gifted man, whose accomplishments are being recognized more and more. But he could never really grow up. He locked onto an older composer, Frederick Delius, as a mentor and model, but the relationship was too one-sided, another sign of his childishness. The younger man lost touch with his own genius as he overplayed his devotion to the established artist. After Warlock's death, Delius's wife wrote: "I see constantly the beautiful lovable incredibly intelligent and artistic boy of twenty—and that tragic figure in a gas-filled room with his face to the wall in the early morning."[50] Her single memory contains the image of youth and the ultimate sign of his dark night.

Perhaps we can learn from Warlock to be both childlike and adult at the same time. Playful habits may need to be hammered into a more livable and workable spirit of the child that doesn't dominate and weaken the personality. There is also the hint in Warlock's life that depression could have been transformed into a spiritual dark night that serves the soul. His friends saw the tragedy of his life, but he remained literally stuck in his fixated youth. A real dark night of the soul might have helped. Instead, he avoided the seriousness of his life until it was too late. There is a crucial difference between confronting the darkness that gets hold of you, and simply letting it take over and ruin you. The idea is to be affected by it emotionally and intellectually, but not literally destroyed.

SPIRITUALITY AND THE CREATIVE LIFE

In a broad sense, creativity means to be who you are; to find words and images for your thoughts and feelings; to translate your inner life into outer forms, whether it be a garden, a painting, a poem, a home, a child, or a way of life. You can be creative spiritually by praying, meditating, and practicing devotions. You can be creative with your wit and humor, by the way you care for your family and friends, and in your travels.

Creativity is the making of a life and a world. It may require the courage to experiment, to stand against society, and to be eccentric in developing your own style of personality and life. You may have to find forms best suited to you, forms that others may not understand and appreciate. You may have to learn to live the symbolic life: Those things that speak to the soul may or may not make sense to the practical world.

The French psychoanalyst Julia Kristeva says, making a fine distinction, that we should find language and images that are "lu-

cid counterdepressants rather than neutralizing antidepressants."
You want to find a way to counter your heaviness without deny-
ing it or even escaping it. You don't want to neutralize your sadness, but you want to find ways not to succumb to it. This is a
fine but crucial line to walk.

Kristeva's suggestion is akin to that of the Renaissance
teacher Marsilio Ficino, who recommends a radical use of images—
paintings, sculptures, pendants—all carefully crafted of materials
that are in tune with your mood and imprinted with designs that
correspond to what you're going through. He wants to counter
depression when it appears, but his methods are not antidepres-
sant. Prayer and ritual can also counter depression without being
its enemy. Jesus prays, "Father, let this cup pass me by. But, let it
be not as I wish, but as you will." [Matt: 26.39]

Ficino recommended playing Saturnine music when you are
depressed. Such an approach would counter your depression
without being against it. Other possibilities are to simply be sad
when you feel sad, to withdraw and find comfortable solitude, to
paint your sadness and write about it, to acknowledge it when
people ask how you are a doing. I found that, when my mother
died and people expressed their condolences, I could listen
closely to what they said. People were sincere and specific about
their feelings. I could enter into the conversation they had initiated with their simple words and share a deep sense of sadness in
them and in me. This may sound obvious, but it is a subtle way
to enter gradually and more seriously into the mood. It is a pro-
depressive action that does not indulge in the emotion, but takes
it further, if only a short step deeper.

A spiritual outlook sublimates the darkness. It takes suffering
as a starting point and as the means for seeing things anew. Creativity begins in a vision that penetrates the status quo. It is life
moving onward. You go forward from exactly where you are in
your thoughts, feelings, and fantasies to a place you have never
known. Living creatively, you don't constantly manufacture a future; you grow the life that is present. You have joy because you

have found something that has life in it. Your soul is awake, and you have some spark of divinity in you.

But if you are going to be creative, you must live the whole story. You have to take the dark nights with the brilliant successes. You have to endure criticism and failure. You have to work hard and remain open to the muse. If you get to the point where you can live the darkness daily, you may come to appreciate the hints of happiness that keep you going. You have to find an enlivening ordinariness that contains the light and the dark with the natural rhythm of days and nights. You can arrange your daily life so that it includes times for the dark and times for routine. The ordinary keeps you humble rather than humiliated, and productive rather than poised anxiously on an illusion of greatness.

Don't work only when the mood is right. Let the dark night come and go, but keep doing your work. Igor Stravinsky said, "Even when I do not feel like work, I sit down to it just the same. I cannot wait for inspiration." He liked to quote Tchaikovsky who said that composing music was like making shoes. In that sense, it was a job.

Creative work is a bold attempt to be like God. You can expect it to take you to the edge of human possibility, where the landscape is as dark as the night sky. You can't know where you are going or what you are doing. You have to have faith and a spirit of adventure that allows you to feel at home in the darkness. As a child of Saturn, you are called to be dark and to be at your best when the emotional and intellectual light is dim. You are an adult, but you are also a child, called to always move gracefully into life—growing up, experimenting, playing, and taking delight wherever it offers itself, understanding that the night is the time of birthing and passaging. To be creative means to be created.

CHAPTER TEN

DARK BEAUTY

BEAUTY FEEDS THE SOUL, wakens it, and brings it to life as nothing else can. Beauty is a deep-seated reaction to some meaningful and stunning presentation of life. It stops you and gives you an instant promise of pleasure. But if you have no soul, you won't even see the beautiful in the thick layers of your practicality and in the density of your own ego. All your senses and your full imagination have to be alert when beauty makes its appearance. If you miss it, it is like going without food.

Everyone knows the beauty of a moonlit night, especially if the moonlight is reflected on a shimmering body of water. That is plain dark beauty of the senses. But a less literal darkness can also be beautiful. Film noir from the thirties and forties, with its night scenes and shadowy sets, conveys the mood of the *soul's* dark night. The paintings of Lucian Freud, Francis Bacon, Frida Kahlo, and many other artists portray the dark side of life and give it a certain stunning beauty. Even the strange stories of the Marquis de Sade, Beaudelaire, and Poe, frightening and devilish, have their attraction. The dark side of life inspires beauty, suggesting that there may be something appealing, if painful and distressing, in dark nights of the soul.

I saw a special beauty in the faces of patients in therapy who were struggling, depressed, confused, and unhappy. The men and women I call on in this book as witnesses to the dark night show remarkable beauty in their courage, faith, and insight, the way the films of Ingmar Bergman are full of dark nights. You might find Bergman depressing in the persistence of his darkness, but you can't escape the beauty of his images and scenes. The beauty in my patients came from their sad plights and their steady courage. As their humanity came forward, I felt they became more beautiful.

From prison, Oscar Wilde wrote, "I now see that sorrow, being the supreme emotion of which man is capable, is at once the type and test of all great art." [51] Not all great art is possessed of the darkness we are probing, but much of it is. It works the other way around, as well: Life often finds its beauty through periods of trial and discouragement. The very depth of your feeling takes you to a place where style and form come into play. You may suddenly become eloquent or at least speak from the heart in such a way that your words have unusual power. When you reach into your deepest resources, you reveal the beauty of your life and personality.

I mentioned before how, during my mother's last illness, my father, my brother, and I began to speak differently to each other. Our gatherings and our words took on new clarity and honesty, which resulted in a kind of beauty. My father says now that my mother's funeral was beautiful because of those early meetings and conversations. There is no doubt in my mind that our farewell to a quite ordinary and yet unusually sensitive woman was rooted in the beauty of the relationships in her family.

Art photography of the past century has shown how much a

tragic theme enhances the beauty of an image. We have seen pictures of children in war, the elderly dying, a town swept away by a tornado or hurricane, a child hungry and vulnerable, and these photographs stir the heart like nothing else can. You can't separate their beauty from the pathos. There is a way in which human life is like that: its tragedies can suddenly make us aware of its beauty.

People often ask how life can be good, how there can be a God, if tragedy is part of it. Maybe an answer eludes them because they are looking for logic. They need to consider the beauty of a human life as an important value. Then they might begin to understand the role of the tragic and see how suffering can be redeemed. The misfortunes, the failures, and the imperfections give life its contours and make it unique, an important ingredient in the beautiful.

BEAUTY RESTORES THE SOUL

Sorrow removes your attention from the active life and focuses it on the things that matter most. When you are going through a period of extreme loss or pain, you reflect on the people who mean the most to you instead of on personal success, and the deep design of your life instead of distracting gadgets and entertainments. You may be more open to the beauty of your world as a relief from distress. Beauty is always present, but ordinarily you may not notice it because of your priorities or your absorption in other things.

In therapy, the way a person talks and acts may change over time. At first, a woman comes in full of tears and recriminations and rage. Later these turn into exquisite stories and subtle feelings. Her language changes as she gains insight. Depth of perception often leads to beauty of expression. Poems, drawings, stories—they all become more aesthetically interesting to her because of a refinement in her thoughts and emotions. People in therapy often have the experience I described of my family at my mother's death—a new, more honest and direct way of talking.

In every hour of therapy I focus on a dream or a memory, partly for the sheer appeal and emotional power of the images, which are often beautiful even when they portray ugly and fearful events. A well-chosen story or dream may not solve the life problem, but it brings order to the chaos. Dark nights are painful because they are often chaotic. They don't seem to have a point, and the fog can be disorienting. A beautiful, if unintelligible image can offer a little relief from the sheer power of its beauty.

BEAUTY IN DISTRESS

We have already discussed, from several different angles, the importance of the words and images you use to describe your experience. It is important that they be suited to your particular experience. You may read about other people going through difficulties similar to yours, and you may borrow their language and their solutions. Because the terms are often discussed in the media, today people may reduce their complicated lives to issues such as codependency or lack of self-esteem. But these are the culture's concerns of the moment, maladies du jour, and, though they may seem convincing as explanations for just about every life problem, they are too simple for your subtle and complex experience. You need your own words, your own poetry, and your own concrete diagnosis.

In talking to a person in distress, I often take my language from the person's dreams or from phrases that emerge from their sincere attempts to describe their experience. A woman says, "The way people around me often act just burns me." So we talk about her "fire." A man says he feels as though he's in a tunnel in his career. We discuss his "tunnel complex."

As a therapist, I have many memories—I wish I had photographs—of people in distress. I don't want to romanticize their suffering, but it gave them a special beauty. They had come out from behind the veil of their comfort and had shown themselves more directly. Their words were poignant and generally without guile. Their stories had a clarity that had been sharpened by their acute feelings. They knew that if they wanted relief, they would have to be open and honest.

In therapy, a person will land on an expression that seems to capture the core of her experience, or a particular dream becomes a reference for months, holding some complex group of events and emotions. A woman dreams of standing precariously on the top floor of a house in the early stages of building. Months later she returns to that image. "There I am," she says, "not yet built and feeling the vertigo of not knowing who I am or what I will become." The image cuts itself into memory and becomes a personal work of art.

An image like this can mark the beginning of an aesthetic development in the process of healing. You need images; otherwise you have only raw emotion and detached ideas. Images give body to your experience and allow you to reflect on it. The more powerful and precise the image, the more effective you will be in dealing with your experience.

A dark night of the soul is not just messy but frightful. Good words and images can provide some comfort. John of the Cross used poetry to transform the unsettling experience of the dark night into positive and clarifying images. Why didn't he just talk plainly about his insight into darkness? Apparently he knew how important it is to value form as well as content. How many poets and painters have transferred their torment into images that come close, at least, to being immortal? There is one answer to our earlier question about why artists suffer: A flat, undisturbed life doesn't usually reveal the beauty of human existence.

Recently I had a conversation with a woman versed in the world religions and interested in science. "It's worth noting," she said, "that religion traditionally presents its teachings about the divine and the mystical in beautiful images: great churches

and temples, elaborate calligraphy and book-binding, extraordinary music, evocative poetry, and transcendent rituals. Science,
on the other hand, focusing on the rational and the knowable,
doesn't appreciate fully the importance of nature's beauty. To the
practical mind, the beautiful is an accessory, as is the soul."

One way science could move closer to religion, thus healing
a split within people between their highest values and their ordinary intelligence, would be by paying more attention to the
beautiful. A sense of the beautiful in nature would inspire us not
only to understand it, but to respect it. Beauty is always immediately within the grasp of the scientist, but his attention is on
other matters—classifying, studying structures and behaviors,
and using scientific knowledge for technological progress.

Fortunately, an artist is frequently in the vicinity of some scientific development, and so we have stunning photographs of
earth from space, but imagine sending an astronaut into space
with the main purpose of getting such a photograph! That would
mark a major shift toward a soul culture instead of a heroic one.
Photographers have been especially attentive to natural beauty,
and filmmakers often bring out hidden beauty in the world that
the ordinary person rarely sees.

PAIN INTO ART

We saw how, in his very last letter, written in the thick of his consumption, John Keats remarked how difficult it was to shape his
experiences into a poem, and yet he could still write an artful letter, surely an adequate form under the circumstances. Letters had
always been occasions for his deepest thoughts and some of his
most elegant prose. In happier days, he had written to his friend
Benjamin Bailey words that have inspired me in all my work: "We
shall enjoy ourselves here after by having what we called happiness on Earth repeated in a finer tone and so repeated—And yet
such a fate can only befall those who delight in sensation rather

than hunger as you do after Truth."[52] Evidently, for Keats, Heaven is an intensification of the bodily enjoyment of this life and is not as abstract or ethereal as some people speak of it.

You can use any form of expression suited to you. We are all poets to our lives in a general sense, but we each have a form that feels comfortable and right. My wife sketches and paints. I write and make music. But you don't have to be a writer or an artist to give expression to your anxiety. You use words every day. You can find the vital words that jar you into awareness. The way you talk to a friend could be your art.

Today there is a special field called "poetry therapy," based on the recognition that carefully chosen words can be healing. Images help clarify emotions, memories, and events. They can connect the past with the present and create a kind of reflection that impacts chronic suffering. It helps to know what you're going through. Often our language is too technical, mechanistic, medical, and psychological, but falls short of our experience. Poetic speech is more personal and more adequately and precisely names the mood.

Some psychotherapists believe that the raw venting of emotion is an important step toward being free of painful memories and static emotions. Certainly healing requires an expression of feeling that is deep and genuine. But a good word or story takes you much further toward a level of meaning that makes the experience human and livable. Today most people look for an explanation and a cure, usually from an expert. But expert advice can be distant and impersonal, not tailored to your specific experience, and it isn't something you discover for yourself in a process of healing.

In a more formal way, the art therapist helps transform suffering into images that heal, but we can all evoke the artist in ourselves for that purpose. At the beginning of his book about his captivity in Lebanon, Brian Keenan makes the point that his writing "is the process of abreaction in art form, both a therapy and an exploration. . . . It has been part of that healing." [53] Abre-action is a relieving of tension through insight and self-discovery. Keenan's writing is full of insight, and, as a reader, you can tell that as he writes he is making discoveries about his feelings and behavior. You feel his art and his reflection as a single act of heal-ing. The fact that he writes well is not insignificant. Good art makes it way directly to the soul and does its job of healing.

You don't have to write a book, but you can tell your story, again and again. Over time, you may tell it more effectively, and its sheer beauty will help you and connect you to the people in your life. You will find unexpected pleasure in the aesthetics of your thoughts and words, and that, too, will keep you going deeper, looking for further insights and language. Beauty is closely re-lated to both love and pleasure, and these spur you on to express yourself beautifully.

On a societal level, artists of all media help people reflect on their communal experiences. Powerful films about the Vietnam War, for instance, help us all sort out our history and keep our memories from becoming vague and gilded. Many Americans were stunned by the beauty of Civil War letters collected and pre-sented by the filmmaker Ken Burns. The simple arts of everyday life, as well as the great art made by the gifted and self-conscious artist, play an important healing role in the life of society.

IMAGE AND MEMORY

The experience of beauty is not just one of pleasantness but of the power of an image to give order and to clarify your situation. John Keats, the master in understanding the connection between beauty and truth, says of poetry that "it should strike the Reader as a wording of his own highest thoughts, and appear almost a Remembrance." [54] This applies not only to an artist capturing a general human emotion in an image, but to the rest of us searching for the perfect word, picture, or sound to give shape to our raw experiences.

In your dark moments you need an image that will compare well with your deepest sensations and your highest thoughts, and you might well have the impression that this image is a remembrance, that it is so perfect that you feel déjà vu in its presence. That is why conversation is so central in the process of therapy, the talking cure. You talk and talk, hoping to find language that will join emotion and thought in such a way that you are relieved. Somehow the raw experience transforms into a mediating image that renews your feeling even as it offers a modicum of understanding.

In the same way, songs and poems and photographs can focus your vague feelings of lostness or despair and give you a little hope. A song such as "Amazing Grace" has helped many people see light in their darkest hours, and it is no mystery that the film *It's a Wonderful Life* gets many people through the Christmas holidays. The hymn "O Sacred Head," which J. S. Bach used in the *St. Matthew Passion*, always keeps me close to my sadness and yet lifts me up with its sheer beauty.

In the 1480s Marsilio Ficino considered this issue closely and said that in moments of deep sadness we should become "devoted to" the source of our pain. For initial relief, he says, you may want to turn to friends and your job, but then comes the serious work: devotion to what is going on in your soul. The phrase he used, *in tota mente se confero*, means "to focus yourself with your whole mind." That is why it is so important for us to have artists who can probe our tragedies and our follies and give us powerful stories, films, paintings, and photographs that take us devotedly deep into the sensations of sorrow. Out of this unflinching experience, focused and attentive, we might become better people and come up from our depression. A dark night almost always has these two qualities: focus and attention.

THE WAY OF HOMEOPATHY

We have already had occasion to consider "going with" the darkness rather than fighting it. I used the word "homeopathy," not in the strict sense of medicine, but as a kind of response. Literally, the word means "like the suffering." Homeopathic medicine uses small doses of substances that in larger quantities would produce the symptoms of the complaint. Modern medicine is mostly allopathic, meaning to work against the problem; it uses substances that attack the cause of the symptoms. To take a homeopathic approach to the soul is to deal with the darkness in ways that are in tune with the dark. Not only is medicine allopathic, but often people take an allopathic attitude toward their emotional distress. They try to cheer up people who are sad and grieving. They like to see people get on with their lives after a tragedy. They appreciate a positive attitude and positive thinking. They want to shed light on the mystery of it all. All of this, in relation to a dark night of the soul, is allopathic.

The homeopathic alternative is to enter further into the darkness and appreciate it through means that are in tune with the dark. "Like heals like," the ancient medical doctors said. In this process images play an important role, either explicit images of art and dream, or slices of life taken as images. Presumably, what is happening to us in our dark night is necessary. We need the change. Images help give focus to precisely how we need to change and what has to happen.

MUSIC AND MELANCHOLY

If we are suffering a dark mood, we might turn to images that take us further into it. Terry Waite reading about slavery, while he was incarcerated as a hostage, is an example. In some cases, the purpose of the image would be to deepen the mood. Each year on Good Friday I listen to the *St. Matthew's Passion* by

J. S. Bach. The sad music draws me deep into reflection on the crucifixion.

Many examples of homeopathic art in classical music come to mind. John Dowland, the famous English lutenist and composer, wrote a piece called "Semper Dowland Semper Dolens" ("Always Dowland Always Sad"), which is part of a series of pieces for viols known as Lachrimae, or Tears. In these he used a pattern of four descending notes, in the Phrygian mode, which is a scale known for its pathos, its plaintive tone. On the title page he writes, "If Luck hasn't blessed you, you either rage or cry." Dowland was a melancholic man living in an age devoted to Melancholy.

Samuel Barber's "Adagio for Strings" is a twentieth-century piece that speaks directly to the melancholic emotions and depicts the dynamics of grief and sadness. It has been used at countless funerals and memorials and was the first piece urged on me when I was compiling a recording of music that especially addresses the soul. Intuitively people who may or may not know much about classical music immediately sense the melancholic strength of Barber's composition. For many, the song "Amazing Grace" has a similar impact.

Whether consciously or not, Dowland's sad tunes are a perfect example of Marsilio Ficino's suggestions, offered two centuries earlier, for dealing with Saturnine moods. Today you are told to get past your mood and get on with life. But art understands how sadness and remorse can give you depth and character. When you listen to strong, melancholic music or contemplate a sad piece of art, you are taking your attention beyond mere sensation to the interior meaning of your mood. You are educating yourself in your emotion, so that you not only get past it ultimately, but you gain from it from having penetrated deep into its nature.

Personally, as a tonic for dark nights I prefer a combination of doing my daily work and listening to music like Dowland's, or Willie Nelson singing "Blue Skies," or Lightning Hopkins expertly evoking the blues upon his guitar. There is something sweet, comforting, and yet strong in these and other pieces of music that use sound to mimic the emotions of sadness. Of course, mimic is not the best word, since music of this kind takes the listener deeper into the experience of sadness and offers a more objective model against which her emotion might be compared and matched. Art can take up your experience and intensify it by deliteralizing it and submitting it to your intelligence and your imagination. The arts humanize the emotion and move it toward the sublime, where it can be brought to a level of perfection. You don't overcome your dark feeling; you take it to its highest level.

In other words, the arts offer a catharsis for the emotion, not through venting but through the transformation of feeling into image. Your emotion blends with the artist's image and your experience is transformed. Art therapy is often presented as a method of clarifying the emotion and giving it form, but it does more: it gives mythic dimension to the particular experience. You find the possibility of a deeper meaning to your feeling, and that discovery offers relief.

John Dowland, Lightning Hopkins, and Willie Nelson are artists who can evoke images grand in scope that rumble from the depths of their inspiration. In that way they provide a homeopathic remedy and give deep background to a personal, ordinary dark mood. That enlargement of the experience is itself a step in the healing process.

WAKENING THE SOUL

The arts also have the power to waken a dormant soul, and there can be no doubt that the chief malady in our time is "sleeping-soul sickness." Ficino put it poetically, saying that Mercury, the foremost patron of the arts, can either waken souls or put them to sleep. When you sit and listen to music or watch a play or follow a dance, your active life goes into eclipse and your soul life takes wing. Mercury, the spirit of art, self-expression, language, and form, brings soul to situations that are otherwise considered only practically.

A thing of beauty stirs the soul out of its slumber first by drawing you into itself. You become interested, struck, and then absorbed. Woody Allen, who has made a career out of creating films of life in New York City, describes his first view of Manhattan: "I was just *stunned* by it all. You'd come up out of the subway at Forty-second Street and walk up Broadway . . . I just couldn't believe it. It took the top of my head off."[55] This is Mercury at work, being reborn by the sight of something wonderful.

I will never forget the first time I saw the Pacific Ocean. I was with a friend just north of San Francisco. We were hiking the hills when suddenly the soft sound of the ocean caught my ear. I have always lived more by sound than sight. But the vision of that living, shimmering sea truly overwhelmed me, and I knew I would need a relationship with it for the rest of my life. I have often thought of living by that ocean, but I know somehow that I'm called to other shores. So I visit it when I can and make every effort to have some quiet moments with it. Things of beauty can give form to your life.

I feel similarly about Ireland's shores. I see the usually gray waters and the rugged headlands, and I feel the strength of nature. I feel its beauty seeping into me, so that every visit is an enlargement of myself. But it all has a pathos to it, like Irish musical laments that tear at your heart. I can't separate the pathos from the beauty.

I remember a morning in 1956. I was a sophomore at a Catholic prep seminary outside Chicago. A new English teacher, a priest, was transforming our building and our lives into art. That day he unwrapped an art print he intended to place on a wall in the monastery part of the institution. He held it up for all us young innocents to see. It was Salvador Dali's *Crucifixion*. I was disturbed by it, not disappointed or offended, but shaken. It was a stylized, unsentimental, very modern representation of the crucifixion; I was used to images that were ultrarealistic, senti-mental, and lacking in style. It represented a world I knew from somewhere but had not been part of my life as yet—a Platonic remembering, not of the past but of what I knew through my temperament and taste. That revelation set me off into a world of music, literature, and painting that has made all the difference.

I am forever grateful to my teacher for introducing me to the beautiful. His simple gesture reached a place in me that was of my essence. He educated me, which sometimes is the same as healing. He knew, as many of us have to learn, that people are not necessarily born with a taste for art. It's important to intro-duce children, and even adults, to the best in art and to show them how to receive it and appreciate it.

Beauty is an experience of the deep soul. You take in beauty with a sixth sense and with a special organ of deep perception. Your eyes pick up physical fact, but your educated interior senses perceive the beauty. Keats said that beauty is truth. It reveals an essential and sometimes hidden quality in things that stirs you in a way far deeper than the mere satisfaction of curiosity. You real-ize that things have a pulse and are alive, and they can offer you a purpose for your life on earth, if only you see deeply enough into them. That deep revelation is the beauty of a thing.

HEALING BEAUTY

A dark night of the soul also reaches deep, usually through sad-ness, emptiness, or anxiety. You can't always explain it in terms of life events, and you can't get rid of it through sheer understand-ing or willpower. It is deep-seated. It may connect up with hid-den memories from childhood and with emotions that are too vague to deal with easily. The great American painter Mark Rothko said he became an artist, rather late in life, only after he witnessed a life painting class and began to appreciate the beauty of the human body. Up to that moment, he didn't know what he was going to do with his life. Just then, his wanderings stopped and he had his vocation. His biographer says it was a conversion experience, not a gradual development.

Beauty is to the soul what truth and fact are to the mind. The beauty of a thing is its depth and meaning being revealed. To perceive that beauty, you need an eye for both appearances and for the invisible radiance of a thing. You also need the capacity to be affected. But many people walk through life defended against all positive influences. They are not open to the invitations and messages coming at them at every turn. They wonder why life feels empty and meaningless, when the problem is not the absence of meaning but their blindness and deafness to it.

Jungian analyst Ronald Schenk, an old friend and a highly imaginative psychological thinker, describes the practice of "aesthetic psychotherapy" as having "a vigilant attitude" and a "complete presencing to the psychological powers at play."[56] "Vigilant" means watchful. You look closely at what is happening in your life. You don't judge everything too soon. You take it in and savor each element. You take note of the most subtle factors. Schenk says that in therapy you notice the unconscious behavior in the person you are speaking with, in yourself, and in the interaction. Similarly, James Hillman says, "You have to listen for what's going on with an ear that is not attuned to the same wavelength as the patient's story. There's a jarring, a discomfort."[57] These suggestions are for a therapist's way of observing, but they apply in every situation.

"Psychotherapy" simply means care of the soul. It's something you can do every day. Especially during its dark moments, you can serve your soul best by being vigilant to what is going on. This is not the same as trying to figure out what is happening. Aesthetics is the realm of beauty. It comes from a Greek word meaning to sense or perceive. Contrary to most modern psychological approaches, which imply that the human soul is a major problem and host to a vast range of illnesses, an aesthetic psychology senses the soul as beautiful, even in distress. But you have to educate yourself to seeing its beauty and then respond to it the way you would to a piece of art. You take it in and become its curator.

INTEREST: A FIRST STEP TOWARD BEAUTY AND LOVE

I have known a few spiritual teachers and psychologists who base their work on this elusive principle of the soul's beauty. Their faces light up when you tell them about some quirk of behavior or some unusual obsession. They are not numb to pain, but they appreciate the many ways the soul shows itself from person to person. They are slow to moralize, slow to diagnose, and very slow to change or instruct. I believe that any effectiveness I may have as a therapist comes primarily from the example of these teachers, who have a wide capacity to consider the manifestations of human life without requiring immediately that they fit certain norms of health and propriety.

Don't misunderstand. I'm not saying we should sit back and enjoy our own suffering or that of others. That would be sheer masochism and sadism. As Ronald Schenk puts it, first you see, then you know. First you have to be present to what is going on, and that requires at least a modicum of interest. You have to be interested in yourself, almost as an object. Things are happening to you that you don't initiate, and you have to look at those things carefully and closely. This kind of self-interest may then turn into a positive kind of self-love, and that is the beginning of healing.

If you can discover your essential beauty, in spite of all your problems and imperfections, you are on the way toward well-being. A preliminary step is simply to accept yourself with all your failures and imperfections. You must get the ego out of the way—the thought that you are so exalted that in your refined state you would be perfect. Acceptance is the beginning of genuine and honest self-love, a requirement for perceiving your own beauty.

Seeing your beauty, without extravagant self-absorption, is the first step in discovering your soul and eventually giving it the attention and care it needs. This is not so much a love of self as a love of your more vast and mysterious soul. It isn't narcissism, but rather the cure of narcissism. First you see yourself for what you are, then you love your soul, and then you breathe easy.

You have to see your beauty in a way that is focused and concrete. You may not be a great athlete, but you may be good at math. You may not make much money, but you know how to live a meaningful life. You may not be highly sociable, but you make and keep friends. Personal beauty is a soul quality. You appreciate your character, a few good decisions and achievements, and ordinary talents, but you don't expect to be completely and extravagantly gifted.

The discovery of your own beauty—and I don't mean this sentimentally—is the foundation of well-being. Your beauty is complex. It is not all good and wholesome. It is not a superficial thing but is the very substance of your being. Truly beautiful people are not necessarily physically healthy, emotionally together, easy to get along with, or productive and successful. Beauty usually requires some imperfection, transgression, or lacuna. The whole of your being, the good and the bad, is the stuff out of which your beauty makes an appearance. A lover may see it. A parent may embrace it. A friend may struggle with it but love it.

DARK BEAUTY

Just as the beauty of nature includes storms, droughts, and geological eruptions, so the beauty of a person includes emotional storminess, dry periods, and occasional explosions. To care for the soul in earnest, you have to learn to appreciate the dark elements as well as the light ones. As you come to appreciate your darkness, you may also understand that some of your lightness may be a defense against the dark. You may present a calm exterior, whereas your interior life is stormy and turbulent. You may not even allow yourself to confront your darkness.

On the other hand, you may realize that your happiness and tranquillity are due to having established a relationship to your dark side. A rich and stable sense of security can arise from appeasement with your darkness. The dark has much to offer your pursuit of happiness. The two work in tandem, one feeding the other.

No one has expressed this better than Oscar Wilde. "I don't regret for a single moment having lived for pleasure. . . . But to have continued the same life would have been wrong because it would have been limiting. . . . The other half of the garden had its secrets for me also." [58] The beauty of a life lies in its fullness, not in a preferred portion that looks superficially positive and wholesome. For Oscar Wilde, as perhaps for any one of us, that knowledge had to be achieved through pain and struggle. Only when you have gone sufficiently deep into your conflict do you understand its necessity.

I was once attending a seminar led by a friend who asked us to tell our first memories. I had been born into a blissful situation. I had great parents and a warm, lively extended family of grandparents, uncles, and cousins. I knew good times, loving friends, and caring relatives. But my first memory was the accident in which my grandfather drowned in a large lake while holding me up out of the water. I was four years old then, and even now I feel that early close linkage between life and death. I feel complete only when I consider both my happy childhood and my brush with death.

Just recently I came into possession of the newspaper account of that day in 1945. It reads:

A boy whose grandfather gave his life to save him was rescued from Lake St. Clair. The boy, Thomas Moore, 4, son of Ben Moore, was thrown into the water with his grandfather, also named Thomas Moore, when a gust of wind overturned their light boat. The grandfather held the boy above his head as he struggled to keep afloat. The grandfather, exhausted by his efforts, cried out for help. Persons in a passing boat managed to pick up all three but two hours' work with the village inhalator failed to revive the grandfather.

My father and I continue to discuss this event, and still, of course, we feel the pain. But then we quickly begin talking about the good times with my big-hearted grandfather. The conversation, like life itself, is bittersweet. We honor the beauty of this man I hardly got to know but who saved my life. And in some mysterious way, that beauty becomes an unfathomable foundation for my life and work. As one of my aunts puts it, "You must have been saved for a reason." The quest for that reason gives meaning to my life.

BEAUTY SERVES THE SPIRIT

Beauty nurtures the soul by serving the spirit. Beauty takes you out of your cramped, merely personal worries and sets you down in a field of eternity. The essence of spirituality is an enlargement of vision. The experience may only last a moment, but in these matters a moment is enough. You need a transcendent sense of things, not one that lets you escape from your situation but one that gives you an added perspective. In this, beauty and religion serve similar purposes, and so it's no wonder that they are often so closely allied.

In a dark night, beauty allows you a glimpse of transcendence and therefore liberation, without allowing you an escape from your situation. In the aftermath of the September 11, 2001 attacks, I felt deep dread and anxiety and was able to find some consolation by staying in tune with the natural world. The beauty of a sunrise or a moonlit night comforted me when no human response seemed adequate.

The connection between beauty and suffering may be even more radical. It could be that only in the beautiful can you really perceive the depth and essence of pain, and only in suffering can you learn how to appreciate the full range of the beautiful. Listen to Samuel Barber's "Adagio" and see if the sheer beauty of the sound carries you to the transcendent levels of suffering and pathos. Read Shakespeare's *Hamlet* slowly and carefully. Isn't the beauty of its language the very means by which you feel the full extent of Hamlet's suffering? If the words were not so artful and pleasing, maybe you would be instructed in a certain kind of pain, but you wouldn't have the same sensual, searing participation in the insights. Beauty takes you down into experience and then up and above all human limitation.

Beauty is not to be found only in suffering. Of course, you can enjoy the beauty of a tranquil setting and a joyful occasion. One would hope that you find beauty more often in bliss than in trouble. But if you avoid the dark side, your sense of beauty may turn sentimental. Just as materialism "coarsens" the soul, according to Oscar Wilde, so sentimentality can "soften" it excessively. The coarse and the sentimental usually sustain each other as opposites. Real beauty solves the split.

EXPOSE YOURSELF TO THE BEAUTIFUL

People often ask, "What can I do during this troubling period in my life?" We have explored many ways to respond that don't go against the darkness. Another effective way is simply to place yourself in the presence of something beautiful. It may be nature, art, culture, or family. You don't have to look for meaning in this beautiful thing, but only trust that beauty can sustain you and even heal you.

I listen to music. Some people sit at the edge of the ocean. Whatever you choose, you have to take it in and let it affect you. In a way, you become this beautiful thing. The moonlight gets into your cells, and the music changes the patterns of your very makeup. You become less an ego trying to understand and solve your life, and more a receptor through whom the beauty of the world radiates. To do this, you have to surrender control and give up particular notions of solution and success. You have to let the dark night happen and change you.

During a dark night, it is best to find something beautiful that is also tinged with pathos or emptiness. I love to read Samuel Beckett, who shies away from anything sentimental. I enjoy a little solitude as well. I read detective stories and tales of profound challenge. You might choose to visit the sick and dying or help out in some kind of public service. There you will see suffering that will distract you from yours. There, too, you will see how beautiful life can be even in the midst of pain and deprivation.

When a dark night takes us to the edge of our reason, it is often useful to stretch the limits and become eccentric. You can do this with beauty. You can "waste" hours painting, singing, and writing in unusual and impractical ways. You can travel extravagantly and perhaps unwisely to beautiful places, when the spirit moves. You can bathe too often or not at all. You can talk to animals and to yourself. You can swim at a beautiful spot in icy water, as Edna St. Vincent Millay did as a cure for her worst breakdown. Like my friend, you can give away old but beautiful athletic shoes to children around the world who need them. You can wear gloves in the summer, as Glenn Gould did, as a sign of your need for human warmth.

You only have to understand this basic point: Beauty nurtures the soul. Expose yourself to the beautiful, and let it do its work. It will accomplish what you could never dream of. All you have to do is trust it and be open to it.

PART THREE
DEGRADATIONS

I stand
And suddenly understand
That you, Deep Night,
Surround me and play with me,
And I am stunned . . .

Your breath comes over me.
And from a vast, distant solemnity
Your smile enters me.

—RAINER MARIA RILKE, "THE VAST NIGHT"

CHAPTER ELEVEN

THE DEEP-RED EMOTIONS

FOR YEARS, night after night, I have told a story to my children about a king and a queen who lived long ago. They have a school of knights whose main job is to deal with fire-breathing dragons that upset the tranquillity of many villages. But this king and queen are quite enlightened. They don't want to have the dragons killed, but only tamed. The knights are taught how to use music to charm the beasts, and kind and beautiful words to make them appropriately civilized. Maybe "tamed" is not such a good word. I don't mean domesticated, but sufficiently charmed and calmed to live peacefully with their human neighbors. They can still breathe fire, but with some consideration for the buildings and people around them.

Maybe this episode with the dragons is a way to talk about anger. All of us, at one time or another, flare up. Fire bursts out of our mouths. We may try to hold it in, because we know that it can get us in trouble, but not getting angry doesn't seem like a good solution. Today, most people have learned from popular psychology that it is important to express anger when you feel it. And yet there are signs of repressed anger everywhere, from road rage to a general lack of civility.

We have seen that the repression of eros and the creative instinct can give rise to a dark night of the soul by suppressing vitality. The same can happen with anger. To be a person with presence requires the power, heat, and force that come with anger. Reject your anger, and you may well feel lifeless and confused. As James Hillman has said, anger tells us what is wrong. It may not tell you what to do about a bad situation, but it indicates clearly that something has to be done.

In general, we are not intelligent about expressing our feelings. We are taught many things in a lifetime, but rarely do we get a chance to learn about emotion and ways of relating to others. We make a great effort to develop the mind, but apparently we are supposed to deal with our emotions instinctively. Without having thought it through, many people think of anger as a negative thing and can't imagine how it could be useful and positive. It's a shock to them when a therapist tells them to show their anger. When they try it, they feel awkward. Or, they notice that the sheer manifestation of anger doesn't accomplish much. After you scream or use harsh words, things are still as bad as they always were, and the satisfaction of making a loud complaint doesn't magically solve your problem. It may alienate people.

Not dealing effectively with anger can stifle joy and make you feel and look only half alive. A dark night of the soul can develop out of this suppressed anger, because, as we saw before, the avoidance of one emotion affects them all. Trying not to get angry affects relationships as well. If you can't get angry, you and those around you don't know who you are. They don't know how you feel, nor do they understand the limits of your tolerance. Anger gives you borders and definition.

ANGER IS NATURAL

There is a difference between venting anger and expressing it. To vent is simply to blow off steam. Play tennis, hit the wall, scream. Venting may release some tension, but it is far from a complete response to the emotion, and it can harm relationships. Anyone in the vicinity of your venting may take it personally and be offended.

To express your anger, on the other hand, is to show your anger about a particular situation or condition. If you are angry at your spouse or partner, hours of workout at the gym are not going to be nearly as effective as letting your partner know how you feel. It may not help to vent, but it may be effective to say, with a degree of passion, what you're angry about. Afterward, you may have to do a lot of talking, and at a later time go through the process yet again.

One problem with merely venting anger is that the raw emotion may contain memories of many violations and humiliations. You may be angry at many people and for many reasons. To vent this conglomerate of feelings in the presence of a single person is to swamp that person with all your accumulated feelings, most of which have nothing to do with him. Rage turning into violence feels impotent and accomplishes nothing, because you aren't dealing with the real object of your anger. You are simply giving other people good reason to be angry at you.

A good therapist once told me that you should get angry as many times a day as you visit the bathroom. I think what she meant was, first, that anger is natural. You may not like it, but it has its place and, depending on your temperament, it may be a constant in your life. She also meant that anger arrives on its own schedule and for its own purposes, and its schedule may be different from yours. Finally, she was saying that anger is part of daily life, and you should expect it to appear often.

Another therapist told me I should be in a relationship only with someone who could handle my anger. Some people seem to enjoy being angry or dealing with someone else's anger. Some relationships are constant battles, a style that seems to work for only a few. Generally, it's important to have the freedom to get angry. You don't want to be judged badly for it or have it held against you. You don't want passing anger to be blown out of proportion, either. Anger builds up, and it is better to direct your mild anger at ordinary situations than to explode far after the fact, when you may have forgotten what you were angry about.

Some people seem chronically angry. They always have a "chip on their shoulders." At the slightest provocation they fly into a rage. Perhaps they never dealt with an injustice from long ago or have a habit of suppressing their feelings, a condition that turns into a personality trait, an eternal dark moodiness. Anger diffused into a mood doesn't look much like anger, but if you don't congeal that mood into something meaningful, it will forever remain illusive and corrosive.

Other people get angry all the time. It takes nothing to cause an explosion of rage. They use profanities in large quantity and throw things and smash them. But they, too, may feel impotent in their rage. Nothing comes of it. It's a habit that accomplishes nothing. They, too, need to know how to *express* their anger, not just indulge in it.

Suppressed anger can transform into violence. Some people have a "short fuse" and blow up at unexpected times. Others find violence vicariously and symbolically. They associate with coarse people who seem to share their generic frustrations. One wonders if the success of violent scenes in the movies is due to a deep anger in the populace. People can indulge their rage by watching violence on the screen without any serious repercussions. But this voyeuristic anger has no effect on the roots of discontent. Watching only prolongs the problem. Occasionally a film offers insight into the dynamics within violence, and in that case the images might help sort out the audience's hidden layer of rage.

But anger always calls for a response that has some effect in the world, because anger is related to power and creativity.

ANGER IS DAIMONIC

When you have been done an injustice, anger flares up before you have a chance to understand what has happened. It's as though someone else is looking out for you and letting you know immediately that you have been wronged. Anger gives you the impetus you need to change conditions that need to be changed. In this way, anger is like a dark guardian angel, a daimonic force—a daimon is an unnamed but felt invisible presence—that offers guidance and spiritual support.

But once this daimonic anger has done its job, you are left with personal decisions. If you don't act soon, you may forget what gave rise to anger in the first place. The first task is to show your displeasure, and the next might be to examine the situation and ask, "Why am I angry? What exactly has happened?" Anger has content, but if you let it dissipate without reflection and action, it may enter a pool of discontent that swells and stagnates over time. This chronic anger is a corrosive emotion that uglifies everything in its vicinity.

Anger can be so suppressed that you feel a vague discontent, but you don't even know that the root emotion is anger. You have to bring this core feeling to the surface and see it for what it is. It might help to remember the stories of injustice done to you and to make some headway changing those conditions. It also helps to find a new reason for being angry, for channeling the rage you feel into a cause worthy of your emotion. Notice that in none of these cases do you try to get rid of the anger but rather to give it a strong reason for being.

You need some insight into your anger so that eventually you can deal with its specific focus. Anger is only partly an emotion. It has an intellectual component and helps make sense of your life. If you know precisely what and who angers you, you know where you stand, some of what is going on, and how emotionally to deal with it. Anger sorts out a complex life and constantly restructures it. It may take considerable anger to change jobs or decide on a divorce. It's obvious that social wrongs are only corrected when the abused get angry enough and resist.

Anger can draw out the knight and warrior in you and transform simple emotion into an effective persona. It can make you a different person. Many men and women going through a dark night describe how they were changed by it, often by becoming more of a warrior. By warrior I don't mean a violent person, but someone who has taken on an edge and has discovered unknown power. In some cases, simply owning your power, your eccentricity, or your creativity is enough to chase away the mood that has kept you dark and quiet.

If you don't articulate your angry feelings in some effective way, you may end up turning those feelings against yourself. This is a subtle way of avoiding the anger—by disguising it as self-annoyance. A habit of self-flagellation can lead to a particular dark night of the soul that is centered on a kernel of anger. You block your feeling, choosing this form of depression over the risk of revealing how you actually feel. But anger wants to flow through your system, from your first awareness of injustice to your final syllable of complaint. That feeling of becoming angry may be nothing more or less than the pulse of life asking for expression. The Sufi poet Rumi once wrote:

> Don't use your anger to conceal
> a radiance that should not be hidden.

Anger is your spirit flashing out of you. It is your presence on earth insisting upon itself. It can be overdone, of course, be expressed in the wrong ways, and be confused with many other things. But it is still the force of your life, your precious daimon letting itself be known.

GIVING ANGER FORM

Medical books of the Middle Ages discuss anger in the imagery of alchemy and astrology. These images link anger to several other qualities and help us stretch our imagination of what anger is all about. Marsilio Ficino said that although anger is a problem, it helps you to *arouse* your feelings and to *purge* them. Anger helps you *confront* your situation. It *stimulates* you and helps overcome any timidity you may have. It *warms* your entire being and gives your voice and your actions a *firmness* and *sharpness* they need. Ficino especially emphasizes how anger can strengthen your "voice" and make your resolve firm and lasting.

These key ideas, which are traditional qualities of the spirit Mars, flesh out aspects of anger that can be useful and even necessary. Firmness, heat, and strength are part of anger. Repress anger and these qualities, too, disappear. Anger might also have a role in other kinds of expression, the toughness in your love or the ground of your compassion, the boldness of your expression or the heat of your passion. Anger is a quality as well as an emotion.

Anger can also become your endurance and strength. It can make you firm instead of flabby, pointed in your speech instead of vague, and direct in your relations instead of indirect. It can inspire you to be more active and to take charge of your life. It can turn your compassion into social action and bring your native creativity into actual life. It isn't enough to have good ideas and values, you have to live them with power and conviction.

Anger transformed into personal strength also helps marriages and other partnerships. Most people want to be with someone who takes responsibility for his own life and offers leadership and support. Relationships begin to fail when one of the partners collapses under the weight of life's challenges. Anger may be the beginning of a creative response, and that is a significant contribution to a partnership.

On the other hand, of course, raw or chronic anger can make

a relationship miserable for everyone involved. Tranquillity, kindness, equanimity, self-possession—these qualities in a family or marriage help create an atmosphere where love can grow and people feel free to be themselves. You have to learn how to give anger its place so that it doesn't crowd out the other feelings that promote intimacy and comfort. Its spirit, Mars, is only one of a pantheon of spirits and emotions. At its best, anger coexists with calm, joy, friendliness, and the feeling of community.

Once again, there is a paradox at work. Real tranquillity in life and relationship doesn't come from passivity, but from an iron-like structure of philosophy and personality. Not that there should not be flexibility as well, but today the importance of strength, a Mars virtue, is often neglected. Getting your anger in place can help create that structure and offer one piece in the security necessary for a creative and loving life.

Your anger may never be understood and yet it can do its work of resolving life problems. Leonard Bernstein's biographer tells how the composer began to get unreasonably angry at his wife of many years, to the point that eventually they split apart. Bernstein immediately went on to explore his bisexuality. Who knows the propriety and morality of this situation, but we can see how anger played a role in bringing Bernstein's deep issues into the open.[59]

GETTING POWER AND SUBMISSION RIGHT

It may sound simple to give anger its place among the many emotions that come and go. But, as I said, anger has a daimonic quality. It has its own will and may have a strength that you simply can't control. Just as love is bigger than any emotion you could come up with on your own, anger is a *source* of strength that you tap into. Anger is often connected with issues of power. You get angry when things aren't going your way or if someone has gone too far in trying to control you. But this issue of power and control has to do with your capacity to let life pass through you, as much as possible, unhindered.

Your vitality is your destiny; it defines you and allows you to be creative. It is your job to cooperate with it. If you don't do your part finding a place for all your strength and promise, it will transform. Instead of being receptive to the constant invitations to increase the life in you, you will start being submissive to other people. The object of your surrender will shift from life itself to a particular person or group of persons. This shift in responsiveness creates a destructive pattern known for decades in psychology as sadomasochism.

The pleasure you would have received by being responsive to life reverses. Now you may find pleasure in being disappointed, emotionally and physically hurt, or betrayed. This is how I imagine masochism and why I think it is so pervasive. It may be perceived in the tone of an interaction. You're late for an appointment, and you berate yourself for your habitual tardiness. You could just take it as one of life's mishaps, but instead, you focus on yourself. You can see in this example how egotism is part of the picture as well. Instead of letting life happen, you imagine the scene as centering on yourself.

When this habit gets deeper and more ingrained, your criticism of yourself may become harsher. You may judge yourself brutally and often. You may even find ways to get hurt or actually cause yourself physical pain. Some people cut and beat themselves. In relationship, you may act out your pattern in sadomasochistic forms of lovemaking, a rather common way of shifting broad issues of power and surrender to sex.

But sadomasochism works in two directions. In one case, the very person who takes pleasure in suffering often has a hidden sadistic side. He may present an image to the world as being powerless, always being beaten down. But in subtle ways, and without owning up to it, the same person may be extremely controlling and harsh. In the presence of a self-deprecating person, it is often wise to look for signs of subtle control and almost invisible force.

The other way sadomasochism shows itself is from the side of the aggressor. When life no longer supports you and gives you strength, you may desperately try to demand strength by becoming aggressive. You may take at least small pleasure in hurting someone you love. You may purchase a sense of power by lording it over others and taking advantage of them. Going through an airport inspection recently, a woman in front of me was having trouble understanding all the procedures. The man in charge told her to lift her suitcase and put it on a belt. Confused by the intricacy of the procedure, she hesitated, setting her bag on the floor for a few seconds. Immediately the young official seized her valise as abandoned luggage and sent it off to a holding room. Then he lectured us all on following the rules. "We're serious about these inspections," he said with exaggerated authority. The rest of us were outraged at the injustice of this little dictator and voiced our objections until the woman was properly attended.

Strength and weakness need not be perfectly balanced to be workable and livable. We've been tracking the difficulties of the writer Anne Sexton. In a letter to the poet Stanley Kunitz she spells out a subtle way in which this particular yin and yang can be coupled: "People are always telling me I'm tough. Maybe because I've survived so much. Inside I feel like cooked broccoli, and I don't mean the stalks which should be crisp and tasty. I mean the heads that fall apart when you cut them. The only time I'm tough in my own mind is when I'm seized by a poem and then determined to conquer it and let it live its own particular life. All my toughness goes into my writing."[60]

Expressing and not expressing anger is a complicated business. Brian Keenan tells a dramatic story of how, after being taunted by a guard named Said, he had an opportunity to shove him against a wall. But his aggression merited harsh punishment for Keenan's companion, John. The next time he was taunted, he felt his rage, but he reacted differently: "Anger roared up in me and I caught it by the throat, choked it and held it back. I said nothing, I merely turned and stared at him with my blind eyes as I had at Said, then turned away. He waited for me to speak. I would not."[61]

But people don't always have such self-possession. A person may act sadistically because of the unknown, simmering anger in his heart. He doesn't know what his anger is all about, and so he inflicts it on anyone he imagines to have wronged him. Often the degree of anger has little relation to the cause of his flare-up. But this is chronic, repressed anger that wasn't trusted when it first arose, perhaps many years ago. There's old anger, and there's new anger. The former needs to be reclaimed, the latter expressed in its proper situation.

In the extreme, of course, people can become violent, but, short of physical conflict, we are all capable of sadistic acts. Parents do it with their children, teachers with their students, doctors with their patients—these roles are particularly susceptible to sadomasochistic expression. Lovers do it to each other in the confusion of their emotions.

Once again, the pattern is complicated. The person who displays his aggressiveness in bullying and fighting, and perhaps with weapons, secretly feels powerless. The only way he can have a sense of his own strength is to reach for a weapon, which is a fetish, a symbol of strength but not the real thing. He may strut and shout, but beneath all the rooster-like display is a weak and ineffectual person. You have to know this about sadomasochism in order to deal with it effectively.

These variations in the use and abuse of power cover a spectrum, from mild forms of control to aggressiveness and violence. The pattern is often at work in suicide, murder, domestic violence, and social conflict. When people are not given the opportunity to respond creatively to the life in them, they may turn violent. On the other hand, we may all fall into mild forms of this pattern in our everyday interactions. A husband and wife try to decide where to go for dinner. It seems a simple decision, but you may sense the underlying issues of power and submission that even such a simple act brings up.

TRANSFORMING PASSIVITY

This sadomasochistic splitting of emotion may be responsible, in part at least, for your dark night of the soul. It may derive from the falling apart and rebuilding that goes on in a dark night, when your emotions are volatile and shifting. You may move frequently from feeling rage to feeling overwhelmed. You may not be certain just what you feel or what is happening in your life.

Often, when someone approaches me with some chronic suffering, I see the pain in her face and sense the tendency to suffer, which is this common-variety masochism I'm talking about. Some people have a habit of suffering every situation, and, true to form, they try to control every situation as well. The way out of some dark nights is simply a change in this attitude. You don't have to suffer your existence; you can enjoy it. You don't have to envy the control and power you sense in others, you can find your own by giving more of yourself to what life asks of you.

Many people transform their anger into self-destructiveness—drinking their lives away or becoming oblivious in drugs or working too much. They make take it out on their children, employees, or animals. They may be passive-aggressive in a number of ways—being silent, uninvolved, offering insincere love and friendship, being available for people but making them suffer for it. When anger is clean, it can accomplish a great deal for a person and a relationship; but when it is camouflaged and indirect, its impact is just the opposite.

People often don't look deeply enough into the power patterns in their lives. They assume that if they feel powerless, they should manifest their strength. They try, but because this is the wrong tactic, they fail. Once, when I was attending some discussion sessions at James Hillman's house, I arrived quite late and disturbed the feeling in the room. The next week I arrived a half hour early. James met me at the door and said, "Ah! Compensation!"

It's always tempting to compensate. You believe that you are a passive person, and so you try to be assertive. What you fail to realize is that hidden in your passivity is some strong, anxious aggression. Here is a perfect place to "go with the symptom." If you are powerless, first learn how to surrender and be receptive in ways that work for you. Almost magically, you will find the power you were looking for. Things are often just the opposite of what they appear to be, and this is because life is made up of paradoxes and opposites.

If you tend to be passive, paradoxically, you don't need to be more assertive but rather more receptive. The difference between passivity and receptivity is the difference between suffering and being open. Maybe you can't tell the difference. When you are passive, you feel the impact of life on you at every turn. You can't see that your passivity is a symptom of your failure to allow, tolerate, and cooperate with life as it comes along. Your very passivity is a form of control.

You see this pattern in people who get married externally but not internally. They live with the person they love, but they never decide to give up their single lifestyle. They constantly complain about having to share their life and temper their will. They are married and not married. Their joy might return if they made the shift, as we saw in the chapter on rites of passage. But that would mean surrendering to the life they have, rather than remaining attached to the one they idealize.

People often feel frustrated and angry because they perceive other people taking advantage of them or having the upper hand. In spite of themselves, these people may cave in under the pressure and find themselves at the mercy of others, who may be in positions of authority or simply forcing their will. To restore a sense of power, the oppressed have to heal the split in their emotions. If they merely compensate and try to be strong when they actually feel weak, there can be no good resolution. But if they can be both vulnerable and strong, they may find an effective way to deal with their frustration—not vulnerable to other people, but open to their feelings and to what is demanded of them.

To put it simply, masochism is an invitation to surrender to life, and in so doing to gain a sense of power and flexible control. This phrase, "flexible control," describes the reconciliation of strength and submission. The *Tao Te Ching* recommends *wu-wei*: achieve things by not trying to achieve. But another quality helps turn masochism into flexible control—intelligence. You have to know when and how to surrender, even to whom to surrender.

Certain kinds of surrender promise vitality, as in the marriage vow to spend your life with someone you love. But even then, surrender can be excessive or poorly handled. The safest surrender is to give yourself to life, to trust in yourself and in the laws of nature. Surrendering to a person or an organization is more dangerous and only makes sense when it is thoughtful, somewhat cautious, and never detached from surrender to your own need.

It is my sense that more people fall into masochism than into sadism. More of us feel victims of society, business, and government. We endure moments in family life and in marriage when we believe that our power has disappeared. These are all moments of promise, when the sense of being crushed and overwhelmed can be transformed into a fuller participation in life. You have to find someone or some group worthy of your surrender. Then you may find new vitality and new strength, precisely because you transmuted your passivity into vulnerability and self-giving.

The best outcome of masochistic behavior might be a marriage in which you are both free and dependent, a job in which you exercise both freedom of decision and the willingness to serve the corporation, or a family to which you devote a great deal of time and energy and yet take care of your own basic needs and desires.

The subtle sadomasochistic patterns of ordinary life account for much of the anger people feel. Some express it too forcefully, violently in fact. Others feel it turned against themselves or so deep-seated and ill-defined that they suffer it daily. Either kind of anger can create a dark night of the soul, a long period of dissatisfaction and unhappiness. In any dark night, it is may be useful to consider carefully where your anger is placed and how you deal with matters of submission and control.

THE NAKED SOUL

The self that you have erected over the years, defensive, controlling, and fearful, may feel this shift in attitude as a death, a dying to life as you have known and loved it. But it is only one layer of death. Every day you have to die, even as you live. The fulfillment of your masochism, and your release from it, may require that you allow it to happen. The desired new life comes into view only when something old dies off.

In his powerful book *The Denial of Death*, Ernest Becker addresses the many complications and ambiguities, as he calls them, in this process, stressing the need of any person to enter life newly cleansed and liberated. "The very defenses that he needs in order to move about with self-confidence and self-esteem become his life-long trap. In order to transcend himself he must break down that which he needs in order to live. Like Lear he must throw off all his 'cultural lendings' and stand naked in the storm of life." "Cultural lendings" may be the many patterns you learn as you grow up, ways that society has of teaching you how to be docile and when you can assert yourself. They also include the many rules you have from your family.

Becker uses the imagery of Jonah—"naked in the storm of life." Jonah-like, we all have to be spit out of the belly of family and cultural assumptions, a new person, freed and unqualified. But this is one of the purposes we have seen for dark nights of the soul: to prune, cleanse, and sort out the essential from the illusory. We have to do something with our anger other than suppress it or vent it. There are a thousand possibilities, but each of them has to honor the emotion while giving it form and meaning. Ultimately, you transform your anger through a channeling of your life force, and this liberated vitality gives you your presence as a unique personality.

If you have ever given birth or attended one, you know the force it takes to shoot into this world in the first place. You need a Mars spirit all your life to keep entering into life as yourself. You will meet up with many obstacles, many people, especially, who would rather have you adopt their views and styles than be your own person. The force you need to thrive and create is your anger turned upside down. Anger gives you all the power and motivation you need to live every minute originally, as yourself. Without it, you will surrender in the wrong places and you will become overwhelmed. Anger both keeps you out of certain dark nights and lifts you out of them once you have succumbed. It is your precious angel, deserving of your attention and cultivation.

CHAPTER TWELVE

TEMPORARY INSANITIES

SOME PEOPLE GO MAD and fall victim to serious hallucinations and dementia. The rest lead relatively sane lives but are sometimes thrown by temporary, situational, and relatively mild insanities inspired by jealousy, envy, fear, rage, or some other basic emotion. It's an illusion to think that most people are normal, rational, and in control of themselves. In fact, most people lose control frequently in anger or in brief periods of unreality. Sometimes a dark night of the soul takes the form of a passing madness.

You certainly know the temporary insanity of falling in love, being jealous, or slipping into depression. Families, spouses, and friends get into deep arguments and conflicts, rooted in madness, about love or money or opinion. Something happens, and you find yourself overwhelmed by emotion that threatens your relationships, but there is nothing you can do about it. There seems to be no reasonable solution, no way out. Anyone who has ever been divorced knows this pit of madness.

Teachers know the scene well. A girl in the class feels rejected by her classmates. She is jealous of the popular girl and doesn't understand why she is not invited to parties and allowed to participate in games during recess. A dark cloud settles over the classroom. The teacher feels responsible for the problem and duty-bound to clear it up. Parents get involved, and their emotions come to the surface in exaggerated tales and hysterical concern for their children. The teacher tries to force equality among the children. Parents meet to find out who or what is wrong. The entire scene is full of dead ends and false victories.

Life is full of these unexpected descents into the thick swampy climate of the soul. There are no exits. You feel imprisoned in what seems to be pure melodramatic emotion. It's difficult to see what is happening and how to get out. The more you experiment with reasonable solutions, the more frustrated you become, because they don't work. People behave unreasonably because they are temporarily insane.

THE LIMITS OF REASON

One reason why you get into trouble like this is that you trust reason too much. Human life is rarely reasonable. You may believe that intelligent, well-meaning people can resolve any conflicts, but that assumption itself arises out of a cloudy image of how things work. Insight usually means discovering the madness hidden in an apparently reasonable situation.

People are always on the cusp between clarity and fog. Pure unreasonableness lies like a shadow at the edge of all transactions. You may wish things were simpler, but they aren't. Your only recourse is to take into account at least a moderate degree of madness in every situation you encounter.

At every moment you are caught up in a story that you can't

make out because you are engulfed in it. You are swept along by events and characters. Eventually you get stuck in a thicket of emotions, and still you think you can get out by the strength of your understanding. Your very misconceptions about how human life works set you up for disillusionment and frustration.

LIFE IS THEATER

Whether you like it or not, human life is a drama, and often full of outlandish characters and outrageous scenarios. Each person appears on his own stage, and somehow you try to make sense of a multitude of dramas. No one has seen the script in advance, and yet each person plays a specific role. Everyone, trying to discover the plot, is a character in search of an author.

It often happens on the job. Workers are acutely sensitive to advancements and romances and raises. It's understandable. The workplace is also a theater where the basic elements of the human drama play themselves out. Every action is both literal and symbolic, every word both practical and theatrical. Theater is the primal language of the soul, and it lies just beneath the surface of the literal issues.

Managers and employees come home from work burdened by the melodramas taking place. It causes some to quit their jobs and others to sabotage their work out of anger and frustration. Others, not knowing how to resolve the conflicts and strong emotions, turn their frustrations against themselves and self-destructively become addicted or withdrawn. The play you are in may not be visible on the surface.

Courtrooms and hospitals are particularly prone to the dramatics of the soul. Maybe that is why they work so well as the setting of movies, plays, and soap operas. There the dramatic elements in everyday life come to the surface, especially around the themes of health, crime, sex, and money. There the situations are extreme, often matters of life and death.

The strength of psychoanalysis is its brilliance at getting beneath the surface and unveiling the stories within the stories. An analyst is like a detective, searching through clues and eventually dredging up a theme so buried as never to have been suspected. The trouble with psychoanalysis as a formal method is that, in searching for a truly primal story, it favors certain sexual and childhood themes. These stories are useful, but they are not the last word.

Still, it wouldn't hurt for you to be a psychoanalyst of sorts in your own life. You can look for clues to deeper stories that account for your emotion. Today some people think of sexual abuse in childhood as the final, enlightening story. Some think a distant father or an overbearing mother is the ultimate culprit. It would better not to look for the one and only person to blame or the ultimate explanatory tale but rather to focus on the stories as narrative. The idea is for you to discover the play you are in, not a theory that explains your life.

As you reflect on your life and nature, perhaps with the help of a friend or therapist, you will find themes that carry weight. It may be a story that you often tell about your past or about the world. It may be a theme that you hadn't thought important before but now makes special sense. The ego, the self, or the "I" is a character in a story, and to know more about yourself you need to know the various stories you are living out.

When I was in the religious order, a colleague kept telling me the story of his father, who left home to be a priest but left long before his planned ordination. His father then married and became a bitter man, feeling that he had betrayed his parents. He was an alcoholic—sweet, complicated, and sometimes violent. My friend came to think that he had to finish what his father had started. He didn't personally want to sacrifice his life for religion, but he felt an overwhelming desire to heal his father's failed life.

Needless to say, my friend also mirrored his father's bitterness and regret. He never felt at home in the religious life and was obviously an unhappy man. It was a short step for this young man to see his father's fate being played out in his own life. His deep story was his father's story. Once he discovered this truth about himself, which was no mystery to his close friends, he could make a decision to live his own life and leave his father to his own fate. At least, he could begin this important work of the soul and spend his lifetime at it.

But stories may lie even deeper, and that is why we place such importance on mythology, literature, poetry, and the other arts. They reveal the deep images at play in a person's life. Time after time, Icarus resurrects in a young person, man or woman, who decides to aim as high as possible and gets burned in idealism and ambition. Madame Bovary haunts many a marriage, as the man or woman seeks an end to boredom in an affair but only slips deeper into meaninglessness. It helps to know who is living through you at any given moment. The less you know about it, the more it dominates and keeps you from other adventures.

THE WAY OF LEARNING

Compulsions are difficult because they block the freedom to consider and design your own life. You are at the mercy of whatever impersonal passion has you in its grip. You can't weave it tightly into all the various considerations needed to make a tranquil and creative life. You can't temper it, and so it interferes with your relationships and your work. The end result is yet another kind of dark night, a chronic oppression that makes life seem impossible.

Mary Wollstonecraft Shelley is a good example—a passionate, confused person who suffered many tragedies and betrayals, and, only after years of effort, found her own way in a demanding world. Early in her life she became obsessed with the poet Percy Bysshe Shelley, traveled with him widely amid scandal, and had children with him. Two of the children died, and then Shelley himself drowned while they were living in Italy. Mary had written her now renowned and insightful novel *Frankenstein*, but the critics and public assumed at the time that it was her husband's work. Because she had gone off with Shelley filled with ideas of woman's independence, which she had learned from the writings of her feminist mother Mary Wollstonecraft, she was denied her husband's inheritance and had to struggle to maintain herself and her son. At this point in her life she was only thirty.

Mary Shelley followed her utopian, free-thinking ideals, but after the deaths of her children and husband, and learning that her closest friends had betrayed her, she fell into deep despair. Her mother had died giving birth to her, and her stepmother always despised her. She idolized her father, who was an author and social reformer, but he was always in debt, preoccupied with money, and angry at her relationship with Shelley. Early in life, she was surrounded by people misinterpreting her actions and withholding their support.

She finally came up with a simple but remarkable solution: She educated herself. She had always read widely, learning from Shelley what and how to read. But now she intensified her education, studying philosophy and classical literature. She also learned about human nature and through painful realizations took firm hold of her life. Her biographer Emily Sunstein summarizes this aspect saying, "She set herself a course of study, not simply for knowledge but for definition."[62]

Mary Shelley offers an extraordinary model for responding to a world out of control and the resulting discouragement. At the turning-point in her life she wrote in her diary, "I must change." And she did. The change didn't come about automatically or at will. She had to work hard at making a life of her own, crafting a presence in the world and a sense of her own character and destiny. She discovered how to move from being passive in the face of circumstances to shaping her own life. She became less gullible with her friends and much clearer about how she wanted to live. Her biographer divides her life between the romantic and the post-romantic periods. The same could be true of us all—to live by passion and by design, not that the two are ever completely split, but it may take years to learn how to do both.

In our rather anti-intellectual age, it may not occur to you that a good way out of despair might be to school yourself in great literature and ideas. Mass entertainment crowds out the pleasures of deep thinking. Yet it makes sense that if the troubles you experience have to do with living life effectively, you should have thought seriously about them. An education of the heart and mind might be the best way to come through a dark night a better and happier person.

PRACTICAL INTELLIGENCE

It is an important lesson: You have to become more intelligent in the conduct of your life. You are surrounded by unreliable advice-givers and shallow experts. To the extent that you do not educate yourself in the mysteries of your existence, you are susceptible to their simplicities. As an alternative to following popular gurus, you could give up the idea that you need an expert and a coach, and simply live your life with intelligence.

You don't have to be highly educated in psychology, or any other field for that matter, to be wise about your life. Intelligence is often a matter of attitude rather than schooling. You have to take yourself seriously. Know what is good and right for you. Avoid the clichés of the day and probe deeply into the behavior of people around you. Generally, people are highly gullible. They are susceptible to advertisers and politicians, and this gullibility is a symptom of a lazy brain. Like Mary Shelley, when life offers endless obstacles and tragedies, you always have your wits—a theme we've seen before—with which you can make a satisfying life.

Also like Mary Shelley, you may be reacting to a period of wildness or a time of tragedy. For me, as these pages show, my early temporary insanity led me to leave home at a young age.

That impulsive act made me who I am, for better or worse, but it also keeps me lonely, apart, always on a walkabout to make heroic sense of my life. I have learned more about the ways of human nature from my practice of therapy than in any other way. I have been schooled by that which I was schooled to do.

Sometimes the catalyzing deed is not your own. I knew a man who as a child was put on a train by the Nazis with his family, to be shipped away to a place unknown. He got off the train during a bathroom stop, and the train started up before he had boarded it. He had to run so as not to be separated from his parents. Fortunately, he got back on the train, and his family eventually found safety. But this crucial moment of separation, the still photo in his memory of that race not to be left behind, stayed with him all his life as a living nightmare. Here the madness was society's and yet it marked him forever with a certain ill-defined fear.

This man, too, while working at jobs far beneath his intelligence, educated himself, and studied literature and depth psychology. He also took his dreams seriously, more so than anyone I have ever met. He educated himself, not in the usual modern way, where mind and life are separated, but for mind and soul. He has always been an inspiration to me and a model of how to deal with a dark night.

The best response to your defining passion and insanity might be to remain loyal to it, even though others will try to persuade you of its negativity. For here lies another paradoxical secret of the soul: That which seems to have twisted your life or personality for the worst is the very thing that will heal you and give you meaning.

Foolishly I entered a religious community too young and foolishly I left it just before completing my preparation. Foolishly I got married too soon, and foolishly I didn't persevere in that marriage until I was mature enough to handle it. This could be a long list of foolish acts, done in moments of temporary insanity, but I can't imagine my life without them. Foolishly I haven't dealt with money well during my entire life; I seem to have a block against it. My insanities define me. Without them, I would be wondering who I am and when my life will begin. My healing requires that I honor the foolishness of all these moments.

Recall the teaching of Heraclitus: "Your daimon is your fate." I might interpret this to mean that when you feel possessed and out of control, you may do things, for better or worse, that define you, that give you the basic structures of your life. Because they are largely unconscious and unwilled, they may come to you as a dark night of the soul. Still, they are precious to you and offer you material for reflection and serious conversation for the rest of your life.

THE VALUE OF SYMBOL AND NONSENSE

The heroic ideal of slaying dragons and overcoming adversity lies deep in the modern imagination. You may feel compelled to solve all your problems and sort out all your confusion. The need for closure may drive you crazy, so that you can't rest until everything is resolved. But there is another way.

The soul is healed more by poetry than by heroics. Symbolic acts and moral victories are more important at the deep level than literal successes. Your lover or spouse may leave you without warning after years of trusting companionship. You may recover your crushed sense of worth, not by proving that you are not to blame, but by finding renewal in that dark night. You may have to learn that passion directed toward another person is always somewhat misplaced, that whether or not you share a life with that person, you have to stay focused on the powerful object that leads you to the fulfillment of your own life in a greater world. You have a destiny that may include marriage but doubtless goes beyond the intimate relationship to an ever-expanding community, and in that series of expanding circles your being is fulfilled.

If you have lost a child to disease or accident, of course you can't recover the life that has been taken from you, but you can live out visions inspired by your loved one. Your imagination can turn despair and grief into a new, perhaps more contributing and unhindered way of life. The implosion of grief can become an explosion of compassion. You may have to go through several stages of grief, but one day you may be able to sense all those emotions settling into place, changing into a new vision. Along the way, you may have to do some crazy things, because, when the soul is touched at its very foundations, only a departure from the rational can restore it.

Temporary insanities, like those of hard loss and grief, are always potentially creative, depending on how you deal with them. The temptation always is to sink too far into self-pity and to find relief in the compassion of others. It's important to feel the sadness, but emotion is always only a partial resolution. Grief is complete only with a shift in being, in the way you live, think, and relate to the world.

You can imagine every emotion having its yin and yang. Grief turns inside out into vision and courage. Sadness reverses itself in empathy and understanding. To live only one side of the emotion is to remain incomplete. You may feel at an impasse with it, stuck and unable to see a way out. You stay with the feeling until it shows its other dimensions. You can't program such a development or demand its revelation, but you can give yourself to the condition of your soul with hope.

Many of the examples of wit and self-possession we have seen among those dealing with horrific dark nights have involved extreme eccentricity. Glenn Gould's exceptional talent allowed him to bring his anxieties about performance, his extreme hypochondria, and his fear of touch into the creative life of a highly fulfilled man, instead of a hospitalized maniac. The difference between the two resolutions was always extremely thin. He teaches us to stand firm in life, crazy, rather than retreat out of it, safe and apparently sane.

Glenn Gould, Oscar Wilde, Virginia Woolf, Emily Dickinson, and many others adopted an exaggerated, inexplicable, eccentric persona as a way of linking the madness of their souls with a minimum of acceptance within society. Anyone can do this. Imagine what you would be like if you allowed yourself your full eccentricity. That might be a perfect way for you, depending on your temperament, to reconcile your dark night and your wish for a life of love and acceptance. Without the zany persona, you might be condemned to darkness, and that would be the tragedy.

I realize that my own taste for the absurd, for slapstick humor, for antiheroes and the generally rejected; my love of certain heavy, dolorous music; my failure to make it both as an academic and as a serious artist—all place me outside the sphere of the normal. As I get older, I recognize and embrace my eccentricity and find freedom in it. The range and intensity of my various neuroses could push me into painful seclusion, but I am redeemed just a little by not caving in to the inferiority. I feel balanced on a fulcrum no less precarious than that of Glenn Gould, midway between exclusion from society and inclusion, between intelligence and absurdity, between profound loss of face and my own kind of creativity.

MONEY: AN OCCASION FOR INSANITY

Gould, Wilde, and Dickinson are outstanding examples of mild insanity corralled into meaning. The rest of us fall into temporary insanities over something as mundane as money. Both an abundance of money and a lack of funds can make life feel completely in order or in total disarray. Both conditions can cause temporary insanities that lead us into strong emotions and disastrous behaviors. Both can take us deep into an emotional slump.

We have to expect many temporary excursions into mild madness, and then have to find our way through them. You have to understand, for example, that money is not neutral. In a world of meaning and feeling it is explosive. It takes you far into the realm of the human soul, and that territory is naturally devoid of reason, full of myth and fantasy, and dark with a forest-like, rich wilderness.

The Welsh poet Dylan Thomas and his wife Caitlin didn't "believe in" money, and yet the poet's biographer says that it was poverty that caused his disintegration and death. Hints about their attitude toward money lie in Caitlin's memoirs: "With money, we spent hours planning all the sensible, civilized things we would do with it; eking it out on moderate enjoyment, like proper people; vowing and swearing before our Holy Maker, never again to indulge in those racketing wastes that wrought such havoc in us; and in which a good half of our lives was spent." [63]

Part of the problem with money is that it bears such a weight of meaning. It may give you a sense of worth and may mark progress in your life plans and hopes. The making of it, the spending of it, and the sheer possession of it may give you a rush of pleasure—and in that way act like a drug—or extreme anxiety. The pleasure may be so strong that it comes to stand in for all other pleasures, and financial concerns may dwarf all other values.

James Hillman makes an important recommendation in relation to money. He says that to avoid its grimy power we may try to outwit it. Voluntary poverty may be such a tactic. But what we really have to do is restore money to the deep soul. The point is not to try to make a life free of the dark nights it brings, but to enter those financial dramas that afflict you with confusion and emotion. The lesson here is simple: Don't try to avoid the emotions of money in fantasies of purity and control. Enter the fray, but keep your sensibilities intact. Don't let money serve only your ego, propping you up and giving you control. Let it take you down into fantasy and memory. Find a part of yourself in your financial dark nights. Keep talking about the place of money in your life. Be creative with it. Don't moralize against it, but let it offer you the dramas that in the end define who you are.

A number of years ago I had a few memorable meetings with the former priest and historian Ivan Illich. Illich always thought for himself, upended the most accepted ideas and institutions, and lived his life with imagination. As I remember, he would be given a good fee for coming to a place and presenting a few lectures. He would take most of that money and buy airplane tickets for colleagues he valued and would fly them to join him in his workshops and classes. He didn't make a big deal about poverty or the intelligent use of money, he simply used his imagination in the unique ways he spent it.

People caught in money complexes often swing from one moralism to another. They find ways to keep money hidden and distant. They wrap themselves in simplicity or indulge themselves in spending. My father tells the story of a woman who kept her money hidden behind the tiles of her kitchen ceiling. People have been found carrying hundreds of thousands of dollars in suitcases they toted daily on city streets. Wills are full of rewards and punishments. Money makes us all crazy, each in our own way.

Part of the dark night for us all is the entropy of culture. Of course, modern life has amazing things to offer, but it also routinely dehumanizes. Go to any American small city or town and see how those places have lost their identity through the insanity of money. The inner, livable, human-scale neighborhoods are decaying, while signs of life appear to flourish on the rim of the town, lined with strip malls, chain stores, and parking lots. Is this a neutral, organic cultural change, or does it represent a decadent society losing its soul?

The materialism of modern times is both an attraction and a worry. Clearly it corrupts children and gives ordinary life a coarse texture and a hard edge. At the same time it is difficult for the most visionary of people to give up the comfort and convenience. Some respond to the materialism by becoming immaterial, highly spiritual and ascetic, but that is just another extreme, a compensation that keeps materialism in place. The world is waiting for us to love it and once again become creative and make it beautiful. Until then, we will live in what is, at least in part, a dark age, where, with both sex and money, we flail about in search of a body and a world. Your dark night could be the sadness you feel for the world, whether or not you are conscious of that feeling.

THE OUTSKIRTS OF REASON

When you live a fairly rational life, accepting what is provable and living by accepted norms, you may encounter the soul as a temporary dip into madness. Everyone has these falls, large or small, into confusion and acting out. Eventually, you may get used to the different climate of the deep soul and live differently. You may weave your temporary madnesses into your way of life. You may be more tolerant of eccentricity and more appreciative of lapses from reason. You may adopt a style that encompasses the mysterious and the unexplained. In your interactions and activities you may be half-reasonable and half-possessed. In effect, you may make your dark night, your temporary insanity, part of life.

Seriously religious people and genuine artists sometimes live out there on the outskirts of reason. They have their mystical moments and their true inspirations. They know they have to be half in this world and half in another, just to do their work. Yes, they teeter on the edge of real insanity, but generally they walk the border and have the benefits of a threshold existence.

Just such a placing of thought and behavior may be what a dark night offers you. It takes you into the twilight, where vision is dim and surrounded by fantasy. The modern person and institution doesn't value the position of the outcast from normalcy. Nevertheless, it is a creative place from which to live and it is potentially full of soul.

You could take your temporary insanity as a sign that you are trying too hard to be in control. If you were to "go with" your symptom, you would become more, not less, nonrational in your approach to life. You would learn how to create excursions from reason that would serve you. I have discovered, for example, that I have to write in the early morning or late evening hours if my words are to have any power in them. I need those liminal moments when I am not terribly conscious to do my work well. Some people need to travel to leave their reason behind. Others use substances like alcohol and tobacco for a similar purpose. Sometimes I wonder if we are too moralistic about these things, rationalizing our judgment of them with scientific studies proving their unhealthiness. At the very least, there is a definite moralism in our contemporary approach to health. Such things may indeed be dangerous, but maybe a completely safe life is not worth living.

INDIGO MOODS

Temporary insanity may take the form of a dark mood, which may come over you, making you feel testy, angry, or depressed. This is usually not a long, black depression, but rather a deep-blue moodiness that is a challenge to the people near you. In those minutes, hours, or days, you are not present in the usual way. When people approach you, they run up against your mood and may not be able to penetrate it.

I have been careful not to equate a dark night of the soul with depression. I believe that depression is too clinical, too general, and too negative a word for all dark nights of the soul. But a depressive mood might well qualify as a particular kind of dark night. You could be a well-adjusted person and still occasionally be seized by a dark mood that is impenetrable. It may not last long, but when it is in place, the darkness is as dense as any other night of the soul.

You may have to endure this mood for as long as it has you in its power. Reason probably won't help. If you are lucky, you will be around people who can accept your mood without being seriously affected by it. Many years ago I fell into such a mood over a breakup. A good friend who lived at a great distance was planning to visit me. She phoned and said, "Tom, you're depressed. I think I'll wait a few months to visit." She was a smart woman who knew how to take care of herself. She didn't visit me to "cheer" me up or get me out of my slump. Sometimes we need to be left alone in our moods.

I think we should allow ourselves these temporary insanities, because even though they may be disorienting, painful, and difficult for our loved ones, they represent an ascendancy of the soul, a moment in which the hardworking ego goes into eclipse and gets a rest. You may catch a glimpse of important things in that moment of self-forgetfulness, and you may have your emotions reset and restored.

Long and repeated deep moods can strain a marriage and spoil a workplace. But if you allow yourself the occasional dive into depression, you may be able to weave it effectively into the whole of your life. The people close to you will find ways to understand your emotional eccentricity, and they will have their own to contend with anyway. A good friendship or marriage doesn't have to be an emotional monotone, and, in fact, it may benefit from the ups and downs that are part of an openhearted life.

You can take a Zen-like approach. When you feel blue, be blue. Don't feign cheerfulness. Speak for the mood. The more you allow it some autonomy, the less identified you are with it. It can come and go like a cloud, without your being attached to it. If external circumstances are responsible, enter into them but don't become obsessed. Keep life varied. We learn this lesson from Jung, who, as we saw, dealt with his breakdown directly but at the same time made sure his home life ran smoothly and kept him anchored.

Know that the current fall into madness is temporary. You might hold back on any serious decisions or actions until it passes. You can get away from the cause and restore yourself in nature or a city walk or even, for some, shopping. You can talk to a friend, but remember that the mood usually isn't going to be much affected by reason. Time, sleep, distraction, small pleasures—they can all have an impact on passing insanities and moods.

Over time, you might get to know these visitations quite well. Jung found a personality in each, tying his various moods to a figure with a name and a face. You might find a way to give your emotional excursions more imagination. I often pay close attention to my dreams in times of unusual moodiness, where I can see hints as to what is going on. You don't have to be a dream expert, especially if you come to the dream with an issue in mind. You might well see it reflected in the images and plots.

In my practice, the most common dream images I have seen in people suffering their various dark nights include descending staircases, going down into cellars, standing in a public toilet while the dirty water overflows, and wandering in a city or countryside that is unknown to them. These dreams may suggest that the dark night takes them to emotional places that are objectionable or unfamiliar. The temptation always is to side with the dream-ego and judge the situation the way he or she does. It often helps simply to reverse that point of view and try to see how the dream might be presenting a necessity or even a healthy alternative.

You may dream of being deep in winter, or a tornado or dust storm may be approaching. A dark night often entails a change of emotional "weather." I had a dream two years ago, when I was about to enter a dark night of my own, in which I found myself in a sprawling apartment building, where the atmosphere reminded me of the 1960s. I got lost and then came upon a rather chubby blonde woman lying in a bed. Playfully she invited me to her, but I worried that I wouldn't be able to satisfy her.

I think of the 1960s as a time of extraordinary vitality and promise. For all its social upheaval, people were imagining a better world and experimenting with lifestyles. I sometimes see myself as someone who has never fully embraced life's invitations. Sometimes, not always, I feel anorexic in the spirit—like my mother, very reserved and hesitant to respond to the life in front of me. I worry that I'm not up to it. I see the dream inviting me to be more involved in the flesh than the mind.

As we have seen, you can turn to nature or art—beauty of any kind. You can let the people you trust know a little about what is happening. Just don't expect any brilliant revelations or resolutions. It is the friendship, and not the help you get from friends, that is important. You can let the fear or anger course through you and pass on, in one attack after another. You are a sieve, not a bottle. You are meant to be porous in relation to the emotions and sensations that come to you. In the best of circumstances you dance with them; in the worst of times you wrestle with them, like Jacob and the angel.

One of the best ways to deal with temporary insanities is to incorporate the nonrational into your daily life. You can note signs of things to come in your ordinary environment. You can take your intuitions seriously. You can even experiment with traditional forms of insight like the Tarot cards, astrology, runes, or the I Ching. In a post-modern world, where reason and fact are no longer the primary sources of knowledge, it shouldn't be difficult to see the intelligence in these traditional ways of spurring the imagination. The more you live in the realm of soul instead of mind, the more familiar you will be with the moods and fantasies that suddenly seize you and throw you into a short-term dark night of the soul.

CHAPTER THIRTEEN

THE ISLAND OF ILLNESS

ALTHOUGH WE TREAT illness as a problem to be solved, it is one of the great mysteries of life. Modern medicine focuses its instruments and attention on nonfunctioning organs and anomalous chemistries and overlooks the *experience* of illness. At the first sign of disease, or at the first word from a doctor that you may be seriously ill, your thoughts and feelings shift. You make a sudden movement into your mortality, which you have probably ignored for years. Life now changes radically. Relationships shift. The things that give meaning are put into a new perspective. You wonder endlessly. You discover new fears. You try to sort out what is important from what is distracting.

It is a mistake to think of illness only as an affliction of the body. Not only is the "whole person" involved, but so is the family and the sick person's life and world. Serious illness is often a dark night of the soul. As such, it requires soul doctors as well as body experts. During illness, the soul comes out of hiding and shows itself in fresh realizations and new priorities. You deal with issues of life and death, and you discover the importance of love and caring from family and from skilled strangers.

A lengthy illness especially may take you into a long and deep tunnel, where you may feel frightened, cut off, and out of control. It helps to understand that illness is an experience of your soul as well as your body. If we understood this key point, our hospitals and clinics would look very different. They would address concerns of feeling, meaning, and beauty as well as good functioning.

THE BODY IS THE SOUL

It's common today to claim that medicine should treat the whole person, and yet we still think of the body as separate from thoughts, feelings, and experiences. When we want to look deep into an illness, we look through a microscope. But the glass lens only intensifies the kind of physical, materialistic viewpoint that is standard. What we need is an eye for the invisible factors that are implicated in disease. We need a soul microscope and a stethoscope that captures the pulse of meaning as well as the beating of the heart.

Virginia Woolf sets out the scope of illness in her brief essay "On Being Ill":

> Considering how common illness is, how tremendous the spiritual change that it brings, how astonishing, when the lights of health go down, the undiscovered countries that are then disclosed, what wastes and deserts of the soul a slight attack of influenza brings to view, what precipices and lawns sprinkled with bright flowers a little rise of temperature reveals, what ancient and obdurate oaks are uprooted in us by the act of sickness . . . it is strange indeed that illness has not taken its

place with love and battle and jealousy among the prime themes of literature."[64]

Illness uncovers a world of meaningful issues that you may have covered over with the lively preoccupations of your active life. Now there are no distractions. You have to look closely at what has been unveiled.

Go to a hospital, and you will see people abandoned in a hall, waiting for an X ray, or sitting in a bed, staring as though catatonic or blankly watching a television screen that has been fixed onto the wall. You would never know that these are people with intense relationships, intelligence, talent, a work life, ideas, strong emotions, and unsettling fears and hopes. For the sake of convenience and economy, they are being fed unimaginative food, nothing like the food they know from home or restaurants. Their families can visit them, but there is no place for visitors to sit. Everything is arranged for the flow of technicians and technology. What do they do with their need for fresh air, a walk under trees, some good music, sexuality?

With a serious illness, you worry about dying. You withdraw from your world, your activities, and your family and friends. You subject yourself to a variety of arcane treatments. In a hospital, you even dress differently, and your attention turns away from your usual interests toward minute developments registered in your physical being. Yet it's extremely difficult to get information about your condition. The medical experts may patronize you, thinking that what you don't know can't hurt you.

You may be probed with intrusive tubes and metallic instruments. You may be shot with X rays and hauled through Frankensteinian chambers and tubings. You are labeled with a variety of polysyllabic Latin words and swallow an assortment of pills and powders and liquids that you would otherwise keep at a safe distance from your mouth. Whenever I see someone in a hospital wearing a plastic bracelet identifying who they are, I think of the way we brand and label animals. It's an expedient practice, but the image is dehumanizing.

You may sit in one waiting room after another, gathered closely together with other people in unusual getup and in various conditions of health. You wonder about them, how long they will live, what illness has captured them, and who they might be in the ordinary world. You certainly wonder about your progress or decline. You may become dependent on people who serve you in your hospital or nursing center all day but have mysterious, ordinary lives at home. As you lie there, you have little to do but fantasize.

While writing this book, I visited my mother many times in her nursing center and became accustomed to a world far different from the home my mother tended for over sixty years. Surrounded by sick, disoriented people, cared for by friendly but hired people, never knowing her real condition or her situation, my mother was a different person in that environment. It worked quite well for her physical health, but otherwise it required a major adjustment for her and her family. Though we had a staff of generous and thoughtful people, the way we imagine medicine in the society made it impossible to give my mother all that she needed.

Illness is always an initiation of sorts. It invites new thoughts and daydreams. It takes you to a special plateau on which you exist in a way different from all that you have known. You have to cope and come to a new understanding of yourself. Your illness fills you with wonder, and perhaps fear. You have to find new resources within yourself and in your world.

THE PHYSICAL LIFE OF THE SOUL

Both the sick person and family go through a shared, though distinct, dark night of the soul. If we had a different cultural philosophy, we might understand the importance of this dark night in both the experience of illness and in its healing. We might appreciate the role of emotions and fantasies in the overall experience of sickness. To be bedridden is to have a forced opportunity to dream and remember and imagine. It's a time of strong impressions and many thoughts, if you are capable of registering your environment.

In a strange and compelling document recently discovered in China, *The Jesus Sutras*, a fascinating blend of Christianity, Taoism, and Buddhism, you will find the following teaching ascribed to Jesus: "Whatever you do in life will have its karmic impact upon your soul and will affect the physical life of the soul." Think about this phrase, "the physical life of the soul." It nicely keeps body and soul together. It's the best formulation I have yet come across. The soul as body is subject to illness, and if we want to understand and treat the illness fully, we have to consider the full life of the soul.

The sutras say that karma is a major part of this soul-body, but what is karma? Buddhist teacher Chögyam Trungpa describes it as a "chain reaction of desire." Desiring something leads to further desire, he says. Planning for the future ties you to it and binds you. Karma is a chain that keeps you bound to both the past and the future. Through karma, your life takes shape through your choices and the way you imagine your situation. It makes sense that illness might be connected to the karma you have gathered over the years.

The soul is affected physically by the choices we make and by the way our desires keep us bound to what Chögyam Trungpa calls a spiderweb.[65] In this age of individualism, you may not think radically enough about the network of relationships that define your life and have a role to play in your sickness and in your healing. You may not take seriously the web of ideas, memories, stories, and teachings that have made you who you are, including the sick person you might be today. There may be something "sick" in these areas that shows up in your body.

This is not simply blaming a person for the illness that has entered his life. The American philosopher Susan Sontag sharply criticizes the effort to find meaning in illness, saying that it is always moralistic. But if you are careful, without moralizing, you can see how the way you have lived expresses itself in illness. It follows that healing could involve all those nonphysical areas that are part of the larger picture.

Still, Sontag's warning is an important one. People sometimes blame the sick for transgressing certain moral and religious values. Dr. Daniel Baxter, a compassionate and gifted physician and author, gives a disturbing example of just such an outrage in the New York hospital where he worked. A young man was dying of AIDS. Dr. Baxter brought his parents to see him in the last moments of his life, and his father waved a Bible at him and shouted that it was his homosexuality that brought this curse on him.[66] As it so often happens, the healthy ones put an even heavier burden on the sick person, blaming him when they should be exorcising their own bigotry.

I want to distinguish clearly between this kind of moralistic blame and the search for meaning in illness. In the latter there is no blame, but you do take into consideration the entirety of your life. You may even find relief from your disease by responding to the actions and feelings that you sense are tied up with it. Even if it is too late or otherwise impossible to find physical cure, you can heal your greater self by dealing with these important issues.

The sixteenth-century physician Paracelsus puts it this way: "The spirit in the body can suffer from exactly the same diseases as the body." It is not only your body that has a cold or cancer, but your spirit and soul. To be healed, you may have to deal with a key relationship in your life, or confess to certain indiscretions, or, in a more general sense, feel the joy of life flowing through your entire being.

CARING FOR THE SOUL'S
PHYSICAL ILLNESSES

Illness is a dark night of the soul, which needs as much attention as the purely physical aspects. To consider the dark night is to look at a particular facet of the illness and to be concerned with the experience of it. Intuitively people have always understood this connection, but in recent decades the focus on the isolated body has changed the very nature of medical care. No longer do we go to spas for an extended time for our health. No longer do we spend weeks in a hospital recovering. No longer do we think about fresh air, good food, and nature as central to the healing process. Instead we go into sealed, labyrinthine buildings and submit to procedures that shield us from all these things.

If you understand that your illness is simultaneously a problem for the soul and the body, you will perhaps give more importance to the role your family has in your care and healing. You may pay attention to your environment, making sure that it gives you the emotional support you need. You may also intensify and modify your spiritual practices in relation to your illness and cure.

If you imagine that illness is only a physical thing, you will probably not respond to it as a dark night. You will reduce the entire experience to the material plane, splitting your mental and emotional needs from your physical requirements. You may not give yourself adequate support on these levels, simply because you don't see how they could be connected.

If you doubt that illness is a form of dark night, visit a hospital and look closely at the faces of those who are sick. Then look at the building for signs of joy and humanity. Finally, look closely into the faces of the attendants, the nurses, doctors, and staff. In all these areas you will find dedicated people and the occasional happy ward. But you will also see emptiness and frustration, behind which may lie a painful personal dark night.

You will see many defenses against the soul: "busyness," routines, vacant expressions, machines, empty conversations, and boredom. Medical professionals for the most part don't understand that theirs is a spiritual calling. Even their technical expertise could be in the service of their sacred vocation. But today, in the modernist West, people have sold their souls to technology, expertise, and quantification. It's unfortunate, because only by daring to address the dark night of the soul can we truly heal each other. Protecting ourselves from deep engagement with the mystery of illness, we are left only with the mechanics and instrumentation of medicine, which are increasingly effective but irrelevant to the soul. They treat the shell of the body, but not the meaningfulness that is loaded into it.

CARING FOR THE SOUL OF THE SICK

Modern medicine is rooted in the values of modernism, an unspoken but powerful philosophy that values speed, cost-efficiency, technical methods, expertise, evidence-based research, and medications. The modern person firmly believes that all these hardware methods offer the best response to illness. Doctors are ready to medicate and perform surgery, and hospitals are prepared to get their patients home as soon as possible.

The realm of soul, the intense experiences of emotion, worry, fantasy, and relationship, considered peripheral in the realm of medicine, has great impact on suffering and on healing. Nurses especially will tell you that given two people with the same condition, one will improve and the other will fail, depending on subtle and mysterious factors that aren't considered by medicine. Medicine doesn't have a language for this invisible world that is implicated in illness and healing.

People still confuse the idea of psychosomatic illnesses with the belief that sickness is only in your mind. But the connection between soul and sickness is not just mental, and it is by no means a delusion. What goes on in the life of the soul has its impact on the body, or it is expressed physically. Therefore, treating the soul could have a beneficial effect on the body's illness and pain.

Looking for the connection between mind and body, some use the word "psychogenic," meaning that the cause of the illness is in the psyche. I would put it somewhat differently: the body in distress reveals the state of the soul. In William Blake's language, the body *is* the soul. From that perspective, it makes no sense ever to treat the body as though it were only physical. I might prefer the awkward but telling word, pathopoetics, meaning illness as poetry. Illness expresses what is going on in the world and in the soul.

In a highly intelligent and sensitive book, *Give Sorrow Words*, psychiatrist Dorothy Judd tells the poignant story of Robert, a seven-year-old boy with leukemia, and his two years of painful treatment. [67] In her conclusion she mentions the importance of a medical staff providing clear and honest information, so that people can decide whether agonizing treatment is worth a few more months of life. She also describes how important it is to care for the emotions of patient and family, noting that the ending of a life can be meaningful for everyone involved. Dr. Judd is clearly a doctor of the soul.

"Those working with the dying," she writes, "those who face the death of one they love, and those who survive a life-threatening illness, often find that they gain insight into parts of their psyche that previously were inaccessible; that they can emerge strengthened." About Robert, she writes: "I feel that in health he must have been a passionate child, with a great zest for life, and with an ability to form strong relationships. Even on the brink of death he seemed—for some of the time—steeped in life." Strengthened by illness—this is one way of expressing the truth of a dark night. The darkness does something positive to you, and you are the better for it.

HOSTING YOUR ILLNESS

In the past several years, advocating a more humane approach to medicine, I have visited many medical centers and hospitals. I don't argue against modern methods, which are often miraculous in their own way, but I do speak in favor of tending the soul as a way toward healing. I recommend quality food, good relationships between professionals and patients, accessibility to nature, and the opportunity for patients to talk about their illness to family and professionals.

The word "hospital" is related to many words like hotel, host, and guest. Originally, it referred to a place where you might find rest and entertainment. Both are in short supply in modern hospitals, which are places of busyness and hard work. Often the only entertainment is the ubiquitous and narcotic television set, more a symptom than a source of pleasure. Sometimes I miss the old days when in such a place they might set up a sixteen-millimeter projector and show one film to the gathered community. There might be conversation and conviviality afterward. Today the television set serves as a means of isolation, just the wrong thing for people going through the fearful rigor of illness.

You could imagine a hospital as a place where you might take the dark night of your illness and nurse it. You could have peace and rest. You could enjoy water—baths, streams, fountains—nature and the friendship of fellow patients, as in the old spas. You could find beautiful surroundings and buildings and attractive, nutritious food. You could have a staff that understood the importance of your mood and the atmosphere of the place. You could enjoy the colors, sounds, and tastes that heal. A hospital would be a special oasis set apart from the demands of a harsher, less supportive world.

The city of Bath in England shows graphically how the ancient Romans constructed a real health center, centered on deep hot springs that were believed to be the gift of the great goddess

Sulis Minerva, a name that blends a Celtic and a Roman goddess. These springs now lie underground, but above them is the celebrated Pump Room, a sumptuous dining and entertainment spot that still today offers a refuge from life's busyness with good food and music. There the idea of healing soul and body within a religious context is still palpable.

A few years ago, while visiting friends at Bath, I had dinner with my family in the Pump Room, while a young man played Chopin on the piano. I sat there thinking of the connection between our simple pleasure in the restaurant (a word that means "restore") and the ancient health springs just below us. I seemed to be in a great metaphor—in a place of restoration, feeding body and soul, supported by ancient and divine springs of health in the underworld beneath. If only every hospital had such depth of imagination!

SOLAR MEDICINE

During the excavations at Bath, a fascinating ancient image emerged from layers of generations—a striking sun-like face, a golden version of the familiar Green Man, who represents nature. This sun figure is the Genius Loci, the resident spirit of this place of healing. I can imagine him having his special place of honor in any contemporary hospital, along with Asklepios, the Radiant Healing Buddha, and Jesus the Healer. A hospital needs a green and solar attitude, a constant and informing awareness that illness and healing are both the work of nature, that nature has to be consulted seriously in the work of healing.

The sun heals not only with the material components of its rays and with its physical warmth, but also with its power to affect the imagination. It is a sign of hope and life. Marsilio Ficino wrote a little book about the sun as a source of personal power, in which he says that the sun is the world's soul, offering vitality and purification. As the font of soul, he says, the sun "generates, warms and moves everything with a vital heat."[68]

These are good reasons to build hospitals in ways that invite patients to be in actual sunlight and to have solar images around them. Ficino would recommend sending a sick person a get-well card with the image of a sun, or the patient wearing a sun image and having sun-like colors around him. To evoke the sun is to create an atmosphere of health and hope.

Compare a hospital influenced throughout by the image of the sun with one shaped by the image of a scalpel or a CAT scan. There is no reason why hospitals today could not foster a spirit of health and well-being, rather than efficient handling of body parts and smooth functioning. The care provided by nurses and attendants can heal more effectively sometimes than the technical methods of doctors and specialists. But they, too, can choose either to be automatons in service of a science and industry, or skilled yet visionary professionals who don't jettison their humanity.

The solar spirit, both literal and metaphorical, could be an important part of hospital design. Workers and patients need to see the sunshine. As Ficino says, it makes you feel alive. I once visited a hospice in Dublin where building was in progress. Patients' rooms were designed for good window exposure and fresh air. A nearby stream was directed under the building so the patients could see and hear its assuring sounds. The staff was extraordinarily friendly and open. I suppose it makes sense that an Irish hospital would be sensitive to the goddess Sulis and her deep healing waters.

THE SPA MENTALITY

The ruins at Bath are full of mysteries. The water travels to a depth of almost eight thousand feet on its way to the baths, where it is 115 degrees Fahrenheit and bubbles escaping gases.

Before the Romans arrived, Druids made offerings and believed they could communicate with the underworld there. The Romans built a temple and a structure for the baths, made offerings and sacrifices, and worshipped at the temple.

It is perhaps significant that not far from the baths sits the abbey, on the façade of which is a sculpture showing angels climbing ladders into heaven. One angel is going down. This ascension of angels is the inversion of the baths, where the religious feeling takes people into the depths and heals them with hot waters from the lowest region. Both directions are necessary, and both are forms of spirituality.

Why not return to the fantasy of the spa, a place of healing waters, of time, solitude, and society? A hospital affords a certain kind of solitude and withdrawal, but there aren't many hospitals you would call spas. It could have a crypt of deep healing waters, and natural places to walk in, and opportunities to chat leisurely with people also in search of healing. It would focus on the needs of the soul and address its dark night directly, and in that way it would be a place devoted to, of all things, hospitality.

In his book on Asklepios, the ancient Greek god of healing, C. Kerenyi says of the spa at the island of Kos: "The patient himself was offered an opportunity to bring about the cure whose elements he bore within himself. To this end an environment was created which, as in modern spas and health resorts, was as far as possible removed from the disturbing and unhealthful elements of the outside world. The religious atmosphere also helped man's innermost depths to accomplish their curative potentialities."[69] This passage could well be carved on the entrance to any modern hospital. Cure is in the hands of the patient, who needs to withdraw from busy, practical life. This kind of cure would be in tune with the dark night, which is a kind of enforced, often internal withdrawal.

Let's not pass too quickly over these central ideas. Cure comes from deep within yourself, a depth mirrored in the wells and springs and temple cubicles for incubation, or night dreaming. If this is true, then in your dark night of sickness you have to find ways to go deep. There, water is not just emotion, but a central core of fluidity and solution. There, your memories and habits can be dissolved and reshaped. There, you might realize how deep is the spring from which your feelings and thoughts flow. There, you will be cured of any superficiality left in you. This source is so deep as to be religious, beyond reason and control, not entirely human. In the deep well of your reflections you may find an opening beyond yourself, where you are in touch with nature, and where your healing really happens.

Illness lies as deep in the soul as the healing waters of Bath. Other dark and deep waters attest to the depths of illness and healing: the rituals in kivas of the American Southwest, the holy wells of Ireland, the medicinal lapis lazuli used by Buddhists and taken from mountains, the Greek Asklepian underground chamber of dreams. Illness is a mystery that lies deeper than the tiniest and most hidden molecules, atoms, and genes, far into what Jung called the psychoid reaches of human life, where soul and body are indistinguishable.

How do you get to that crucial interface between your illness and your healing, your life and the secrets of nature? The way is through the darkness of your moods and thoughts. You need sunlight for your everyday spa recovery, but the crux of the healing takes place in darkness. Kerenyi says that the sunrise had no place in the Asklepian temple, which was dedicated to the night. You have to let your darkness shape your journey to the place of healing. You have to go deeper than your mood, far beneath your emotion, and down into the underworld of the very meaning of your life.

You don't have to manufacture any of this. Your illness will shake you up and provide you with the necessary anxieties and hopelessness. You have to own up to these and let them be. You have to speak for them and about them. You have to track their roots in your dreams and in your history. You have to talk to your loved ones about them and learn as much as you can. You have to gather your depths, and in the resulting darkness penetrate through the skin of meaning that has kept you healthy so far. Now you have to transcend yourself in a downward direction and have a glimpse of your fate.

DISCOVERING THE LIMITS OF HUMAN EXPERIENCE

One thing you might hope to learn from your illness is a basic law of religion: As a human being you have limits. Your soul is vast and participates in the infinite, but your life is bound by time, place, and the laws of nature and humanity. Hubris is the great sin that threatens the spiritual lives of individuals and societies. Traditional stories warn of flying too high to overhear the whisperings of the gods. When you stretch beyond your appropriate limits, you suffer the consequences emotionally and physically.

In his passionate book *Medical Nemesis*, Ivan Illich made a great plea to live within humane limits. "Act so that the effect of your action is compatible with the permanence of genuine human life."[70] Don't put chemicals into the air that will poison your grandchildren. Don't put off clean-burning automobiles until you have destroyed the atmosphere. These seem like intelligent and reasonable limits, and yet we don't take them seriously. The cost of health care goes up in proportion to the rise in world pollution. But who talks about a connection between illness and hubris?

We are keeping the great dark night of Earth's fatal illness at bay. But individual men, women, and children are bearing the illnesses generated by the collective hubris of modern society, for whom "the sky is the limit." We don't see the importance of human scale and local life. Globalization threatens to destroy what local culture remains, and one wonders if cancer, runaway cell growth, is not a mirror of runaway economic, political, and cultural ambition.

This connection is not merely theoretical. If you live in a society in which growth is the measure of happiness, then you might expect to be saturated by values associated with ambition and craving. For many years now, I have been advocating ordinary life as the proper arena for care of the soul. The extraordinary, the image of unlimited growth and success, is not characteristic of the soul, which is not satisfied with speed and striving. Growth is a fantasy of spirit, as you see in psychologies in which personal growth is the primary value. The soul thrives more in small, local settings, where ambition is toned down by other values like those of family, place, nature, and peace.

Is it going too far to say that modern illnesses specifically reflect modern values and hopes? Depression sets in when there is no immediate source of joy. Heart attacks multiply when the heart is no longer given its due. Cancer enters when your body can't slow down and take life step by step, when you can't be satisfied with the amount of money, things, and experiences you have. These are not mystical connections but direct ties between lifestyle and sickness.

The dark night of illness sets severe limits on what you can do. It forces you to slow down and focus on the things that matter. It keeps you in one place and on your back. It prevents you from eating what you want and doing the things you are used to doing. This particular dark night has special lessons to teach, and it is tempting to see it as a corrective to a life abandoned to ambition.

HUMOR AND LAUGHTER

Living close to the dark is entirely compatible with good humor and a positive attitude. The darkness completes the picture.

Without it, you would be left with only a happy face, and your sadness would be repressed. In such a condition, happiness can only be feigned and humor only a show. To escape from sadness is to fall into chronic unhappiness. Sadness is a positive, fluid emotion that keeps the other feelings in perspective.

Norman Cousins is famous for his work in medicine and especially his idea that laughter can heal any kind of illness. He complains of physicians who gave him little hope that he would get through his major sickness, a problem with the connective tissue in his spine. With relish he tells the story of meeting one of these doctors after he had recovered, shaking his hand and squeezing it tightly, to make his point. Don't make any pronouncements of doom, he advised.

The nobility of the human spirit lies in its refusal to accept defeat. You go on living and trying even if the odds are against you. People who have been diagnosed with a fatal disease sometimes claim that they have been healed but not cured. They mean that they have come to grips with their situation. Their attitude has been resolved. Whether they survive or not is not the issue. They have been cured in their soul.

There are many kinds of laughter, some cynical and some giggly. There is also a laughter that comes out of the darkness. It is based deep in the heart and gut, where it finds its source. Many kinds of humor and laughter can be healing, but especially this kind that is close to the dark. It is trustworthy because it is connected to the whole of life and is in no way defensive or superficial.

I learned this lesson about humor from many people, but especially from a man I got to know just a year before he died. Philip Simmons was a writer and teacher who suffered the gradual impairment of ALS, Lou Gehrig's disease. Phil and I worked together a couple of times, and he completely won me over with his combination of sharp, penetrating humor and his coming to terms with encroaching death. In the few times I had the gift of being with him, I felt the exquisite melding in him of sadness and comedy.

In his book *Learning to Fall*, Phil Simmons says he had become "a seeker of the dark way." "I've grown suspicious of perfection," he writes, "seeking not a perfect life but a full one." He tells a simple story about going to a piano recital of his son and daughter, a ritual he might rather have skipped. He describes the "ordeal": "I endured a stretch of terror watching her march solemnly to the front, climb on the piano bench, and play a flawless rendition of that immortal classic, 'Fuzzy Baby Bird.' "

About that recital, Phil says he was surprised to have such a good time, but he also felt sad, knowing that he could no longer play the piano or the guitar. Later, he felt better, knowing that the children could play and could carry on with the music. And then, finally, he had the sense that the children and he were all playing, together, the feeling of separateness having been lost.

In the thick of his illness, which he himself understood to be a dark night, he was able to keep people laughing. He could say serious, even sad things, and still be funny. That, to me, was the critical sign that his illness had sanctified him, had fulfilled whatever it was that needed to be brought, not to perfection, but to fruition in him. His deep humanity was revealed in his sophisticated wit and his simple, heartfelt humor.

Gritty sadness and guileless humor are blood brothers. One may often be found in the company of the other. Together they keep the soul intact. They are a kind of yin and yang that heals by spreading emotional glue on the many splits and divisions that show as pain. You may win this deep humor by your pain, suffering, and endurance.

BE YOUR OWN HEALER

While one of the great and inspiring mysteries is the fact that we care for each other, befriend each other, and heal each other, this can be accomplished only if we also care for ourselves, are friendly toward ourselves, and heal ourselves. If we don't do these things for ourselves concretely and wholeheartedly, then in each case we will feel a painful gap between ourselves and those who care for us. Jungian psychology speaks of a "split archetype," a harmful distance between the one who suffers and the one who heals. The sufferer as well as the healer has to help heal this split. The gap can be bridged if each of us has alive within us the spirit of caretaker, friend, and healer.

Ivan Illich, whose insights into medicine unfortunately haven't had the impact they deserve, stresses this point about taking responsibility for your own well-being. He lived this philosophy himself and always called for a local, familial, humane participation in all phases of life. "Healthy people need minimal bureaucratic interference to mate, give birth, share the human condition, and die," he wrote.[71] Modern institutions tend to distance us, whether they intend it or not, from the primal experiences of being humans on this earth. Yet the secret to health, happiness, a sense of security, and meaning is to live close to the natural processes of life and to your own innate nature. We all need a minimum of interference in accomplishing that important task.

A small but dramatic example of taking health into your own hands is the dark night that dominated the later years of the brilliant and spunky American poet Edna St. Vincent Millay. Nancy Milford's spicy biography tells how Millay struggled all her life with an absent father, demanding sisters, a plethora of eager lovers, a satisfying but contentious "open" marriage, and an up-and-down career. She became heavily addicted to alcohol, and then, after an automobile accident, to morphine. Most devastating of all, at one point she lost her ability to write.

After some years of struggle she spent a month in a hospital dealing with her addiction, and then, as Milford says, she and her husband tried their own form of therapy—swimming naked in the cold waters off a small island in Maine, living without electricity, and memorizing long and difficult poems. Milford says, in language close to our theme, "It was as if a black cloth had been lifted from her." Her one-time lover and constant friend, the literary critic Edmund Wilson, visited her during this time and noted in similar imagery that "she was just emerging from some terrible eclipse of the spirit, . . . groping back *in luminis oras* [into the light of day] from the night of the underworld." It's worth noting how people spontaneously use the imagery of the dark night for a particularly intense kind of breakdown.[72]

In a typically crystal clear yet profound and paradoxical poem of this time, on chaos, she writes about the attempt to contain the chaotic, which she tried to do in her extravagant life and personality and in her poems. At the heart of the sonnet are these two lines about Chaos:

> *I hold his essence and amorphous shape,*
> *Till he with Order mingles and combines.*

It is an alchemical image, finding an effective container so that the opposites of chaos and order can meld into something livable. Millay was not able to accomplish this, except in her poetry, until the last years of her life. The entire passionate, topsy-turvy process led her deeper into her dark night of the soul, and she emerged from it more by magic than by medical effort. A month in a hospital doing nothing in particular and a period on an isolated island swimming naked gave her the containers she needed for her chaos, her illness.

PHYSICAL MALADIES OF THE SOUL

Faced with illness, you have to see through its physical manifestations to its soul. You have to see it for what it is, a dark night that gives your entire being a tincture of the *nigredo*, the darkening of your fate and your very life. You have to address that soul with as much imagination and as many concrete experiments in living as possible.

The ancient Greeks said that the archetypal wounded man, Philoctetes, was forced to live alone in a cave on an island. Edna St. Vincent Millay lived this myth quite literally when she retreated to her Maine island. She separated herself from life so that she could finally heal her soul. We have seen this theme over and over, how the dark night is fulfilled in some form of withdrawal from active life.

I'm tempted to say that every illness is primarily a soul malady and only secondarily a physical problem. In sickness, the soul comes into the foreground. It asks for attention. If its wounds are addressed, then perhaps the physical manifestations will no longer be necessary. But care of the soul is not a surface activity; nor is it easy. It demands that you finally confront yourself and decide to live fully rather than halfheartedly. It asks that you learn to love with your whole heart and get over any self-pity or cynicism that may still remain in your heart. It asks that you transcend yourself in genuine concern for others and in a feeling of community that knows no boundaries. This is not an easy task, but it is the only way, finally, to health.

Every physician is a doctor of the soul and every nurse a psychotherapist. The word "therapy" comes from the Greek word for nurse. The patient is also a doctor, and the doctor a patient, as everyone concerned tries to evoke the spirit of healing that will accompany the illness. The great physician Paracelsus said that the medicine is the wife of the illness. All try to create the conditions under which healing may happen according to the will of God or the course of life. In the face of illness, you have to honor the deep laws of nature.

The religion scholar Mircea Eliade explores in his journals what he calls "the spiritual, 'religious,' functions of illness." "Illness," he writes, "is the point of departure for the process of personality integration and for a radical spiritual transformation."[73]

Illness is also a kind of poetry. It expresses the course of life, but it doesn't explain it. It invites you to reflect on your way of life, spotting the gaps where your soul is neglected and complaining. You can think about where the disease came from and how it reflects the way you live or the ways of your society. Eventually, your sickness may cure you of your misconceptions, as it speaks its poetry on behalf of nature, guiding you deeper into union with the source of your own life. The more you are emptied of your physical abilities, the more you are filled with the strength of soul.

CHAPTER FOURTEEN

THE TWILIGHT YEARS

O N A COLD, rainy morning in Boston, eleven years ago, I stood at my wife's bedside, holding my daughter. She had just been born, and my happiness was boundless. Yet a disturbing thought crept into my mind. We had given birth to this beautiful girl, but we had also introduced her to the world of human mortality. One day she would die. In the fullness of my delight at her arrival, I couldn't help but think, for only a second, of her leavetaking.

At every moment you are living and dying, coming further into life and going out of it. At any given moment, you may feel your youth or sense yourself aging. Age is a way of imagining yourself, and though it has a literal dimension—the number of years you have been alive—the experience of age depends on how you sense yourself now.

This idea of imaginal aging, or the age of the soul rather

than the body, is one of the central ideas in James Hillman's writings. In one of his earliest essays he describes the image of aging, using the ancient Roman word for old man or old woman, *senex*.[74] As he presents it, age is a quality in people, places, and things. Young people may feel old, and old people young. You may have a momentary realization of your advancing years, but then immediately you go on living the way you always have. Age is always what we imagine it to be.

Aging is not imaginary. You do grow older, but you are not bound by the number of years you have accumulated. Some children seem quite old, and some ninety-year-olds have an amazing youthfulness. As you age, you don't want to deny your years—an old person trying too hard to be young often looks uncomfortably out of place. But you don't want to lose touch with your youth, either. Maybe the best way is to keep aging and youthfulness in creative tension, one always influencing the other. And the only way to do that is not to take either literally.

It was popular during the European Renaissance to make images showing the paradox of youth and age. You find a turtle with a sail on it, a butterfly on a crab, a figure with the head of an old man and the body of a baby.[75] People wore medallions with cryptic sayings etched onto them, such as *senex-puer* (old-young), *matura celeritas* (mature-lively), and speed-patience. A popular motto, *festina lente* (hurry slowly) was applied to the progress of the Church. One of my early childhood memories is of one of my beloved aunts crying inconsolably, telling her mother how sad she was about getting old. She was sixteen.

THE IMAGE OF AGE AND
THE DARK NIGHT

Your birthday comes along yet again, and you feel the passing of years and especially the symbolic nature of the numbers. Thirty carries a person from clear and undeniable youth into maturity.

Forty ends the identification with young adults. Fifty marks a major turn toward old age, though it is the prime of life to those in their sixties and seventies. Receiving an invitation to join the American Association of Retired Persons may in itself feel like a shift into old age.

Each turning point is a passage that brings memories and melancholic thoughts. You may think of people you knew at the age you are now and can't believe you are in their position. You may well feel that a good portion of your life is behind you and that you have lost something that you never realized before was so precious. You may even relate to your body differently in those moments when you lean toward the side of the old person and disengage from youth.

Some people go into a deep funk at their birthday or at any signal that they are getting old. It isn't a reasonable, thought-out sensation, but a mood that sweeps over them. Aging can generate a dark night of the soul, and it may seem that there is no way out of it because you can't reverse the process. But in fact, you can. There is, after all, a fountain of youth. You can restore your feeling of being alive and stop identifying with death. Usually when people look for immortality or eternal youth, they take it literally. Or they deny their age and their mortality. In the imagination, however, you can rediscover your youth without pretending that you will live forever. You can be old-young, mature-lively, patient-speedy.

What I am saying here goes far beyond the old saw that "aging is all in your mind." Aging is more than your idea of it. It's a quality of being itself, an aspect of life and the world. To enter the archetype of old age is to bring an entire world of feelings, images, and thoughts to your awareness. You would never say that you have entered the dark night of youth, but you would say it of age. As you age, you may feel increased melancholy, and you may become more fascinated with the past and your personal memories. I keep telling my children stories of my childhood, just as my parents and grandparents told them to me.

One story I tell is how when I was a child I would go to the movies a few blocks from home with a gaggle of friends. My mother would give me a quarter. With that quarter I would watch two features, two serials, ten cartoons, and a long string of trailers. I would buy candy and get a "grab bag" stuffed with treats. Then, when I got home, my mother would ask for change.

I love telling this story. It makes my children scream with outrage, which is pleasurable in itself. But it also contains a degree of melancholy, a yearning for the good old days, and some anxiety about the present, when life in a rapidly advancing society is expensive and not terribly generous. The story reaches a bit deeper, suggesting that children are now at the mercy of the profit-making mania, and that we pay stiff emotional prices as well just to get along among people who don't seem to have as much plain, human feeling as they used to.

My little story also links, but at the same time distinguishes, the old man and the young children, age and youth. It is a way in which the old guy connects with the young people, giving them some images of aging, while they, simply as responsive audience, vivify the old gentlemen in his reminiscences. He brings the spirit of the old into the world that is coming in.

When I was twenty I met a man in his seventies who became my friend and mentor. I was living in Ireland, a monastic student in a priory studying philosophy in a two-year program. I wanted a piece of art from Ireland, and so naively I wrote to the public relations department of the National Gallery in Dublin. The director himself, Thomas McGreevy, wrote back, inviting me to come and see him. For almost two years on several occasions we met and talked mainly about his friends, an amazing roster of writers and artists that included W. B. Yeats, Jack Yeats, D. H. Lawrence, James Joyce, and Samuel Beckett.

When I returned to the United States, he wrote me a touching letter that is one of my personal treasures. It captures the idea I am sketching here about how youth and age intersect: "The least I can hope is that, forty years on another Tom Moore will walk in unexpectedly and put new heart into you, make you feel that your apostolate is not necessarily over and that in some way you respond to a need of his as he to a need of yours. Just as my Tom Moore, blessings on him, walked in unexpectedly on me."

Now I am approaching that time of life, waiting for some young person to present himself or herself innocently to find some mentoring and to restore some youthfulness to me. We can give these precious gifts to each other. The cure for the dark night of aging is a taste of youthful immortality. The young possess the plant of immortality that Gilgamesh sought, found, and lost. They have it in their illusions of immortality.

THE ETERNAL SELF

You have no doubt noticed that as you get older, your body changes but something in the way you feel about yourself doesn't change. To yourself, you seem to be the same person you were twenty years ago. Of course, you've learned a few things and have changed some opinions, but something in you is constant. Some part of your existence isn't determined by time.

In your dark night associated with growing old, it might help to make the most of that immortal kernel of personality that may appear like a whisper in an otherwise noisy world of old age. Life is short. The old realize this bitter truth. The actor Marcello Mastroianni once remarked that a man from Naples described life to him as "an appearance on a balcony." Eventually, too soon, the shutters close.

But that microcosmic life is full and rich and long, if you look into it closely, as you might inspect a drop of water through a microscope. Though it is a mere appearance, life is also infinite in its richness. Telling your stories with loving detail is a way to bring that richness to the foreground and to accent the broad arc of your life. It helps to evoke your immortality and ease the burden of your life's brevity. You don't want to be dishonest about any of this, but neither do you want to sulk in your wish for more time.

You can also identify more with the immortal self than with the passing one. I am not suggesting any denial of death or time or difficulties in the aging process. The immortal self is another aspect and could be made more of. You could live from that deeper, vaster place, as Rainer Maria Rilke recommended to his young poet: "In the man, too, there is motherhood, it seems to me, physical and mental; his engendering is also a kind of birthing, and it is birthing when he creates out of his innermost fullness."[76]

You can live from your soul rather than your self. This means to be less in control, less certain of the truth of things but more in touch with your intuitions and emotions. It means to be less focused on the self and more identified with others. It means to understand that you are part of nature and that your soul, which is the source of your very identity, is a piece of the world's soul. Your roots reach downward, not into the brain, but into the soil.

Living from the soul, your actions are more in tune with the root of your experience and less influenced by passing social fads and your personal views. Your life has a primal quality, some of it going back beyond your birth to your ancestors and your far distant primitive source. As you age, you sink more into the earthiness of your identity and become less interested in the surface glitter of culture.

You don't have to understand this deep level of your existence, but you do have to trust it. You may discover over time that the deep self has a wisdom that you could never muster on the surface. It seems to take in experience and ruminate on it even as you go about your business. Insights arrive from that deep place, and you can trust it to offer help in making decisions.

In your youth you may live from your new knowledge and your passion to get on with life, but as you age your center may shift downward and the quality of your thoughts and ambitions changes. You may be slower to make decisions, to move about, to think about future careers and circumstances. You are more present, because the future doesn't necessarily hold any more drastic developments.

All of this may feel sad, but that disappointment may be the experience of your youth, which is always present, at least as an echo. If you can understand that you are made of up many personalities, youth and age being merely two of them, you may identify less with the disillusioned youth and more with the insightful old person who can now enjoy relief from the mad pulse of life in its prime.

The melancholy that often characterizes aging may have to remain as a tonality in everything you do. But melancholy is not the same as depression. It is a mood and a coloring that doesn't necessarily compete with happiness and vitality. It is more a quality than an affliction, and it has many gifts to offer you.

The melancholy of aging can make you reflective and even occasionally wise, as you advance in years. It can keep you quiet and allow you to slow down in appropriate ways. It can give weight to your thoughts and your pronouncements and can allow you to be the advisor of youth, a significant way of offsetting feelings of irrelevance that may come with the breakdown of your physical powers.

REGRET AND REMORSE

When people grow old, they are sometimes consumed with regret. They wish they had done more, seen more, and accomplished more. They feel that their lives are not justified, and they wish they could merit the esteem of their children and their communities. They feel that they wasted too much time and didn't seize opportunities in ways they can now see. They wish life had taken a different turn.

A good example of this aspect of aging appeared in a story in the *New Yorker* magazine. Forrest Tucker was a thief. He got into trouble at sixteen and cultivated a life of gentlemanly crime for the next sixty years. As an old man, after escaping from prison many times, having been married three times, he pulled off his final bank robbery and was caught. Everyone said he was a master thief but also a stylish, modest, and nonviolent man. From prison he told a reporter about his life and concluded, "I wish I had a real profession, something like the music business. I regret not being able to work steady and support my family. I have other regrets, too, but that's as much as one man can stand. Late at night, you lie in your bunk in prison and you think about what you lost, what you were, what you could've been, and you regret."[77]

Maybe Forrest Tucker's feeling is more remorse than regret, though it seems to be a mixture of both. Regret is usually a stale, stillborn emotion that gets you nowhere. It is empty because it is full of ego. "Why didn't I do these things? Why didn't I become somebody?" Regret can be a kind of whining, or it may develop from the sheer failure to have sufficient insight into your life. It begs for change, but it usually leads to repeated, unredeemed behavior. It doesn't have deep roots, and though feelings of regret can be intense, they lack an intelligence and bite that motivate a significant shift in attitude.

Remorse is different. It has long been associated with conscience, with a deep, guiding voice. It is full of content and power. The word "regret" means to weep, but remorse means to bite, as in the word "morsel." Remorse pricks you into awareness and stimulates new and fresh behavior. Regret keeps you stuck in feelings that are sufficient in themselves and have no bite. Remorse doesn't have to change your life, but it will change your attitude.

As you age, then, you might not allow yourself to feel and express regrets. They are cheap and don't do much for you. But if you feel remorse, you may express your insights with effect and you might even change something in your life. It is never too late to reimagine experience and tell people who mean something to you how you think and feel. You can even make a new life for yourself based on what you learn from your remorse.

A dark night of the soul, in this case brought on by the mere fact of getting older, offers an invitation to live more from the soul than the self. Remorse chips away at actions done from a place of insufficient wisdom and gives a fresh imagination to them. You discover, full of feeling, how to live your life differently. Remorse serves you. It doesn't merely make you feel guilty. It tugs at the old way of understanding and allows a new style of thought and feeling.

JUSTIFYING YOUR EXISTENCE

Now, what about this idea that you have to accomplish something in life in order to make it worthwhile? People have this thought at different times in their lives, not only in old age. It represents a certain degree of anxiety and comes from a voice that is not entirely your own, a voice more like that of conscience. It isn't an encouraging voice but is usually judgmental. It makes you feel that time is passing and you don't have all the time in the world to accomplish what you desire.

This voice is a call to heroism of a sort, perhaps the egotistical kind. It urges action, self-improvement, and sometimes fame. It makes you feel inadequate and demands that you be other than who you are. It hyperactivates the ego by calling it into question, and in that way it works against the deep soul.

When regret turns neurotic, then according to the rule that neurotic symptoms reveal what has to be deepened, it hints at a greater heroism, one that is not so allied with the ego. Compared to fulfilling your destiny, justifying your existence is a rather negligible project. If you feel justified, then you have done what *you* think is required to be a person of worth. But to fulfill your destiny, to live out your fate with openness and heart, may not justify anything. You may be an antihero, doing less than the ordinary person, and yet being yourself.

Where you fit in the scheme of things is not your choice.

Your job is to deal honestly and generously with the fate given to you. It may be a brief life of sickness. You may or may not be overflowing with obvious talents. You may be the most ordinary of people. On the other hand, you may be called sometime in your life to make an extraordinary act. Your task is to be prepared for the invitation offered, the chance to define yourself by an important choice.

One of the greatest things a human being can do is raise a child to be happy and wise. One of the most altruistic things you can do is be a good neighbor and an involved citizen. The soul is fulfilled by the ordinary. If you know people of high accomplishment, you may have noticed how they treasure the ordinary life, and how that life serves as a base for their more visible activity. Something highly spiritual in you may wish for wondrous success, but the deep soul longs for ordinary connection and engagement. It wants friendship and family and community. It longs for the simple pleasures, and from its perspective, the idea of justifying your existence is a dangerous distraction.

Self-justification is also an image, a narrative and a fantasy that gets hold of you. It is not literal and may not be supported by the facts. I know a woman who raised a large family and wrote several successful books by the time she was thirty, and at that point she wondered if she would ever do anything with her life. Self-justification is a fantasy, a highly emotional notion that has its roots in some other issue. Maybe she was raised to constantly prove herself or to become a celebrity. Maybe she feels so bad about herself that this need to be justified will never be satisfied. Maybe the complex is only a way to keep her moving until she finds a way of life that satisfies her.

In any case, the torment a person suffers from such a preoccupation qualifies as a genuine dark night of the soul. It is beyond reason and can't be argued away. People get attached to the idea and don't want it taken from them. Evidently, it has something to give them, but that gift may be hidden for years before the torture diminishes and a satisfying way of life shows itself.

In old age, self-justification joins forces with both regret and remorse, and one can only hope that the idea, like a buzzing fly or mosquito, will disappear with a change in climate. The required shift in attitude may be a Zen-like acknowledgment that the meaning of life consists in whatever small task lies before you in this instant. If you want to justify yourself, do what you are doing. Be present to it. Shunryu Suzuki said that the true practice of Zen is like drinking water when you are thirsty.

The story is told in Zambia, in Africa, of a woman whose name was Liulu, meaning Heaven. She had the ears of an elephant and was despised by her family for her ugliness. But the great King Mukulumpe heard about her and had her brought to him. He didn't know what to think of her ears, but he saw something in her and married her.

The story is told as one of reconciliation with the divine and has relevance to our theme. It may be your fate to have, metaphorically, elephant ears, and yet, with the proper vision, you may see the beauty in your essential anomaly and understand that it comes from Heaven. You may be graced by it, whatever it is, even though it may seem to be entirely out of context. You may have to stretch your imagination to appreciate it, and yet you can base your life on it.[78]

Your dark night has something to do with the elephant ears. It doesn't seem to fit, and yet it is of the essence. Sometimes you have to look beyond it for some hope, but you never deny that it's there. You have to be a special person to love it, but if you do, you may know what the notion of Heaven is all about.

THE TWILIGHT OF A SELF

Growing old tends to take you into a place of relatively dark feelings and atmospheres. It isn't bright like youth. But it would be a mistake to take this dimming of the light literally and give up hope or think that the central matters of life are now over. You never know what you will be called to do. The great ending of a life, which may endure for years, is full of adventures that may not be as obvious as they were in your younger years. But they are no less important or challenging.

The failing of your physical strength and capacities may only make for greater powers of mind and imagination. Certainly, you will be called on to live even more vigorously with an open heart. People will need you and benefit from your care more than ever. The elderly have immense gifts to offer their families and communities.

When my mother was lying in her hospital bed, stricken by a major stroke and lucid for only a few hours every other day or so, her lifetime of caring and spiritual intensity didn't diminish. It came to the foreground, and I felt her new powers as near miraculous. She could hardly speak, and yet she was more eloquent than ever. Every word counted, and she made good use of her diminished speech. I thought she was a fulfilled human being, revealed now in a way never seen before. In her soul, she had more powers than one ever suspected previously.

Growing old can be a matter of growing deep. It doesn't always happen, but the opportunity is there. It helps if the person has lived a life of preparation for it, but apparently it isn't necessary to do so. People sometimes change radically as they age.

There can be no doubt that as you grow old, you must come to terms with the arc of your life, its rising and setting. You have to see its elephant ears as things of beauty and signals of a divine design. You have to move gracefully with that downturn and dimming so that you will benefit from its special powers. Then all your dark nights will begin to make sense and fold themselves into the ultimate passing of the light. You will enter the darkness knowing something about the territory. You will understand that it has its own luminosity and beauty.

CHAPTER FIFTEEN

NAVIGATING A DARK NIGHT

WE HAVE CONSIDERED many kinds of dark nights and many ways to deal with them. Now it's time to put it all together and find a pathway through the murky feelings and foggy thoughts. We have talked about a slender shaft of light as offering a way through the darkness, and we'll now consider other kinds of luminescence. But John of the Cross, our model and primary teacher, says that it is the darkness that offers the best way—not the light, but the darkness itself. I want to restate this principle, because it is the one most misunderstood and is the key to this entire exploration of dark nights of the soul.

Today, of course, there are hundreds of ways offered for dealing with your dark night—pills, psychotherapy, expert and not so expert advice, spiritual guidance, books and tapes, workshops, churches, communities, government guidelines, and spas. You may be advised to get out of the darkness quickly, to act and do something rather than passively suffer it, or come to a level of understanding that will dispel the mood. You may also be encouraged to "go with it," learn from it, get what you can from it, and by all means don't deny it.

But when you look closely at all these contemporary approaches, you see the hero's shadow in the background—Superman disguised as the mild-mannered Clark Kent. You may still believe that a dark night, though possibly beneficial in the end, is basically an anomaly, something that shouldn't be, an aberration to deal with. Many people claim to have integrated their shadow sides, but that effort is itself a work against the dark. To integrate it is to co-opt it into the light. The real task is to live in, and with, the darkness, appreciating its unredeemed value and loving its irreversible qualities. What is needed is a view of life that includes the dark.

I have tried to go beyond ordinary therapeutic methods to a different way of thinking about the dark night altogether. Accordingly, you may have to give up all notions of growth, success, change, progress, and enlightenment. Instead, you allow all experiences to have their place. Your job is to be affected by them, letting them do their work on you. You can then see life as a process in which your understanding and will are step by step defeated by the thrust of vitality, by life always wanting to transform you. You are always the caterpillar in the cacoon and occasionally the butterfly flying free.

This isn't literal masochism, in which you give up and indulge in the suffering. You surrender to life, not to pain, and still you struggle to survive. The examples we have seen are of strong men and women who suffered much, often against great odds, but who constantly fought whatever or whoever was oppressing them. They may have used more imagination than force, but they were full of energy, fighters all. They were all different in their approaches and in the degree of their surrender.

Brian Keenan constantly looked for ways to outwit his captors and beat them at their game, at least morally. Oscar Wilde suffered greatly, but he allowed his dark night to waken new thoughts and possibilities in him. Anne Sexton never won the immediate battle, but she boldly transmuted her suffering into poetry that will last for many generations and will help many deal creatively with their dark nights.

You can see from these few examples that the end result is not a final victory nor an end to suffering. It is a moral development, the result of an initiation in which the mysteries of life stamp themselves into you more deeply, not necessarily making life easier or happier, but allowing it to take place more intensely. You are more fully who you are. You engage life more energetically and in that engagement discover a level of meaning that dissolves any discontent you may have.

In other words, a dark night of the soul can heal, where healing means being more alive and more present to the world around you. It heals by opening you up, sometimes to the point where you might feel dismembered. It opens the doorways between you and the world that heretofore have been closed. It reinstates the flow of life through you, for human beings at their best, remember, are porous—like an artist open to inspiration, a mystic open to mystery, a physician open to the healing power within her, a parent open to the dramas of transformation that constitutes family.

This initiatory process is more difficult and sometimes more painful than treating your dark night as a problem needing a solution. It is never easy to accept more life, never easy to become more of who you are. It is challenging in the extreme to really live life instead of taking it in portions that are comfortable or convenient for you. Often it may feel preferable, though this preference is rarely conscious, to be depressed than to allow life to flow. This is one reason why the darkness is so tenacious and takes forever to vanish: At some level you prefer it and want it.

All the many kinds of dark night we have explored here want you to live. That they come to you with sensations and images of death is not so odd. To some degree, new life always requires the termination of the old. Death is an appropriate image. And that is exactly what it is, an image. It doesn't mean you are going to die, although you may feel the sadness of ending in the midst of your dark night. It means that life wants to go on differently. Real, vital life doesn't repeat itself.

You have to experience this dying. Sometimes it will be more difficult than at other times. In each case, you can't cheat the process by knowing that it will all turn out right eventually. It may not, in fact, turn out in a way that you would wish for. Your mother may die, your friend may commit suicide, you may lose your job. The new life may depend on painful endings. You have to look through and beyond the literal facts. Failure and tragedy may be the only means by which life can continue.

GOING FOR DEPTH

Many years ago I was stunned by the simple idea of caring for the soul. It seems like an easy thing to do. Yet it requires that we stop taking life so literally and at a surface level. We have to understand that we have a profound, underlying existence in emotion, fantasy, and dream. Here our values are formed and the gist of our lives takes shape. The dark night of the soul will introduce us to this world and let us know that nothing is as simple as it appears to be.

Anatole Broyard complained that when his witty and irreverent friends visited him in the hospital, they were too serious and too extravagant with their good wishes. "They looked at me with a kind of grotesque lovingness in their faces," he says. He didn't like the falseness in their optimism. They had become emotional literalists, fundamentalist friends. They had set aside their wit because they couldn't deal with Broyard's situation as well as he could.

A dark night of the soul may favor you with a revolution in consciousness. You may be a different person because of it. You may finally give up the simplistic persona you have been compelled to use in the world of society and institutions. You may be free now to be the complicated person you are. This complexity doesn't have to be worrying, it can be enjoyable and interesting. It gives you a sense of humor, which often is nothing more than seeing double, noticing contradictions and paradoxes. The Three Stooges prefer to throw pies at the well-dressed and mannered upper crust rather than at ordinary people. The fun lies in the contradiction. A dark night is a little like a pie in the face—it relieves you of the stuffy ego you have been wearing.

THE HUMAN COMEDY

The rule is: Don't become one-dimensional in your dark night. Keep your sense of humor. Broyard says, "When you're lying in the hospital with a catheter and IV in your arm, you have two choices, self-pity or irony." He wants a doctor who can appreciate the ironies in the situation. His experience agrees with Norman Cousins who recommended laughter as a tonic for disease, but Broyard wants to take the humor deep. Not the dumb chuckle at a cheap joke, but a profound sense of the irony that accompanies all illness and distress. It's one thing to joke about your situation but another to laugh from a deep realization about what matters.

Anne Sexton makes many dark jokes in her poetry, reflecting the new vision given to her by her suicidal compulsions. Here the press between laughter and tragedy gets tighter, but the humor remains, right up to the moment of death. She captures the idea in a palindrome she once saw on the side of a barn: "Rats live on no evil star." Rats, backwards, is star. The image of the rat was her sickness, which had in it, by some kind of magic, a star, which she saw as a divine mother. "Live," she notes, is backwards for "evil." Opposites are wrapped up in each other.

This is not just brittle wordplay. The poet sees through the play of language to a truth about being. The acting out of evil may be literally destructive and is a tragedy of humankind's blindness. But there is a more subtle kind of evil, a moral darkness that you have to own and keep. When it is subtle, it is an essential part of your goodness and your shining, just as "rats" turns into "star." In *Care of the Soul* I noted that the minotaur, the beast that lives at the heart of the labyrinth and feeds on young men and women, was named Asterion, Star. The luminosity to be found in a dark night is not the sun, not ordinary light, but a special radiance that doesn't undo the night.

You can find your life's poetry, words and images that express the contradictions and ironies that shape you. One of the simplest expressions of this mystery are the Irish knots and spirals, images that go back thousands of years, showing the complexities and circularities of every human life. Modern science prefers the straight line of evolution as the energetic principle. The Irish spirals complement the Taoist idea that a thing is always entangled with its opposite; yin always looping into yang.

Nicolas of Cusa, the brilliant early fifteenth-century theologian, described the divine as a coincidence of opposites. Whatever you say about the nature of things has its opposite, and so you are always turned back into the questions you ask, always faced with mystery. The same is true of the dark nights of the soul. They are full of contradictions, and the main paradox is that as much as they seem to plague you, they are your salvation. They can heal in a way nothing else can. They can erase the false logic by which you have lived your life.

ON NOT PURSUING HAPPINESS

James Hillman has observed that depression may be a special problem in a society hell-bent on happiness. But let's examine this connection more closely. It is possible to imagine that the situations life offers may not be happy ones and yet may be the most desirable of all. An example is romantic love and marriage. Today people believe that you have to be with the exactly right person in order to be happy, and that the thrilling illusions of romantic love are the best prelude to a life together. You expect your infatuation for another person to be a sign of your entire future happiness.

But what if, instead, you look for other signs in your search for a lifelong partner? I have written about soul mates as people in various kinds of relationship who enjoy a deep, perhaps fateful connection. But some see a soul mate as the one individual destined to make you happy. This romantic notion may work for some people, but others feel deprived and lonely all their lives because the promised perfection of a person never arrives.

Happiness is more a temporary sensation that things are in place and Heaven seems to have blessed the moment. But life is always complex, a mixture of pain and satisfaction, the proportions different for each person depending on destiny and grace. Weaving the dark into the light in your expectations and personal philosophy might temper the role of happiness and offer a way to appropriate the dark night with style and wisdom.

The word "depression" is too broad. People begin to think that anything that is not cheerful and joyous must be depressive, and that is something to avoid. But no, there are many ways not to be happy that do not equal depression. You can have a critical view on life, seeing its tragedy and its evil, and not succumb to the mood or emotion of depression. The actress Susan Sarandon once observed that though she is moved to political action by feelings of empathy for a suffering world, basically she is a joyous person.[79] Woody Allen's films, though often witty portrayals of life's daily anxieties, are comic and celebrate life.

A dark night of the soul may make you more serious, and that is a good thing, because becoming more serious can have the effect of deepening your humor. As everyone knows, all laughter is not the same. It can be cynical, manipulative, and egotistic, or it can be joyous and guileless. You can feel the weight of a confused and murderous world and still know at a far deeper level that life is basically good. You can have a broader viewpoint, even in the face of tragedy. You can laugh and cry simultaneously.

Many of the men and women we have heard from in this journey through darkness have made a distinction, in one way or another, between literal disaster and moral tragedy. They make it clear that you can be physically imprisoned or assaulted, and yet your soul is free and unaffected. A dark night of the soul is not exactly the same as physical injury or oppression. Let's not be Pollyannaish about this. Oppression and deprivation affect your feelings and outlook. But you don't have to succumb completely. Sometimes a sliver of moonlike bliss is all you need in the midst of darkness.

On the other hand, the sensation of darkness may be linked to your failure to live your life onward and make the necessary decisions and changes. Many times I have sat in therapy with a man or woman suffering a profound impasse in their lives. Usually it has to do with a relationship or with work. They feel strongly that they have to move on and cut ties, but they can't deal with the emotions of loss. Often they wait, hoping that the other person or fate will force a change, and they won't have to take the responsibility. They may feel absolutely balanced between two options and feel unable to make a clear decision. The varieties of impasse are many.

In these instances, I don't like to recommend willpower or activity for its own sake. An impasse can be a creative time for the imagination. But the failure to act can also be rooted in a mistrust of your own thoughts and emotions. A decision need not be full of will and ego. It can issue from the ripening of a feeling or a thought. It asks for trust and imagination, and it invites a generous engagement with life.

Maybe your imagination is too limited. Sometimes people feel stuck because they don't have the range of imagination needed to deal with their problem. As a therapist, I often see my job not as providing options, but as educating the imagination so that solutions are visible. That's why I have studied literature more than psychology, which expands the imagination rather then reduces it. For the same reason, spiritual ideas are more valuable to me than the usual therapeutic ones. Literature and spirituality offer a broader range of imagination for the human condition.

A dark night of the soul has its own poetic qualities. As we have seen, it is a drama in its own right. It was always a specific dark night, with its own themes and rhythms. Although it may seem odd to say so, a dark night is a fiction. It's a narrative in which we find ourselves and in which our imagination of it is as important as the facts of it. Primo Levi makes it clear in his memoirs that although hordes of people were with him in the prison camp, each one was living a special story, with slight but defining nuances.

It's helpful, then, during a dark night, to constantly broaden your imagination of what is happening to you. If your only idea is that you're depressed, you will be at the mercy of the depression industry, which will treat you as one among millions, for whom there is only one canonical and approved story. Maybe you're overwhelmed but not depressed. Maybe life has sent you a great challenge, and you may need a vast spiritual vision to deal with it.

According to the machine image of the human being, we are brought up to be well-adjusted, to work hard, and to obey the laws and conform to expectations. If and when that process breaks down, we have mechanics at the ready to patch us up. But that story of a human life is minimal and allows nothing of soul and spirit, meaning or deep experiencing. An alternative is to see human life as a continuing invitation to be more of what it is capable, to be individual and deeply connected. The Irish writer John Moriarty, describing a moment of intense transformation in his own life, writes, "If nature can handle the destruction and reconstruction of a caterpillar into a butterfly, why shouldn't I surrender and trust that it can handle what is happening to me?"[80]

If nature can handle what you are undergoing, you should be able to find confidence and security. It helps to see yourself as a piece of nature and not as an isolated ego. Stand back and look at yourself from a distance. See yourself as part of the same world that changes a caterpillar into a butterfly, a storm into the increase of life, and a forest fire into an opportunity for new growth. You don't have to be sentimental about it, but you can have enough distance from your intensely personal thoughts and sensations to allow yourself the experience. The distance doesn't take away any confusion or pain, but it does make the experience tolerable. Meaning allows you to go through almost any form of change, no matter what the costs.

The black of the dark night comes from ignorance, not knowing what is happening and where life is taking you. This is as true of a divorce as it is of a terminal illness. The only choice, as Igor Stravinsky said of the artist, is to remain in the present, not bound or deluded by the past and not imprisoned in a fixed and defensive idea about the future. The worm has to let the transmutation take place. It would do no good for him to plan his wingspan and colors or to wish to remain in the snug safety of the tiny world he has known. The most difficult challenge is to let the process take place, and yet that is the only release from the pressure of the dark night.

When the pianist Leon Fleischer suffered a mysterious failure in his hand from overworking it, he became a teacher and a conductor. He played all the left-hand repertoire, but it was the expansion of his musical vision that saved him. When Glenn Gould realized that emotionally he couldn't play the piano in public, against all convention and advice he gave it up, becoming passionate about recordings and television. What I particularly appreciate about Gould is that he had no good reason, apart from his neuroses, for quitting the public arena. He referred to his audiences, people who paid to hear the music they loved played with genius, as voyeurs. Did he expect them not to watch him? If only the rest of us could so honor the twisted demands of the soul!

The butterfly metaphor carries a degree of sentimentality, perhaps because of the beauty of the insect. But you don't see the sentimentality in the examples of Gould and Fleischer. They changed their lives from felt necessity. Fleischer says, "I coped with it very badly. I went into a deep funk for almost one and a half years. . . . For almost seventeen years there were countless hours of examinations, psychiatric and psychological sessions, an operation, and muscle therapy."[81] Such dark nights, even when they eventually turn out well, tend to be long.

Frida Kahlo said she would never want to return to this life after years of pain and struggle. I remember my grandmother once saying, in one of the saddest statements I have ever heard, that she wouldn't want to live again and have to go through the Depression of the 1930s. There need not be a final solution to the dark night of the soul, no ultimate redemption or certainly no victory.

The dark night is the soul shining through with its lunar luminosity. It is the deep, dark discovery of roots and cellars, the opposite of enlightenment, but equally important and equally divine. It is the pulling apart of meaning so that mystery can be revealed. It is the disappearance of an ego so that life can eventually move in its own time and its own way.

The best way to deal with a dark night of the soul is to be made luminous by it. Not enlightened, but translucent. You are not the eye seeing in the dark, you are the candle being burnt for its luminosity. It is not your luminosity that issues from a dark night, but the dim light of existence itself. Your dark night tells you that life is never as bright and successful and meaningful as you might imagine. If you never learn this lesson, the essential moonlight, the Claire de Lune, will forever be hidden from you.

Your dark night teaches you the truth of the moon. Life is not intended to be only solar, and indeed the cool, blue shadows of the moon have a special beauty. You can live in that beautiful glow, that light shaded by painful experiences and doubts and lack of understanding. Life is often more buoyant there than it is in solar brilliance.

SCINTILLA

Simone Weil, the extraordinary practical, personal philosopher and mystic, made a distinction between suffering and affliction. The former is simple pain, the latter a condition of being much like what I am naming a dark night of the soul. To be in pain is not necessarily to be in a dark night. The two states require different approaches. Weil recommended intelligence, genuine piety, and a profound and active empathy with the suffering found in the world.

At times, she lived this extreme empathy by not eating, so as to be in tune with the hungry people of the world. This act may seem more than extreme, neurotic at best. But whatever its roots, it symbolizes the seriousness with which anyone might respond to affliction by identifying with those who are more afflicted than you. I suspect that something of this fantasy inspires many to enter the medical world and to become psychotherapists. I don't mean that they will or should literally go so far in their empathy, but Simone Weil's example shows that their desire to be present to suffering is in itself unlimited. They can go as far as they want in their identification with affliction.

Simone Weil made another observation that fits well at the end of our discussion of the soul's dark nights. First, she makes a close connection between beauty and affliction. I tried to make this linkage in an earlier chapter. Being open to the beauty of the world and of life, you become susceptible to the divine force that lies at the very quick of life. By being open to the dark nights of your soul, you transcend the tight limits of your self and discover what it is to live religiously.

The alternative, says Weil, is not absence of health but mediocrity. Today, psychology and spiritual teachings explore every corner to help you live a healthy life. But do they ever help you overcome mediocrity? Are they concerned about it at all? And yet, millions of people have suffered and have lived painful and emotionally unfit lives while still evading mediocrity. Many, like Oscar Wilde and Anne Sexton, have apparently fallen to the very depths in the entropy of their existence, and yet they have erased all mediocrity from their lives. They shine brilliantly in the history of humanity because of their exquisite crystallization of soul in the midst of turmoil.

What is mediocrity in life? It is the failure to let the inner brilliance shine. Medieval theologians described this personal brilliance in the Latin word *scintilla*, the spark that lies at the heart of a person. When that inner genius shows itself in personality, way of life, values, and expression, mediocrity disappears. It is the cloud that prevents the spark from being seen. Mediocrity is the attitude of "do only what is necessary and sufficient," the feeling of not having an essence worth showing. It involves giving up on the possibility of living an outstanding life. It is being stuck in what we discussed earlier as the Jonah complex, the refusal to follow your calling.

Dark nights of the soul play a role in transcending mediocrity. They force you to consider your situation and to feel the dark material out of which the spark arises. Jung writes pages and pages about the spark, concluding with what may at first sound like an obscure statement of the mystery: "Numinosity entails luminosity." The numinous is that mysterious power of life, seen in nature, people, and works of craft and art, that inspires a sense of awe. It is the heart of religion and involved in the experience of falling in love. Something deep in you perceives something of immense value in the world. This extraordinary quality also has about it a brilliance and light that you can't overlook. You must feel the awe when you walk into an ancient cathedral or ascend Mayan steps. You stand mesmerized at the sight of a panther or at a rainbow forming over the plains. You meet a person who shines a light deep into your heart and in spite of any intentions to the contrary you become that person's friend or lover.

Mediocrity covers over this life-giving scintillation in yourself and in your world. But the person alive to life and calling and love responds and shows herself. She makes every effort to let that light shine, whether it is within her small family or in the greater world. The arc of the scintillation depends on fate and destiny, but the spark is important to everyone. It makes life worth living.

Go to a bookstore or library and look over the many volumes of biography. There you will see how differently the spark shines in people. There you may also discover, as in a mirror, your own spark, and you may find the motivation to unveil your own numinosity. Too often the modern man and woman allows that spark to remain outside, in someone else's life—the cult of personality and celebrity. When you discover your own spark, the god within you, many elements that you have felt are wounded will suddenly be healed.

I believe that the best way to deal with a dark night of the soul is to use the emotional and intellectual darkness to help you see your own luminosity, to discover exactly how you shine when you are at your best. Modern psychology is minimal in its goal of helping people adapt and feel normal. We have to press beyond psychology to a spiritual vision in which your life is redeemed by the discovery of the spark of divinity in you.

This was a popular theme among gifted writers of the European Renaissance. Marsilio Ficino recommended wearing glittering jewelry to remind you of your inner spark. He said that jewels and sparkling stones contain the light of the stars, as do our very souls. In the East we are taught to learn from the Lapus Lazuli Radiant Buddha, who represents spiritual healing. The great magus brought the infant Jesus gold, frankincense, and myrrh, all special substances representing the shine and aroma of the numinous.

I realize that I am far out of step with the times in recommending numinosity rather than health as a goal. Ours is still a therapeutic society that values the removal of symptoms over the soul's sparkle and shine. But just as the unicorn's horn was valued for its inspiring beauty and yet guaranteed health and beauty, so letting your spark light up a dark and dangerous world is a way of healing both you and your world.

Nothing could be more precious, then, than a dark night of the soul, the very darkness of which allows your lunar light to shine. It may be painful, discouraging, and challenging, but it is nevertheless an important revelation of what your life is about. In that darkness you see things you couldn't see in the daylight. Skills and powers of soul emerge from your frustration and ignorance. The seeds of spiritual faith, perhaps your only recourse but certainly a valuable power, are found in your darkness. The other half of who you are comes into view, and through the dark night you are completed.

You become the wounded healer, someone who has made the descent and knows the territory. You take on depth of color and range of feeling. Your intelligence is now more deeply rooted and not dependent only on facts and reason. Your darkness has given you character and color and capacity. Now you are free to make a real contribution. It is a gift of your dark night of the soul!

NOTES

1. Thomas Moore, translation.
2. Merlin Holland and Rupert Hart-David, eds., *The Complete Letters of Oscar Wilde* (New York: Henry Holt and Company, 2000), p. 912.
3. *The Ink Dark Moon*, transl. Jane Hirshfield with Mariko Aratani (New York: Vintage Books, 1990), p. 107.
4. Ananda K. Coomaraswamy, "Akimcanna," p. 6, n. 14. Quoted in Joseph Cambell, *The Hero with a Thousand Faces* (New York: MJF Books, 1949), p. 92.
5. A. M. Sperber and Eric Lax, *Bogart* (New York: William Morrow, 1997), p. 290.
6. Ralph Waldo Emerson, *Essays: First and Second Series* (New York: Gramercy Books, 1993), p. 205.
7. Emily Dickinson, *Selected Letters*, ed. Thomas H. Johnson (Cambridge, MA.: The Belknap Press, 1986), p. 303.
8. James E. B. Breslin, *Mark Rothko* (Chicago: University of Chicago Press, 1993), p. 497.
9. Shunryu Suzuki, *Zen Mind, Beginner's Mind*, ed. Trudy Dixon (New York: Weatherhill, 1970), pp. 75–76.
10. *Letters and Papers from Prison*, ed. Eberhard Bethge (New York: Collier Books, 1971), p. 362.
11. R. F. Foster, *W. B. Yeats: A Life* (Oxford: Oxford Univerity Press, 1997), p. 87.
12. Robert Gittings, ed., *Letters of John Keats* (Oxford: Oxford University Press, 1970), pp. 396–398.
13. Martha Amora, ed. *The Letters of Frida Kahlo* (San Francisco: Chronicle Books, 1995) p. 30.
14. Sigmund Freud, *The Interpretation of Dreams*, transl. James Strachey (New York: Avon Books, 1965), p. 436.
15. Annie Dillard, *The Writing Life* (New York: HarperCollins, 1989), p. 37.
16. Brian Keenan, *An Evil Cradling* (London: Vintage Books, 1993), p. 76.
17. *Unholy Ghosts*, ed. Nell Casey (New York: HarperCollins, 2001), p. 113.
18. R. Kearney, *On Stories* (London: Routledge, 2002), p. 142.

19. Ibid., p. 138.

20. C. G. Jung, Mysterium Coniuncionis, *C.W.*, vol. 14, trans. R.F.C. Hull (Princeton: Princeton University Press, 1970), p. 364.

21. Hillman, *The Dream and Underworld* (New York: HarperCollins, 1979), pp. 49–50.

22. Barry Till and Paula Swart, *Art from the Roof of the World* (Victoria, BC: Art Gallery of Greater Victoria, 1989), p. 42.

23. Oscar Wilde, *De Profundis and Other Writings* (New York: Penguin Books, 1973), p. 152.

24. Hillman, *Dream and Underworld*, p. 40.

25. Patricia Berry, ed., *Fathers and Mothers* (Dallas: Spring Publications, 1990), p. 100.

26. *The Tibetan Book of the Dead*, transl. Francesca Freemantle and Chögyam Trungpa (Boulder: Shambhala, 1975) p. 81.

27. James Knowlson, *Damned to Fame: The Life of Samuel Beckett* (New York: Touchstone Books, 1996), p. 400.

28. Brian Keenan, *An Evil Cradling*, pp. 204, 266.

29. David Chadwick, *Crooked Cucumber: The Life and Zen Teaching of Shunryu Suzuki* (New York: Broadway Books, 1999), p. 301.

30. Otto Friedrich, *Glenn Gould: A Life and Variations* (New York: Random House, 1989), p. 301.

31. Martin Green, ed., *Gandhi in India* (Hanover: University Press of New England, 1987), p. 101.

32. Jacob Boehme, *The Way to Christ* (Montana: Kessinger, n.d.), p. 81.

33. Anne Carson, *Eros the Bittersweet* (Princeton, Princeton University Press, 1986), p. 4.

34. Linda Gray Sexton and Lois Ames, eds. *Anne Sexton: A Self Portrait in Letters*. Boston: Houghton Mifflin, 1977. p. 375.

35. R. C. Hogart, *The Hymns of Orpheus* (Grand Rapids, Michigan: Phanes Press, 1993), p. 121.

36. James Hillman, *The Myth of Analysis* (New York: Harper Colophon Books, 1972), p. 94.

37. David L. Miller, *Three Faces of God: Traces of the Trinity in Literature and Life* (Philadelphia: Fortress Press, 1986), p. 122.

38. C. G. Jung, "Marriage as a Psychological Relationship: The Development of Personality," *C.W.* v. 17 (Princeton: Princeton University Press, 1954), p. 341.

39. Fred Kaplan, *Dickens: A Biography* (New York: William Morrow and Co., 1988), pp. 381, 384.

40. Adolf Guggenbühl-Craig, *Marriage Dead or Alive*, transl. Murray Stein (Zürich: Spring Publications, 1977), p. 113.

41. "Ghost in the House," in *Unholy Ghost*, Nell Casey, ed. (New York: Harper-Collins, 2001) p. 169.

42. C. Kerenyi, *Zeus and Hera*, transl. Christopher Holme (Princeton: Princeton University Press, 1975), p. 103.

43. Margaret Atwood, "Axiom," from *The Animals of That Country* (New York: Oxford University Press, 1968).

44. Kathleen Raine, *The Land Unknown* (London: Hamish Hamilton, 1975), p. 104.

45. Jan Morris, *Conundrum* (London: Faber and Faber, 1974), p. 14.

46. Ibid., pp. 156, 158.

47. Henry David Thoreau, *Walden and Other Writings*, ed. Joseph Wood Krutch (Toronto: Bantam, 1981), p. 111.

48. C. G. Jung, *Memories, Dreams, Reflections*, ed. Aniela Jaffé, transl. Richard and Clara Winston (New York: Pantheon Books, 1973), p. 174.

49. Barry Smith, *Peter Warlock: The Life of Philip Heseltine* (Oxford: Oxford University Press, 1975), pp. 86, 135.

50. Ibid., p. 285.

51. Oscar Wilde, "De Profundis," p. 160.

52. Keats, Letters, p. 37.

53. Brian Keenan, p. xiii.

54. Robert Gittings, ed., *Letters of John Keats* (Oxford: Oxford University Press, 1970), p. 70.

55. Eric Lax, *Woody Allen: A Biography* (New York: Alfred A. Knopf, 1991), p. 21.

56. Ronald Schenk, *The Soul of Beauty* (Lewisburg: Bucknell University Press, 1992), p. 144.

57. James Hillman, *Interviews* (New York: Harper & Row, 1983), p. 49.

58. Oscar Wilde, "De Profundis," p. 164.

59. Humphrey Burton, *Leonard Bernstein* (New York: Doubleday, 1994), p. 437.

60. Anne Sexton, *Letters*, p. 375.

61. Brian Keenan, *An Evil Cradling*, p. 246.

62. Emily W. Sunstein, *Mary Shelley: Romance and Reality* (Baltimore: Johns Hopkins University Press, 1989), p. 231.

63. Constantine Fitzgibbon, *The Life of Dylan Thomas* (Boston: Little, Brown and Co., 1965), p. 204.

64. Virginia Woolf, *On Being Ill* (Ashfield, MA: Paris Press, 2002), p. 3.

65. Chögyam Trungpa, *Cutting Through Spiritual Materialism* (Boston: Shambhala, 1987), p. 200.

66. Baxter, *Least of These My Bretheren* (New York: Harmony Books, 1997), p. 122.

67. Dorothy Judd, *Give Sorrow Words* (Binghamton, NY: The Haworth Press, 2nd ed. 1995), p. 209.

68. "The Book of the Sun," *Sphinx* 6, p. 142.

69. C. Kerenyi, *Asklepios: Archetypal Image of the Physician's Existence*, transl. Ralph Manheim, Bollingen Series LXV.3 (New York: Pantheon Books, 1959), p. 50.

70. Ivan Illich, *Medical Nemesis* (New York: Pantheon Books, 1976), p. 268.

71. Ibid., 275.

72. Nancy Milford, *Savage Beauty: The Life of Edna St. Vincent Millay* (New York: Random House, 2002), p. 468.

73. Mircea Eliade, *Journal III: 1970–1978*, transl. Teresa Lavender Fagan (Chicago: University of Chicago Press, 1989), p. 211.

74. James Hillman, "On Senex Consciousness," *Spring* (1970), pp. 146–165.

75. Edgar Wind, *Pagan Mysteries in the Renaissance* (New York: W. W. Norton & Company, 1968), p. 99.

76. Rainer Maria Rilke, *Letters to a Young Poet*, transl. Stephen Mitchell (New York: Random House, 1984), pp. 40–41.

77. David Grann, "The Old Man and the Gun," *The New Yorker* (January 27, 2003) pp. 60–69.

78. Harold Scheub, *A Dictionary of African Mythology* (Oxford: Oxford University Press, 2000), p. 161.

79. *Modern Maturity*, November/December 2002, p. 44.

80. John Moriarty, *Nostos* (Dublin: the Lilliput Press, 2001), p. 533.

81. Elyse Mach, *Great Pianists Speak for Themselves*, Vol. 2 (New York: Dodd, Mead & Company), pp. 112–13.

A Religion of One's Own

Own

A Guide to Creating a Personal Spirituality in a Secular World

Thomas Moore

Bestselling author of *Care of the Soul* and *Dark Nights of the Soul*

"[Moore] offers a new vision of how seekers can fashion their own connection to the sacred out of the materials of ancient faiths and everyday life."—Psychology Today

Intelligent, thought-provoking, and beautifully written, Moore points the way to creating an amplified inner life and a world of greater purpose, meaning, and reflection.

Also available in hardcover: 978-1-59240-829-0, $27.50

GOTHAM BOOKS